CONT

Some Introductory Notes...........

Apartheid: The Blame – Past and Present...............

The Afrikaner Nation and Apartheid

Birth of the Afrikaner Nation: My People 12

The British Occupation of the Cape 32

Apartheid from Beginning to the End 72

Living in Apartheid South Africa

People of Colour; Suffering under Apartheid 100

Are Africans Less Intelligent than Europeans? Why? 136

My Career in Civil Defence; Protecting People 153

Post-Apartheid, Reverse Discrimination

Liberation: Eight Southern African Countries 178

Democratisation and Reverse Discrimination........................ 206

South Africa Today, Post-Apartheid.. 235

Payback for Imperialism and Colonialism

Politics Post Imperialism.. 277

Political Manifestations in South Africa................................... 310

South Africa, Decolonisation: The Future

Decolonising and De-Whiting South Africa 331

South Africa: A Way Forward... 342

Epilogue: South Africa Today in Turmoil:................................ 352

Acknowledgements.. 354

The Author - Jan Cronje 356

References & Resources... 358

SOME INTRODUCTORY NOTES

I make extensive use of internet reports, websites and publications. I acknowledge the full list of resources, used in research; all included as per the Index. Should you wish to do an in-depth analysis, the websites and books contained in the reference list will provide ample guidance.

I write the book as a biography. The contents are reflective of all the colours of the South African Rainbow Nation; it is not all about me.

You might not like what I write! We all have our opinions. I trust that you will find the book informative and enjoyable.

Six Players That Changed South Africa

1652 - Dutch Colonial Administrator Jan van Riebeeck: When van Riebeeck met the Khoikhoi they were underdeveloped and vulnerable. The Dutch exploited the Khoikhoi people; they were inferior in and vulnerable with limited defensive ability. Europe occupied South Africa.

Cecil John Rhodes: British businessman, mining magnate and politician and Prime Minister of the Cape Colony. The ardent British maker of Apartheid, Imperialism and initiator of the *Scorched Earth War* method.

Rhodes Memorial

1

Boer Graves Springfontein

The Springfontein cemetery containing the Boer graves; among them some of my ancestors.

Emily Hobhouse: British humanitarian. Campaigned for Boer women and children in concentration camps. Her philanthropic efforts thwarted; the British deported her from the war zone. Emily's Samaritan initiatives changed the Anglo-Boer-War.

Lord Horatio Kitchener: Implemented Cecil John Rhodes Scorched Earth Policy. Concentration camps killed 22,000 Boer children.

Hendrik Frensch Verwoerd: *Fathers of Apartheid shared with Rhodes.* He died in 1966 in a second assault. Unlamented by blacks. Africans suffered cruel Apartheid policies.

President Jacob Zuma: ANC President and the most corrupt politician in the whole-wide-world. A Fraud who can't read or count has five wives and twenty-plus children. It took Zuma just two terms in office to destroy Mandela's dream. A vision for which he sacrificed twenty-seven years in jail. Mandela's Rainbow nation turned into a failed state.

Prologue

APARTHEID: THE BLAME – PAST AND PRESENT

The West Occupied Africa

Europe set foot on the continent of Africa as early as 1652. At the Berlin Conference of 1884, Western Europe divided Africa into colonies. By 1905, Europe occupied the African continent. Few countries spared; Britain and France claimed the most significant geographical stake. Germany, Spain, Italy, Belgium, and Portugal also commanded African colonies. As a result of imperialism, the majority of African countries lost their sovereignty. Today most African countries suffer failing economies and severe poverty. American President Roosevelt and British Prime Minister Churchill met in 1941. They announced the Atlantic Charter. The policy document determined the borders of the Post-Second-World-War Africa. I deal with South Africa as part of the African continent.

I explicitly consider the position of the white Afrikaner. The nation blamed for the atrocity of *Apartheid*. Imperialism and oppression of Africans finally ended in 1994. The people of colour formed a majority black government. I investigate the period of the empire from 1652 right up to present-day Post-Apartheid.

Why this Book? Apartheid: The Blame – Past and Present

Eureka. Finally, South Africa democratised! After more than five centuries of exploitation, the country is free! Nelson Mandela's dream of a Rainbow Nation gave hope to the people. South Africa will have peace and tranquillity. The nation will have a future as colourful as the rainbow.

News Flash: – Two decades of ANC rule, and there is no Rainbow Nation. Today, South Africa is still-segregated. It has a non-white population more miserable than ever. The country suffers arguably the worst inequalities in the world. The situation is worse than under minority Afrikaner Apartheid rule.

Facebook Nov. 2017
As Nelson Mandela so eloquently put it: "Little did we suspect that our own people, when they got a chance, would be as corrupt as the apartheid regime. That is one of the things that has really hurt us" (March 2, 2001).

Accreditation to Facebook posting November 2017

The book *Apartheid, The Blame – Past and Present,* is jam-packed with stories from my life under Apartheid. In fact, my life is a journey within the bubble of Apartheid. It switched discrimination away from black people. Today discrimination focusses on white people. Apartheid did not end in 1994. It just transformed into reverse-Apartheid.

I was born into Apartheid and today we live with reverse-discrimination. I stand by and watch events unfold. I am naturally concerned about the white people's future in South Africa. The African National Congress (ANC) government disturbingly supports communism. It turns a blind eye to black-on-white hate crimes.

I respect all ethnicities, and I support habitation and citizenship to all that qualify. But being an Afrikaner, you need to understand, my prejudice has white people at the core. The unfairness and defiance of the ANC predispose and offend me. I protest against all inhumane atrocities. I love the idea of a peaceful and tolerant *Rainbow Nation.*

Decolonisation and *de-whiting* of South Africa are not only detrimental to white people. It also harms the country as a whole. There are five million white people in South Africa. Do the de-whiting protagonists believe de-colonisation is feasible? And above all, it is ludicrous to lose the most developed sector of the South African nation. Just give it a thought; South Africa will be much weaker?

I do understand the grievance associated with imperialism, colonialization and enslavement. I have a different approach to correcting the wrongs of the past. I am no slave, and I do not own a slave. The time has arrived to shelve old grievances. Payback and retribution are not the answer. *Gandhi truthfully proclaimed: "An eye for an eye leaves the whole world blind."*

Nelson Mandela's Rainbow Nation presents the best solution. Or, have the de-whiting, and decolonising protagonists forgot his legacy? Did Mandela lived and suffered for nothing; are you prepared to murder his legacy?

My solution: Draw a line in the sand and let history be. We are the born-free generation from past atrocities. Reach out a hand of reconciliation and peace.

Get real: We do not have to repeat the wrongs of the past. Do not carve the future from the British imperial tombstone. Do not look at the future through a looking-glass of African anger. Colonialism and slavery is and should remain where it belongs in the Imperial past.

Apartheid: The Start and Demise

The Afrikaner Apartheid nation suffers the blame for Apartheid. A political dispensation, keeping people *apart* and impart *hatred.*

Combined the anti-Apartheid movement coined it as Aparthate. It all started in the 15th century with capitalism, compelling imperialism into slavery and colonialism. In the process, Europe introduced segregation, or shall we call it *Aparthate* to Africa.

The political scenario changed as a result of the Second World War. The aversion to fascism and racism reached a crescendo. British Prime Minister Harold McMillan warned; Britain will not support the Apartheid policies.

The world supported and liberated eight previously colonised nations in Southern Africa. Imperialism rejected, and African freedom took centre stage.

Africa dumped white oppression. Black Africans celebrated their majority rule over towns and cities. But, liberation and decolonisation went seriously wrong with gruesome results. Ferociously, the previously oppressed Africans resorted to violence and corruption with black-on-white (reverse-) discrimination.

Decolonisation and de-whiting murdered more than 70,000 white people in South Africa since 1994. African freedom caught fire as a result of *reverse discrimination.* The psychosis of fear and mistrust took hold of the nation. The Communist-inspired majority ANC Government became an *enemy to the country.* South Africa according to the authoritative *Economist,* turned into a failed state. Is this Nelson Mandela's Rainbow Nation dream?

Another corrupt African Fiasco?

Sins of the Fathers: Blame the Children

During democratisation, the Afrikaner felt an uncomfortable awareness of remorse and self-reproach; the legacy of Apartheid still fresh in their minds. The global community once again sees South Africa as Apartheid, Mandela, liberation struggles, and the oppression of black people. Trevor MacDonald, the black BBC reporter, still remembers the 1976 Sharpeville massacre. Distressed blue eyes ogling white police officers shooting, chasing, and bludgeoning young black people.

Everything had changed, but nothing has changed. People of colour are still the worse-off; shoddier than under white minority Apartheid. Only whites and Asians prosper. They are the ethnicities that migrated to Africa.

Cecil John Rhodes: The Father of Imperialism

Cecil John Rhodes, born on 5 July 1853 in Bishops Stortford, England, was the fifth son of Francis William Rhodes and Louisa Peacock. Based on Rhodes' track record he can be considered the father of Britsh Imperialism and Apartheid policies.

Rhodes developed an affinity for British Imperialism while studying at Oxford. He speculated on establishing a *secret society* of British men. The *secret society* will further the concept of British Imperial expansion. He wanted to put the whole uncivilised world under British rule. His dream incorporated the idea of an Anglo-Saxon race as one Empire. Rhodes admired the *Oxford system.* He stated: *"Wherever you turn your eye - except in science - an Oxford man is at the top of the tree."*

Rhodes, a prominent businessman, mining magnate and politician in South Africa, served as Prime Minister of the Cape Colony from 1890 to 1896. He died at Muizenberg in the Cape on 26 March 1902. I write extensively on Rhodes' Rhodesian colonisation through his British South African Company (BSAC) in later chapters.

The present-day *Black Land First Land (BLFL) and the Rhodes Must Fall Movement (RMF),* still target Rhodes' expansionist legacy. They see Rhodes as the symbol of colonisation and want to remove his legacy from the earth; even within the UK. Twenty-two years after democratisation, Rhodes' imperialism serves as the prime motivation for the *decolonisation and de-whiting* efforts in

South Africa. I write extensively about these manifestations in later chapters.

Is Imperialism the cause of Terrorism Today?

Was the dominance of Europe wrong and out of place? Or did the occupiers earn their loot by superior power? The strongest will survive.

Power breeds bribery, and absolute power produces corruption. Cecil John Rhodes' role in colonialism and imperialism is extensive and real when it comes to South Africa, Zambia and Zimbabwe. There seems to be an altruistic undertone in Rhodes's Oxford speech. An aspiration to uplift and develop the colonised countries. But, when the Western colonisers sniffed wealth, they became ruthless. Genocidal practices, wars and slavery ravaged Africa. Atrocities committed while enriching the European imperialists.

Yes, the colonists did build various shapes and forms of improved infrastructure. But, at what cost? The price paid, amounted to death and extermination of millions; even the partial annihilation of nations. Collateral damage always favours the subjugator, not the conquered. But, the improvements were *burdened gifts*, predominantly constructed to further imperialism. The occupiers did not have the worth of the occupied native nations at heart. Pompous expansionists will attempt to justify imperialism by claiming they added development to Africa.

Imperialism did not award political privileges, human rights, and fairness onto the conquered natives. The reverse happened. Oppression and subjugation *representative and endemic to Apartheid* emerged; reflecting the mandate and legacy of colonialism.

The hatred of African nations, subjugated in the imperial epoch blossomed in the liberation era. Grievances not forgotten nor forgiven. Today, home-grown and migrating terrorism, threaten Europe as the colonisers of yesteryear.

Is Afrikaner Self-Rule Aspirations Justified?

The Boer-Afrikaner nation claimed South Africa as their own Afrikaner land. When the British colonised the Cape in 1806, the Afrikaner was a nation-state. The British take-over did not sit well with the Afrikaner. In revolt, they moved north in the *1838 Great Trek migration*; the Boers established the Republics, Transvaal and Orange Free State.

The discovery of diamonds and gold incited more capitalistic greed and resulted in the British attacking the Boers in the Anglo-Boer-Wars. The British occupied the mineral-rich north. The Afrikaner loathed the British and longed to be free; they craved self-governance.

The ANC did not answer to *Mandela's Rainbow Nation dream*. Because of corruption, South Africa suffers as a failed state.

As recent as September 2017, a state capture attempt happened in South Africa. President Jacob Zuma in cahoots with the Indian Gupta capitalists employed the British Bell Pottinger PR to orchestrate the state capture. After thirty years, and with clients like Maggie Thatcher, Bell Pottinger lost all credibility and went into administration.

South Africa pays, at this stage, a high price. Psychotic fear, the breakdown of democracy and disrespect of the rule of law, are rife. Societal distrust in the governing powers prevails. Will this be the price South Africa has to pay for actual freedom?

The future of South Africa is bleak. But, the track record of the communist ANC government does not promise a prosperous future.

Let's Start the Turnaround:

- Trust in the rule of law and accountable administration.
- Grow skills and expertise and acknowledge the white professionals.

- Accept and cherish the differences. Celebrate harmonies and cuddle the kaleidoscope of colours.
- Engage with loyalty and build the nation, phase out inequalities.
- Invest in the youth; education, education, education...
- Condition the minds and hearts of the people and love your country.

Nkosi Sekelel' iAfrica - God bless Africa

There might be some terms I use that people find offensive. But, I don't include them inconsiderately. I do my best to inform and be authentic. Enjoy the journey. I will appease the dark picture with some entertaining personal experiences.

First, I will deal with the movement of people to and from Africa and South Africa. How exactly did the white man come to Africa?

The student that dubbed me the *African Dude* had all the right in the world to challenge me:

"Sir if you are from Africa, why are you not black?" And, why do you have a woman's name Djan?

Part One:

THE AFRIKANER NATION AND APARTHEID

In part one I will deal with the archaeological discoveries that explain how Southern Africa populated. Which tribal ethnicities came first and who last. Land ownership and citizenship are crucial to land entitlements. The question I ask is; where did man first walk the earth and how did humanity disperse to populate our planet.

I also research the historical origin and development of the Afrikaner nation. It is essential to explain how the white Afrikaner, as the only European nation within Africa, came to be in Africa.

The movement of the Europeans during the Imperial Expansionist era is of vital importance to the cause of Apartheid. White Europeans were different from the Africans in the seventeenth century. The disparity led to the subjugation of people of colour. They were oppressed, enslaved and subjugated. Why were they less developed and vulnerable?

Imperial expansion and colonialism by Europe, ever since the slave trade era gave rise to Apartheid in modern times. The origin and development of oppression and exploitation by the western world I enlighten from 1652 right up to the end of 2017; I elucidate Apartheid from beginning to end.

Part One consists of the following chapters

1. *Birth of the Afrikaner Nation: My People* 12
2. *The British Occupation of the Cape* 33
3. *Apartheid from Beginning to the End* 72

11

CHAPTER 1

BIRTH OF THE AFRIKANER NATION: MY PEOPLE

The Afrikaner nation constitutionalised the political dispensation of Apartheid after 1948. It shocked the world into a revolt giving rise to the imposition of isolation and sanctions. First of all, who is this white Afrikaner nation, within a predominantly black Africa? How did it all start, and how did it develop? I will establish how people moved from and to Africa and specifically South Africa. What is the origin of the Afrikaner nation?

Identity is core to who I am.

Being the native to a country is an ambiguous concept. Many centuries ago, the world did not belong to anybody. The world became an open arena for citizenship once humanity started roaming the earth. Man only developed after the planet formed or created; whatever your belief may be. Before that the world was barren. No shape or form of Homo sapiens lived in Southern Africa. Naturally, my conclusions rely heavily on modern science. I consider scientific assumptions and accept them as the reality.

Once the Southern sub-continent of Africa populated all those centuries back, more and more people migrated to South Africa. People emigrated in their sprawling expeditions of imperialism. Europeans set foot in Africa in the 15th century when Vasco da Gama, discovered Africa.

Based on the first come first claimed, people of colour appear to be the owners of the land; even though African tribalism does not consider ground as private ownership. To them, the area is communal property and cannot be owned privately or stately.

But, people living in South Africa as descendants, for close on five centuries, have a claim by birthright. Time turn migrants into citizens, irrespective of who came first and who last; it is an internationally accepted principle. The only qualification is migration policies; when there is no law governing migration, the land is open to all.

Some stereotypes developed within the vast spectrum of ancestry. Africans are black, even if they live in America, they are African-Americans. Europeans are white, also if they live in Africa. Do they now become Euro-Africans? I research the movement of people within Africa. Even from Africa to the rest of the world. And also from abroad to Africa and South Africa. My objective; to establish a perspective of the South African nation.

A white-skinned man, laying claim to be an African will raise an eyebrow in the broader world. Especially for people with limited knowledge of African history. Challenged, as the author of this book, I had to explain my African identity. People questioned my confusing skin and eye colour. The following incident I recall to account for my European appearance. I introduced myself as a South African living in England.

Since arriving in the Midlands, I've worked as a supply teacher. I covered classes in Business Studies, Maths and Science. That is when teachers are absent or otherwise occupied.

The Student that Dubbed Me the African Dude

I arrived at a secondary school in Bakewell, Derbyshire County, for a day of supply teaching. A young man enthusiastically informed his friends, "That is the African Dude." He was one of the senior boys, quite audacious and outspoken, one of the year elevens; bottom set. These students are forthcoming and confident, maybe a bit challenging, but not that inspired. I get along with them well. They remind me of my school days. Skiving and time spent in the snooker parlour instead of attending class. It takes a rebel to recognise one. Some of us have been there, a lifetime ago.

The student approached me and tossed a question in the early morning air.

"Hi Sir, will you be teaching us today?" he asked.

"Maybe, I have to pick up my teaching plan But, I will see you when I see you," I responded. As it happened, I caught up with the students in the fifth period, teaching Maths.

The student tested me once more.

"Sir, if you are from Africa, why are you not black, and why do you have a women's name, Djan like in Djanice?"

It is a mystery where he found out about my first name. But, trust me if there is something to uncover, these young lads will. He did not beat around the bush, he cut straight to the chase, anything to avoid school work. I had to humour them and find a way to bring them back to task. Strike a deal. That might be the solution.

"Okay, I replied, I will explain my perplexing skin colour and confusing name. But, after that, we get on with Maths, all right?"

"Cool," he replied with a smile as broad as the surf on the beach. His hair colour and highlights reminiscent of sea sand. The spontaneity of the youth is fascinating.

My plot to humour them started with Queen Victoria, I told my story to be gripping and sinister.

"Do you remember Queen Victoria, the British Monarch? She conquered the whole world while she established the British Empire. And, then the rest of Europe joined in, creating colonies all over Africa."

The student appeared doubtful, this sounded like a history lesson, too much academia, just school all over again. A frown wrinkled the young man's brow, like corrugation on a dirt road. A quizzical look flushed his mistrusting face.

"Yeah, what's that to do with you being a whitey?" he probed.

"Hold your horses mate; I'm getting there," I responded.

I prolonged the story with unfolding seriousness. These guys do not want to return to academics. Stories need to intrigue. They thrive on mysticism, something long, long ago and far, far away. Especially far, far away from school work.

I continued.

"Britain conquered Africa and sent thousands of white Brits to Africa. They had to manage Britain's new-found treasure of colonies. South Africa turned into a proper British Colony. Britain reaped the harvest of African gold, diamonds and precious minerals. The loot was for the coffers of the British Crown. The aim was to enrich Britain and turn it into a prosperous state. That is the Britain we enjoy today, isn't it?

Almost every European country followed, populating Africa with white European faces. The Europeans were dominant and well advanced in industry and warfare. They could just overpower the native tribes and reap the harvest Africa offered. The African Tribes did not resist. The Europeans over three centuries turned into Euro-Africans. Their African bodies covered in white skins.

After Queen Victoria died, Britain and Europe realised their mistake. They should never have colonised Africa. The Colonists returned to Britain and Europe. They handed Africa back to its rightful owners, the black African tribes. That was the proper thing to do, wasn't it?

However, they left my white ancestors in Africa; we became the first Euro-Africans. I am one of them, white-skinned with blue eyes. Moreover, calling me Djan, you should spell it Yan for correct English diction; a Dutch version of John. It is just the English that turned it into Djan for Djanice.

Do you think the European Colonists gave back all the African treasures they harvested? Nope, the Star of Africa is still in the Queen's crown."

I thought to myself: *'Yes, and my African arse is still in my white European skin; I am a Euro-African.'*

The student was not impressed, his ploy for missing the lesson thwarted. His bored response: *"Whatever"* with accompanying body language, all interest lost.

I concluded. "Well open your books, we will be doing percentages and fractions today, okay?"

The Real Reason for me being in Africa

However, let's return to the events that gave rise to the Afrikaner being in Africa. They are white skinned among the majority black people. European colonialism is an epoch in time that brought the white man to Africa after centuries black African habitation.

Ever since my memory surfaced, I was in the presence of black African people. They were part of my life in a way that was different from being with white people. Black Africans had a different standing; they were of a different class. Present in servitude to white people. There was no equality, no integration and no sense of national unity.

America, Australia, Canada and New Zealand historically were not white man's land either. Europeans conquered and claimed the land as their own, new white man's land. Imperialism brought segregation and imparted separatism to the world, especially to South Africa. How did this come into being worldwide? The people of colour were the original and native people, the original first occupants. Africa seemed to *belong* to the Africans, equal to America *belonging* to the Native American Indians. In later chapters, I write about the disparities in *intelligence* between Europeans and Africans; I endeavour to explain the difference in development.

Even though the Dutch established a refreshment post in 1652, the British were ultimately the de-facto colonists, the occupiers and the invaders of South Africa. It sounds wrong; the Dutch were the first to occupy the Cape of Good Hope. The Dutch did not formally colonise South Africa. They only established a refreshment post to provide supplies to their passing ships.

The Afrikaner nation developed over one and a half century as an extenuation of the Dutch, French, and German settlers that migrated to Africa. The composite Boer nation as immigrants became known as the Afrikaner nation with an own language, culture and religion. They are the people that claimed South Africa as their colonised Afrikaner-land. The question is, was it colonisation and by whom; the Dutch or the Afrikaner?

The scope of my book is Apartheid, as blamed on the Boer-Afrikaners, the people that fled from the British colonisers. But, let's not get ahead of ourselves. Colonisation transformed South Africa from a Black African sub-continent to a multicultural and racial society. The South African nation became known to the rest of the world as the *Rainbow Nation*. The Nelson Mandela dream after the 1994 democratisation, reflecting the many skin colours of its people.

The British Empire: Significant Influence on South Africa

I cannot consider the founding of the Afrikaner nation without taking into account the impact of Britain on Africa. British imperialism not only changed Africa and South Africa, but it also had a determining and lasting effect in the broader world.

The tale I told might have messed with the mind of the young student that dubbed me the *African Dude*. It might also reflect a grievance on my part with Britain. That is not the case, the people that were arseholes and criminals were the people from Europe in the colonial years. Today we are born free of the colonial carnages, in the same way as all my Afrikaner compatriots, we are all born-free generations. In fact, I admire these small British Isles; they conquered the world in their British Empire heydeys. When the opportunity arose, they seized the moment. Britain did just that, *carpe diem,* captured the moment. Africa had the chance to resist occupation and retain its sovereignty, but they could not ward off the colonial onslaught. The colonists were advanced in technology and warfare. The imperialistic expansion was an accepted principle from the 15th to 20th century, gaining wealth and expanding territory. Historically British imperialism first became the British Empire and later the British Common Wealth; the dispensation that returned the occupied colonies to the original African nations.

During the colonial era, developed European nations occupied countries of lesser evolvement; the strongest will survive and conquer. Colonisation was inevitable and in touch with the times, particularly in the epoch of slavery and imperialism. The Imperial expansion was the political norm of those times.

How Great was Britain at the start of the 20th Century?

The British Isles are small compared to South Africa. The most modest province in South Africa, the Orange Free State, is more extensive than England; the biggest of the four British nations. Britain was ambitious in its land grab mission. It is doubtful whether the British world stature of today would have been as impressive was it not for Imperialism. Britain would probably have had less authority in the world. Just imagine Britain without the British Empire and today's Common Wealth. What colonialism accumulated, enriched not only Britain but also Europe. Capitalism with its money and land grabbing enthused expansionism and imperialism.

Just consider the size of the British Empire at the beginning of the 20th century. The British Empire covered fourteen and a half million square miles. An astonishing quarter of the world's landmass. The British Isles by itself covers only eighty-nine thousand square miles; only 0,61% of the Empire. Probably the most significant empire worldwide at any time in history.

What about the population of the British Empire? Queen Victoria, by 1900, reigned over five hundred million people. The British people totalled only thirty-eight million; they account for just 13% of the Empire population.

Studying the evidence, it comes to no surprise, Britain was the mightiest nation, and it had the most powerful military force at the beginning of the 20th century. Suddenly it was not only a British force but a British Empire military force. Britain excelled in its colonial aspirations. If that is not mind-boggling, what is? It will surprise me if any country ever broke this land-grab record. This result is impressive, and Britain should be granted its title as *Great Britain.*

However, this magnanimous achievement brought about some severe collateral damage. Colonialism played a decisive role in African development, in some ways it caused severe destruction in Africa. South Africa as we know it today, would not be the same as it was before colonisation. British occupation affected and influenced black and white Africans. Apart from the magnanimity of the British Empire, colonialism had a significant impact on me as a young boy.

Childhood Afrikaner Perspective: German-British Split

I have to consider the influence of Germany in South Africa and specifically about the Afrikaner. In fact, Germans constitute more than a third of the root genetic make-up of the Afrikaner. In later chapters, the inference of Germany will surface more prominently. However, even though the British genetic contribution to Afrikaner genetic makeup is only five percent, the influence of Britain on me as an Afrikaner was enormous.

My early memories rekindle thoughts of a division in the composite Cronje / Carsten families. Mother Carsten married father Cronje, resulting in an almost West-side Story fairy tale. The Cronje family originated from France while the Carsten family originated from Germany. World War Two was ongoing when Mum and Dad got married in the late 1930s and raised a family; their countries of origin were at war.

Even though the parents were not that active in politics or the war, there was a noticeable split. The war affected whom they supported, opposing loyalties into the broader family. As a young child, ever since memory surfaced, the family on both sides visited. When the Carsten family paid a visit, not a single English word spoken; English was forbidden. They would scorn, Anglicization was unacceptable and taboo.

My uncle, Hendrik Carsten, was a member of the *Broederbond (Afrikaner Brotherhood)*, an organisation set on imparting Afrikanerism and opposing Anglicisation. He joined the *Ossewabrandwag* (OB), I suppose it can be translated as the *ox waggon guards*, formed in 1938. The OB evolved on the model of the German Nazi political structures. The OB mission, according to the following extract was: *"To formally represent the rising Afrikaner nationalism inspired by the Great Trek centenary celebrations."*

The OB was closely related to both DF Malan's *Herenigde Nasionale Party (HNP – Reformed National Party)* and the *Afrikaner-Broederbond (AB) Afrikaner Brotherhood*. The OB rapidly evolved from a cultural organisation into a highly motivated, political voice. By 1941, its membership had risen to approximately 350,000. During the early years of World War Two, the OB became more militaristic. It created an extreme right-wing paramilitary sub-group, the *Stormjaers*. They were modelled on the *Nazi Sturmabteilung, (Storm Division or Brown Shirts)*; implying a strong affiliation to Germany. As a protest against Jan Smuts' British loyal United Party government, the *Stormjaers* carried out raids of sabotage. All in all, it suggests that the Afrikaner (HNP) would have preferred to be an ally to Germany rather than Britain.

In her younger days, my mother joined the *Kappie-Kommando* (Bonnet Commando), a ladies support group to the OB. The bonnet was a symbol of identification with the Boer nation. The commando of women demonstrated against the British and the United Party; the Afrikaners did not like the British.

Pictures that hung in our family home reflected the struggle of the Afrikaner. In fact, mother died a staunch supporter of Apartheid and the Nationalist Party. She can be considered a racist, in an *empathetic* sort of way. In my mind, she never meant any harm. She was part of the brainwashed white people of South Africa. I love her to bits, bless her soul, she was a super Mum; she had her reasons and convictions.

When the Cronje side of the family visited, the language approach was the complete opposite. They were posh, and English inclined. In fact, the more English, the more pompous. The terms like *darling* and *sweetheart* were ever present.

Father was not into politics but a social person and a member of the Free Masons movement of British origin. The Cronje strain of the family supported General Jan Smuts' United Party, loyal to Britain. Father was a construction worker. He toiled away from home on construction sites. Therefore Mum Carsten's sentiments dominated and established our youth life perspective and political make-up.

There was no real drive to turn us into political foot soldiers. However, raised as Afrikaner-Nationalists, we were groomed and conditioned into Apartheid. At that stage, Apartheid was as standard as breakfast and sex. Maybe, not sex, but rather teasing the girl next door. Apartheid was the way of life, the ordinary, the routine.

Some historical research is needed to determine the Afrikaner's genetic roots. Europe introduced white people to Africa. This warrants a closer look at how people moved to and from Africa.

Science has it that the Southern part of Africa was early-on not populated. In fact, at some point, it belonged to nobody. The question is, who came first to lay claim to the land, and how legitimate was the entitlement? The map inserted, gives an impression of the movement and migration of humanity.

Homo-Sapiens that remained in Africa developed into the Rhodesian man (Homo Rhodesiensis). Africans, therefore, originate from the Rhodesian man. Homo Neanderthal, also coined as *intelligent man,* is the European variant that migrated to Europe. Europeans, lived in Eurasia from 200,000 to 30,000 years ago, during the Pleistocene Epoch. But, what happened in Southern Africa.

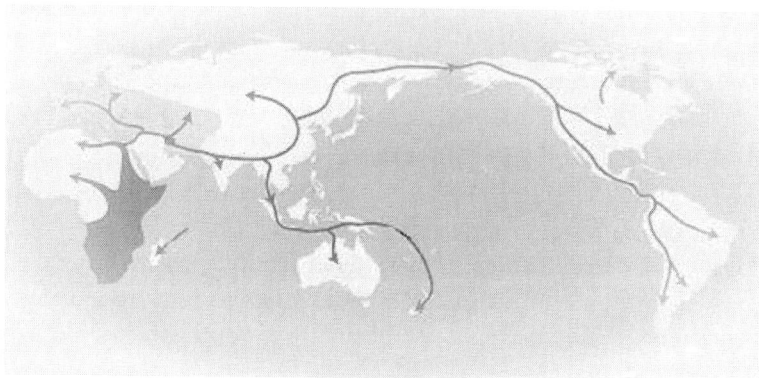

Migration from Africa and to South Africa

Most scientists accept, that man evolved over two and a half million years. According to archaeological finds, man, *Homo-Sapiens,* first walked the earth in Africa. Tanzania and Ethiopia uncovered the first archaeological discoveries of humanity. From here the first people moved north. One hundred and thirty thousand years ago the Neanderthals moved to Eurasia, down and across the southern hemisphere.

The diagram shows the movement of the *Neanderthal man* to Europe while the *Rhodesian man* evolved within Africa. Rhodesian man, in Southern Africa, resembles the Eurasian Neanderthals, but they are not Neanderthals. They identify as the Rhodesian man *(Homo Rhodesiensis).* Rhodesian man existed long before the Eurasian Neanderthals. According to anthropologists, the

Rhodesian man had a more modern set of teeth. Two thousand years ago the Rhodesian man settled in Southern Africa. For my research, I will join the migration in Botswana; the origin of the Khoikhoi that populated the Cape.

Migration from Botswana: The San Tribe

This image portrays the typical San people as the native people of Botswana that migrated to South Africa. The San people moved in search of better land for food propagation and better grazing for their livestock. Re-identifying themselves as the Khoisan, they moved and populated Namibia and the Northern Cape.

The people that migrated even further south to occupy the Western Cape and the Cape of Good Hope identified themselves as Khoikhoi to show pride in their past and culture. They also distinguished themselves from the Botswana San, and Namibian - Northern Cape Khoisan. The image portrays the Khoikhoi; their appearance differed from the Dutch settlers; they are distinctly different. The Khoikhoi appears to be a weak people, not as equipped or well dressed and fortified as the Europeans of the seventeenth century.

The Khoikhoi as a tribe in present-day South Africa is somewhat unknown. One can even think them to be extinct. If you ask people in the Cape Province to point out a Khoikhoi, it is doubtful that you will find anyone. Few people even remember the Khoisan and Khoikhoi, even though the Kalahari Bushmen are direct descendants from the San as the Khoisan.

The Khoikhoi dispersed within the population of the Western Cape as a mixed-race ethnic group. They are known as the Coloureds, an ethnicity and a people of colour with original heritage as Khoikhoi.

It is well-known that Vasco da Gama and his Portuguese sailors were the first Europeans to set foot in Africa. Portuguese and Dutch ships traversed the oceans to source spices from East Asia. There was a powerful capitalistic drive behind colonising Africa. The Khoikhoi were already settled in the Cape when the first European Colonists arrived.

The Dutch Migration

When the Dutch migrated to the Cape of Good Hope only the Khoisan-Khoikhoi people inhabited South Africa. They populated South Africa from the north, across Namibia and into the Western Cape coastal regions.

In the larger spectrum of time the Nguni Bantu arrived shortly before the Europeans, while the Dutch arrived at the Cape four centuries after the Bantu-Nguni tribes moved into South Africa from the North.

The Nguni-Bantu tribes moved along the eastern African coastal areas, from the present Cameroon area. The Nguni-Bantu tribes speak Nguni languages which differ from the Khoisan languages, known for their klick sounds.

The Nguni are the Xhosa, Zulu, Ndebele and Swazi people domiciled in the Eastern Cape, KwaZulu-Natal, and Mpumalanga. Shaka kaSenzangakhona, more commonly known as Shaka Zulu ruled the Zulu Kingdom. During the early nineteenth century, the Nguni tribes had numerous conquests in South Africa and exterminated large portions of the original Khoisan people in a conquest for settlement.

When considering the matter of land entitlement the Nguni, Khoisan and Dutch migrations are of great importance; especially when considering private land ownership.

Black tribal custom always regarded land as belonging to anyone and everyone. It seems that the Europeans introduced private land ownership first in South Africa. Cecil John Rhodes passed the Glen Grey Act in 1894; I deal with Rhodes extensively later on.

It was not the Portuguese but the *Dutch East Indian Company* as the first European settlers to the Cape. The company crossed the oceans in three ships, the *Dromedaris, Reijger,* and *Goede Hoop.* The commander, Jan van Riebeeck was a Dutch Colonial Administrator; the denomination implies colonialism. On 16 April 1652, van Riebeeck set foot at the Cape of Good Hope, today's Cape Town. Deaths with the first voyage were high, one-hundred-and-thirty of the crew perished.

A supplement of colonists followed with two ships, the *Walvisch and the Oliphant.* The Dutch interest in the Cape was to establish a halfway refreshment station for passing ships circumventing the Cape Horn, sailing from the Netherlands to the spice-rich regions in East Asia.

The Dutch belittled the native Khoikhoi, calling them *Hottentots* because the sound of the Khoikhoi language was different from any European language. They could not pronounce the European words and sounds. Belittling the Khoikhoi and downgrading their status, the Dutch brutalised them and endeavoured to make them extinct. They enslaved the Khoikhoi, dispossessed their land for farms, and exterminated them. The Dutch settlers in time turned into Afrikaners. They are my ancestors of three and a half centuries past. The typical characteristics of what Apartheid represents were prevalent during the Cape occupation.

Migration changed the demography of South Africa. The question is, who were the migrants and who were the natives? Over centuries all migrants become citizens of Africa. Irrespective of geographical and ethnic origin, skin colour or culture; all European settlers became Afrikaners.

However, when the Dutch migrants arrived, were they welcomed by the Khoikhoi? No, the Dutch as colonisers settled in the Cape uninvited. African tribes and the Khoikhoi did not consider land as privately owned. The land was communal property and not restricted to any identifiable group of people.

Another European company, the *British South African Company (BSAC)* of Cecil John Rhodes, occupied land in Africa and called it Rhodesia. The occupation had corresponding features, on par with the *Dutch East Indian Company*. In later chapters, I deal with the Rhodesian invasion. Is it a coincidence that the Rhodesian man *Homo rhodesiensis* shows a correlation with Cecil John Rhodes? I doubt that there is any correlation. Rhodes ties in with the *Neanderthal man* originating from Europe.

Company rule, which ultimately became colonisation, underpins the capitalistic nature and drive behind colonisation, the motive being greed, wealth and enrichment for Europe. The occupation happened with the support and blessing of the European governments.

The Dutch settlers infringed on the land and intermarried with the Khoikhoi. In time they became known as the *Boers*, a term attributed to a person working the land. The Boers were an advanced nation and coerced the Khoikhoi into labour on their farms. Over a century and a half, they became the Afrikaner nation.

The Khoikhoi were vulnerable, not able to challenge colonial expansion. This oppressive behaviour of the Dutch motivated the Khoikhoi to flee from oppression into the harsh deserts. Today ancestors of the Botswana San tribe, still live in the Kalahari Desert.

The loss of Khoikhoi as slave workers enticed the Dutch to traffic slaves from Dutch Colonial Malaysia. Malaysian people were introduced to the Cape and are to this day a prominent ethnic group.

The geographical and strategic locality of the Cape was essential to the Dutch; they needed to expand production. Farming was a prerequisite to produce supplies for passing ships. The Dutch needed proficient farmers to work with the Khoikhoi and Malaysian slaves.

When the western world liberated the colonised countries, the colonial masters allowed their people to return to Europe.

The exception is the Netherlands; the Dutch did not allow any of their people in the form of Boers and Afrikaners to return to Holland. The Afrikaner just had to deal with the consequences of imperialism and colonisation.

French Huguenots Migrated to the Cape

The Edict of Nantes was revoked in 1685, exposing Protestants to persecution by Catholics. Before 1685, the Protestants were granted religious tolerance under the Edict promulgated in 1598. The people that fled from persecution became known as French Huguenots. Persecution drove many of the French Huguenots out of France.

An influx of French Huguenots migrated to the Cape in 1671. The Dutch welcomed an advanced nation, they supplemented the Dutch Boer farmers and managed to boost farm production. The South African wine industry originated predominantly as a result of the French Huguenot migrants.

Among the French Huguenots were two brothers Pierre and Estienne Cronje. They migrated from Normandy France, in 1678, and settled in the Cape of Good Hope. They were the first Cronje migrants as my French ancestors and namesake to the Cape with the family motto; En-garde *ma Foi*, meaning Guard my Faith. The Cronje families settled on the farm *Wamakerskloof* in the Wolseley District of the Western Cape.

Pierre Cronje, shot two Khoikhoi men when they stole cattle from him. He had to appear in Court. As punishment, they banished him from the Cape. Due to the administrative incompetence of the Dutch, the court did not execute the order. Pierre returned to his farm, and he carried on farming. The crime not punished, resulted in the Khoikhoi not having effective recourse to justice. The negation serves as an example of the inferiority of the Khoikhoi; they were at the mercy of the invading settlers.

The Cape Colony expanded into areas to the North to provide produce for passing ships. The fertile land catered well for the plant material imported by the French Huguenot settlers. As the Boers moved further north, the soil changed to less arable land forcing them to convert to livestock farming on marginal land. The Boers in time replaced production for passing ships with self-preservation. They became farming communities in their own right, divorced from the *Dutch East Indian Company*.

In moving north, the Boers encountered the Xhosa tribe. They were able to challenge the Boers' advance into their native land. They were a developed people with robust central structures, already trading with Arabs and Europeans. Xhosas were also cattle breeders, bringing them in direct competition with the Boers. The Boers found their first opposition in their land and wealth grab. As the conflict between the Boers and the Xhosa developed, they were forced to establish defence units in the form of Commandos. An uneasy frontier era dawned on the Boers and the Xhosa people to the North.

The Xhosa tribe is the tribe of Nelson Mandela and is presently one of the largest tribes of the South African Nation. Civil Defence measures became essential for protection on both sides, the Boers and the Xhosa. I deal with Civil Defence extensively in later chapters. The early Boer expansionism era did not establish a social integrated South Africa. It instead imparted conflict and segregation.

The Afrikaner and the Afrikaans Language

I explained that the contemporary Afrikaner derives from Western Europeans that migrated to Africa and settled in the Cape during the 17th century, where they came into contact with the Khoikhoi as descendants of the Khoisan.

Employees of the Dutch East Indian Company, mostly Dutch and Germans, eventually over time retired from service of the company. In the middle 17th century they became the first *Free Burghers – free citizens* as European natives of South Africa. They became independent farmers trading with the *Dutch East Indian Company*. Later they would separate from the *Dutch East Indian Company* to become entirely independent.

We also ascertained that in the late 17th century, a group of French Protestants, French Huguenots, decided to leave France; they settled in the Cape. The Free Burghers inclusive of French Huguenots became some of the earliest ancestors of the Afrikaner nation. However, Afrikaner identity materialised as early as 1707, when Hendrik Biebouw-*Bibault* declared himself to be an *Africaander*.

Dutch settlers and the resettled workers as slaves were the first to speak *Afrikaans; African,* when translated from the Dutch. Slaves were introduced to the Cape by the Dutch East Indian Company from 1652 onwards. The enslaved workers were Malays from Indonesia and the indigenous workers similar to the Khoikhoi people as native people to South Africa.

In 1925, the world acknowledged Afrikaans as a language in own right that developed from colloquial dialect. Afrikaans originated as a means of communication between the Dutch settlers and their African and South Asian slave workers. Early on Afrikaans as a language acquired the identity as *kitchen Dutch* because it was the dialect spoken by slaves in the kitchen. English strongly influenced the style and contributed to Afrikaans. The genetic roots of Afrikaans speaking people are set out in the pie diagram. Afrikaans, also known as *Cape Dutch*, belongs to the West Germanic branch of the Indo-European language family. In South Africa, seven million people speak it as a mother tongue, and ten million inhabitants speak Afrikaans as a second language. Afrikaans is also a spoken language in Botswana, Lesotho, Malawi, Namibia, Swaziland and Zambia.

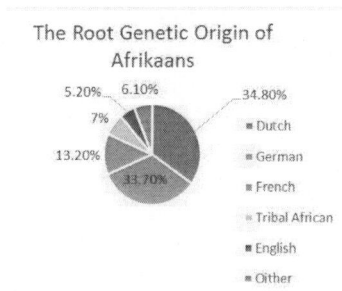

The Root Genetic Origin of Afrikaans

5.20% 6.10% 34.80%
7%
13.20%
33.70%

■ Dutch
■ German
■ French
■ Tribal African
■ English
■ Other

Afrikaners living Abroad

■ Australia 29%

38310
41676   155690
78616
227000

■ United Kingdom 42%
■ United States 15%
■ New Zealand 42%
■ Canada 7%

According to census figures, more than a million South African-born Afrikaners migrated to other countries. The pie-diagram reflects the dispersal. The 2006 census indicates that over five million Afrikaners lives in South Africa. In South Africa, the Afrikaner nation, inclusive of the *Cape Coloureds*, the citizens of Namibia, and all the countries that Afrikaners migrated to, can and do speak Afrikaans. The total number of speakers of Afrikaans decreased over time.

The Afrikaner nation developed over a period of one-hundred-and-fifty years with an own language, national identity, history and religion. By the time Britain colonised South Africa, the Afrikaner was a fully developed nation. They contrasted from the indigenous San and the Bantu-speaking peoples.

Conclusive Comments: Afrikaner or Euro-African?

Peoples of different ethnicities migrated to South Africa to populate an ancient barren land, at first vacant from any humans. The Khoikhoi and Bantu speaking people of colour came first. Followed by the imperialists. Early-on the Dutch in 1652, and then the French Huguenots in 1671. The British colonised the Cape in 1806.

The Afrikaner developed as a result of imperialism into an acknowledged nation in own right. For South Africans, colonisation and expansionism are realities; you cannot go back in time. The San, Khoisan, Khoikhoi, Dutch, British, Germans, French, Indo-Asian slaves, all played a part to form the South Africa of today. We need to accept and acknowledge the realities of life and history to move forward.

White Afrikaners are what we are, and I am what I am. We have the appearance of Europeans, but we live as Africans. Our ancestors over three-and-a-half centuries are African born. Even the South African Communist Party acknowledge in their constitution: *"South Africa belongs to the people living in the country."*

All the ethnicities of South Africa, past and present contributed and influenced my life. They made me what I am; a white-skinned Afrikaner and Euro-African. Do I resent my past, who I am, being an Afrikaner and descendant of the Boer nation? No, I do not. What I dislike I will consider in the next chapters, especially the Apartheid debacle and the Anglo-Boer-War.

There are some that would argue that colonisation started too late, and ended too early. Expansionism in countries like the USA, Canada, Australia and New Zealand resulted in western governments. Dream-on; the European nations that migrated to South Africa at no point constituted the majority.

In the following chapter, I will deal with the British colonisation of South Africa and the atrocious effects it had on the Afrikaner nation and South Africa.

CHAPTER 2

THE BRITISH OCCUPATION OF THE CAPE

The arrival of the British in Africa changed the continent. Especially South Africa and its peoples transformed and suffered as a result of British colonisation. The Anglo-Saxon way of life imparted on South Africa to this day rule and regulate society.

From Dutch Expansionism to British Colonialism

Previously I researched the establishment of the Afrikaner nation as a result of European expansionism. The imperialists in the form of first the Dutch and later the British affected my life from early on in my formative years. In fact, the incidence of Dutch imperialism lies way in the past. Even though it forms most of the DNA of my being, British colonialism has a more recent and identifiable effect on who I became.

The first British Governor of the Cape was Lord Charles Somerset. The Netherlands fell to the French, during the Revolutionary-Napoleon-War, which led to the British occupation of the Cape. The fall of the Netherlands rendered the Dutch holdings in the Cape vulnerable. British political leaders responded to the weakened Dutch position; they occupied the strategic and vital Port of the Cape in 1806. There was little resistance from the Dutch.

In 1814, Britain paid the Dutch six million pounds for the *Refreshment Post*; delighted with the harbour, a business transaction. The British Government, contrary to the Dutch East Indian Company, effectively introduced colonisation to Africa. They valued the Cape as an essential port on route to East Asia; also a valuable colony in their imperialistic expansion.

The 1820 British Settlers were an attempt by Britain to boost the English-speaking population of South Africa. Britain suffered severe unemployment after the Napoleonic wars; many white Britain's were impoverished. The Cape colonial government needed to defend the eastern frontier against the neighbouring Xhosa peoples. It led to the establishment of Albany, an Anglo-Saxon island in a predominantly Xhosa and Afrikaans-speaking Eastern Cape. Ninety thousand prospective British Settlers applied of which four thousand were approved. They arrived in the Cape between April and June 1820. The settlers were given farms, supplies, food and equipment and settled near the village of Bathurst.

Their lack of agricultural experience forced many of them to settle in Bathurst, and towns like Grahams town, East London and Port Elizabeth while a group continued onto Natal. They obtained permission from the Zulu King Shaka to stay on the land in return for advanced technology related to firearms.

Even today the white people in the Eastern Cape are predominantly English speaking. The names of towns and cities still reflect the Anglo-Saxon heritage.

Boer-British Clash and the Start of Boer Migration

The Boers gradually migrated far inland from the Cape, not thoroughly acquainted with the British colonial masters in the Cape Colony. The British proved to be better governors with strict laws and sure to clash with those of the Boers. The Boers did not appreciate the interference of the British. The manner in which the Boers' managed their slaves did not meet with the approval of the British.

Interference by the British with the Boer slavery might be perceived a bit rich; themselves being active in the slave trade. In the 17th century, they moved forty-two thousand of the eighty-thousand chained and shackled African slaves to America.

To be fair, the British Empire abolished slavery, by the Slavery Abolition Act of 1833, shortly after the occupation of the Cape Colony. The British frowned on the ill-treatment of slaves by the

Boers. Their interference is understandable; the Brits needed to show that they moved on from slavery.

The Boers however, were not beyond reproach when it came to handling their slaves, they treated their slaves like animals. Slaves were the Boers' property. They received Western names and their native cultures displaced for western cultures.

The self-proclaimed Khoikhoi leader Hennie van Wyk is an example of the name change. Even though he claimed to be a Khoisan, he has a Dutch name. Slaves had to become an extension of their owner. Boers punished slaves when caught stealing, or doing something untoward in the eyes of their masters. Chastisement varied from cutting-off fingers, noses and ears along with branding them with red-hot irons on their cheeks. Like you would brand an animal.

The British interference with Boer slaves changed the matters in South Africa. The hanging of five Boers as slave-owners by the British in 1815, at *Slachters Nek*, was a defining act that drove a wedge of hatred between Brit and Boer. Boers refused to appear in British courts leading to the execution of five Boers. The hanging resulted in the first *Boer martyrs* under British rule. A painting of the execution structure is on show in the Slachters' Nek Exhibition at Somerset East, Eastern Cape.

The following is a quote from the Slachters' neck web blog: *"Four of the nooses broke during the procedure as the hangman who came to perform the execution had not realised there were five to be hung; he had to use old ropes. The four whose nooses broke, as well as the public, pleaded for their lives. British General Jacob Glen Cuyler ordered that they hang a second time, and they swung one by one. The names of the five who hung were Hendrik Prinsloo, Stephanus Bothma, Abraham Bothma, Cornelius Faber and Theunis de Klerk. The clash between the British and Boers would continue for years to come. On 9th March 1916, exactly 100 years after the execution, a monument was unveiled on the spot where the hanging took place."*

The execution resulted in the intense hatred among the Boers against the British and also contributed to the Great Trek of 1838. The oppression and subjugation of the Boers by the British ultimately culminated in the Anglo-Boer-Wars. The desire for self-governance intensified as a result of the rift between Boer and Brit. Did the self-governance-desire lead to the atrocity of Apartheid? Probably.

Apartheid and colonialism excluded non-whites from the political process right from the outset. Neither the Dutch, British nor Afrikaner wanted to share political power with the people of colour.

The British land-grab did not end in the Cape, it extended far to the North, along with the Fish River up to Grahams Town. Cultural assault on the Boer Nation intensified with Anglicisation in 1827. British missionaries replaced the Dutch ministers. Ministries took cause with African cases of any Boer slave masters' injustices. Boers became irritated with the interference of the British.

The Great Trek: Afrikaner Boers Occupying the North

Compensation for liberated slaves was only available in London. Due to the distance and cost, the Boers were not able to turn their claims into pay-outs. In revolt, Piet Retief led three thousand Boers away from the Cape to the North in what became known as the *Great Trek*. The image portrays a typical ox waggon used in the Great Trek.

The Boers established their own Republic of Natalia with Pietermaritzburg as the capital. The British claimed that the Cape Colony's jurisdiction applied in KwaZulu Natal. The Boers responded by moving back over the Drakensberg Mountains. They moved further north to the Transvaal High Veld crossing the Orange River, away from the British.

I traced the Cronje family history, back to the time of the Great Trek. My ancestors settled in the North-East of the Orange Free State. My grandfather lived on a farm called *Wolwehoek* and incarcerated in the Springfontein concentration camp as a ten-year-old.

The Great Trek of 1838, resulted in the establishment of two independent Boer Republics named the *Transvaal* and the *Orange Free State*. Britain, recognised the republics as ordained by the Sand River (1852) and Bloemfontein (1854) Conventions.

Cecil John Rhodes: Pioneer of Imperialism and Apartheid

Cecil John Rhodes is well known for his beliefs as an architect of the British Empire in Africa. He made his imperial views known when he proclaimed: *"I contend that we, the British are the first preferred race in the world and that the more of the world we inhabit, the better it is for the human race. Just fancy those parts that are at present inhabited by the most despicable specimen of a human being, what an alteration there would be in them if they were brought under Anglo-Saxon influence. If there be a God, I think that is what he would like me to do; paint as much of the map of Africa as British Red as possible."*

A most despicable specimen of a human being?

History might pardon Rhodes for his derogatory comment. The Africans were under-developed and crude in the late 19th century. Maybe there was a noble endeavour to develop and uplift the African people. But, in the outcome, the non-white peoples of South Africa are still impoverished. They are today the neglected ethnic groups.

Although Rhodes' imperial aspirations are well known; his Apartheid views are not that well known. He voiced the first proposals on legalising Apartheid in 1889. It is fitting that the legacy of Rhodes be unravelled to understand modern time social ills like *democratisation, de-whiting and black-on-white hate crimes.*

As Prime Minister, Rhodes enjoyed the support of English-speaking white and non-white voters, along with that of Afrikaners. Rhodes's British South African Company (BSAC) served as an active sponsorship in his election.

Rhodes bought the farm Vooruitzicht, from the brothers, De Beer, in April 1888. The purchase culminated in the De Beers Consolidated Mines with his partner Rudd. Rhodes became the secretary and invested 200 000 pounds in the venture; he owned the majority shares.

Barney Barnato, the owner of the Kimberley mine, wrote the following about Rhodes: *"When you have been with him half an hour you not only agree with him but come to believe you have always held his opinion. No one else in the world could have induced me to go into this partnership. But Rhodes had an extraordinary ascendancy over men: he tied them up, as he ties up everybody. It is his way. You can't resist him; you must be with him."*

Rhodes became an incredibly wealthy man and understood the relationship between money and power; it was the power he sought. In conversation with Hans Sauer, while looking over the Kimberley diamond mine, Sauer asked of Rhodes: *"What do you see?"* Rhodes answered with a slow sweep of his hand: *"I see power."*

The Cape Colony in 1877 incorporated Griqualand West as part of the British colony. The Cape Colony allocated six seats in the Cape House of Assembly to Griqualand. In 1880 Rhodes entered public life. Rhodes stood for the constituency of Barkley West. At age 29 the Barkley West constituency elected Rhodes as its parliamentary representative. Rhodes continued as the Barkley West member until his death.

It is reasonable to consider the *Glen Grey Act,* promulgated by Rhodes in 1894, as the portent to Apartheid. Tribal Africa did not believe in the land as owned individually. Africans held the political belief that land belonged to the peoples as a nation; it is the property of anybody and everybody. The Act of 1894 changed this tribal partisan custom. The Glen Grey Act legalised individual land tenure. The ruling replaced tribal and communal ownership with private ownership in favour of white people.

Glen Grey is situated in Lady Frere, in the Eastern Cape and became part of the Transkei. The Act levied a labour tax, forcing the Xhosa into employment on commercial farms or in industry. In July 1894, Rhodes introduced the *Native Bill* to the Cape Parliament. The *Native Bill for Africa* forced more Africans into the wage-labour market. The *Bill* would provide forced labour for Rhodes's mining in Kimberley and the Transvaal.

Rhodes believed innate idleness among blacks does not contribute to the wealth of the country. He preferred not to impart the United States' forced labour problems in South Africa. According to the Civil War Trust of America, the cause of the war was differences between the free northern states and slave states in the south. Abraham Lincoln, the Republican president, wanted no slavery. The southern Confederate wished to retain their slave labour; their economy was dependent on slavery and forced labour. More than three million soldiers fought on both sides in the American Civil War of which six-hundred-and-twenty-thousand died. One-hundred-thousand more than in both World-Wars combined.

Naturally, Rhodes realised the extremes of the war in America caused by slavery. He wanted to put the people of colour to work but not to repeat the mistakes of America.

Rhodes addressed Parliament by stating that the indigenous African issue should not be a concern of anxiety. He alleged that people of colour could be a source of help to white people. He based his reasoning on the supposition that the whites maintain their position as the supreme race. Rhodes retained that the Europeans should be grateful to have the natives in their midst, primarily as a source of labour. That should remain the proper connexion regulating the black-white relationship.

Rhodes arrogantly accepted responsibility for the about two millions of people in the Colony. When Rhodes considered the present state of people of colour, he concluded that Africans multiplied excessively. The solution to this he suggested was to allocate specific land areas to Africans. Within these demarcated regions they will be herded together. Africans will live on the land but hold no title of ownership. Rhodes proclaimed that the people of colour would not share in the government; he believed that was the correct thing to do. The African should not have any; *"… interest in the local development of their country."*

In 1894, Rhodes's constitutional promulgations represented the first initiative giving rise and effect to Apartheid. Verwoerd held the same beliefs more than a half-a-century later. Verwoerd addressed the Apartheid Parliament on education when he voiced almost verbatim the same sentiments.

Rhodes believed that the natives would be useful in building civil, industrial and agricultural infrastructure. He pointed out that the government do not employ the native labour force in the present time adequately. Rhodes concluded that instead of fighting among themselves in civil conflict, putting them to work would occupy their minds. He believed a labour addition would be much more productive. Rhodes considered it the responsibility of the Colonial powers: *"… to teach them the dignity of labour, instead of loaf about in sloth and laziness."* He affirmed his stance by pointing out that Africans do not go out to work. Rhodes specified that it is a failure of the government not to consider the native population as a source of labour.

Rhodes vociferously emphasised that there should be no white men in the African allocated areas. Rhodes stressed that the natives should not be part of white people. There should be no intermingling. In Rhodes's words: *"The Government looks upon them as living on a native reserve…"* Rhodes specifically excluded blacks from political rights to the transfer and alienation of land.

He considered it a failure of the government to put the natives on equal footing with whites.

Rhodes in an address to Parliament concluded by saying:

"If we deal with them differently and say, 'Yes, these people have their own ideas,' and so on, then we are all right. But, when once we depart from that position and put them on an equality with ourselves, we may give the matter up. As to the question of voting, we say that the natives are in a sense citizens, but not altogether citizens they are still children."

Cecil John Rhodes and Hendrik Frensch Verwoerd might have lived more than a half-a-century apart. But, they sang from the same hymn sheet. The content of the *Glen Grey Act along with the African Native Bill* reflects pure racism. The Act is as crude and discriminatory as the Afrikaner Apartheid government's legislation. In all honesty, I believe that Verwoerd was not that innovative. He took his cue from Rhodes when he designed the Apartheid policies.

The *Act and Bill* reduced people of colour to sub-human beings; it stripped them not only of their political rights but efficiently of their human rights. By 1895, Rhodes was dominant and the master of South Africa. He ruled over the nation white and black, controlling nearly all of the world's diamonds and much of its gold. Rhodes governed three colonial dependencies in the heart of Africa.

Cecil Rhodes and Alfred Beit orchestrated the Jameson Raid of 1895. The Raid lasted only five days and started on 29 December 1895. The British colonial statesman Leander Starr Jameson led the failed attack. Rhodes' *British South Africa Company (BSAC) police* in the employ of Beit along with the Bechuanaland police forcefully marched against the Boer Republic of the Transvaal. The objective was to start a revolt by British expatriate mine workers; named as *the Johannesburg conspirators*. Rhodes and his plotters incited the mine workers to concoct an insurgency against the Boer Republic. Paul Kruger was president of the republic. The ex-pat mine workers in the Transvaal failed in their rebellious effort; no uprising happened. However, the consequence of the Jameson Raid served as an incitement to the Anglo-Boer-Wars and the Matabele Wars.

Rhodes fell from power when his role in the Jameson Raid became public knowledge. Rhodes resigned as Prime Minister and head of the British South Africa Company (BSAC). Rhodes had many friends among the Afrikaners for many years. The Afrikaners saw his support of the Jameson Raid as an overthrow attempt of the Transvaal Boer Republic government. The Bondsmen of Afrikaners saw this as a complete betrayal.

Rhodes continued his political activities. In mid-1896 the Shona and Ndebele attacked the colonial oppressors in an effort of liberation from oppression. Rhodes took charge and attacked the Ndebele and Shona. He was grossly malicious, resorting to a *scorched earth policy*, destroying the Shona and Ndebele villages and crops.

In the *Anglo-Boer-War, Lord Horatio Kitchener took the Scorched Earth Policy* of Rhodes a step further. He introduced the British concentration camps. He incarcerated more than hundred-thousand Boer women and children, starving and killing more than forty-thousand.

Rhodes, in the end, decided on reconciliation with the northern tribes. He negotiated a peace settlement with the Ndebele and Shona. During talks, Africans explained their uprising against the colonial powers to Rhodes. The Tribal Chiefs complained that for decades, Africans had been humiliated by white colonists and pushed into forced labour. Rhodes promised an end to the derogative treatment. Africans conceded they would end hostilities. The Ndebele and Shona chiefs believed that their grievances would justly be recognised. Africans seized attacks against the colonisers. The Africans praised Rhodes as the *Umlamulanmkunzi;* Ndebele for the peacemaker.

The Anglo-Boer-War broke out in October 1899. Rhodes endeavoured to organise the defence of Kimberley. With his health deteriorating he travelled to Europe. Shortly after his return to the Cape, he died on 26 March 1902 at Muizenberg near Cape Town. Reportedly some of his last words were, *"so little done, so much to do."* Rhodes' burial took place at the Matopos Hills in Zimbabwe.

Rhodes' never married, his legacy included £6 million. Most of his wealth donated to Oxford University. He established Rhodes scholarships for students from the United States, the British colonies, and Germany.

Considering Rhodes' African legacy, relating to the harm done to Africa, his bequest is much less philanthropic and moral. Remembered as the architect of so many evils in the eyes of mainly the African, but also the Afrikaner. *Par excellence,* Rhodes enhances his contribution as the father of British Imperialism and Colonialism along with Apartheid and the Scorched Earth War method.

The Newberry - Prynnsberg Estate

It is just astonishing how history is like a wheel. What happened in South Africa, around the 1890's diamond exploration era, came about within my life today in England. My British friends in England, Graham and Jenny Newberry, uncovered a connection dating back to the 1890 diamond era of South Africa. The discovery of diamonds and gold is the age when my ancestors opposed the British in the Anglo Boer War. I write about the Cronje family in the Anglo-Boer-War later in this chapter.

I met the Newberry family when I relocated to England in January 2000. Graham recently introduced me to the South African connection. I do not know whether Graham and Jenny were aware of their ancestral links to South Africa when they immigrated to South Africa in the 1960/80's. They lived in Cape Town for some time. Graham and Jennie's two children, Nick and Kate, were born in South Africa. Today the Newberry and Cronje families are inter-related in more ways than in the nineteenth century.

Charles Newberry, an ancestor to Graham Newberry, played a significant role in the diamond exploration era of South Africa. Charles Newberry emigrated to South Africa in 1864. The Kimberly Mines opened in 1872. Charles joined his older brother John on the diamond fields, between 1881 and 1884, in the hottest Kimberly sun. The Newberry brothers dug for diamonds in Grey town. Charles gained sufficient holdings to become a shareholder in Cecil John Rhodes's Central Mining Company. Rhodes consolidated all the independent claims to create De Beers Mining Company. Today, De Beers Mining Company holds a significant share in the South African Stock Exchange. Later, I will explain the Rhodes's holdings that became the Anglo-American Company, in more detail.

Charles Newberry and his brother John attained substantial assets in Rhodes's De Beers Mining Company. John Newberry became a director of the newly formed De Beers Mining Company. By that time, Charles Newberry gained enough fortunes in the Kimberly diamond mining industry. He moved on from active mining to property ownership.

While on a trip to the Eastern Free State, Charles fell in love with Elizabeth Daniel, the daughter of Rev John Daniel. Rev John headed a Lesotho based British missionary. Charles decided to make the Eastern Free State his home. Along with his new wife, he set about the fulfilment of his dream. Charles wanted to build a classic English country estate in the African wilds. He purchased the property from a man named Prynn. In 1881, Charles Newberry built his mansion. He christened it Prynnsberg.

The estate in its heyday covered over 20,000 hectares of land on the edge of the Maloti Mountain. Situated under a sandstone cliff in the Thaba'Nchu District, the house turned into a Manor of national esteem in later years. It started off as an original single-story farmhouse and became a three-story, twenty-room mansion. Constructed out of finely crafted sandstone in the African veldt, it included two churches, a vicarage, a gamekeepers' lodge, stables and various outbuildings.

The Prynnsberg Manor, built in the style of old-world grandeur, became a national gem. The London firm James Shoolbred and Company, of Tottenham Court Road, decorated the estate. Adornments to the interior included large rooms covered in gold leaf and flocked wallpapers. Part of the decorations incorporated intricate oak parquet, pressed leather panelling, rococo plastered ceilings, gilded cornices, elaborately tiled fireplaces and teak doors. The windows embellished with Victorian style stained glass with ornate friezes. The energy supply to the manor was a 700-Volt D.C. – Dynamo, powering the machinery and refrigerators.

From 1884 to 1900, Charles and his wife Elizabeth established a private museum with many cultural artefacts. The collection included the most exquisite Nguni, Zulu and other tribal sculptured art. The Egyptian relics on the Prynnsberg estate came from the famous English Egyptologist Guy Brunton. Guy married Charles' eldest daughter Winifred. Winifred made a name for herself through her art. She created many murals and paintings within the house.

When Charles was head of Prynnsberg, he employed seventeen Europeans on the estate. They included a horticulturist, forester, tutor, two farm managers, stone cutters, masons and other functionaries. Prynnsberg welcomed members from the African Elite as guests to the Manor. Under the dignitaries counted: Lord Milner, the Duke of Westminster, President Steyn as President to the Orange Free State Boer Republic and Rudyard Kipling. Kipling painted a frieze of Noah's ark in the night nursery.

Interesting, Lord Kitchener, as co- executioner with Lord Milner of the Scorched Earth Policy during the Anglo Boer war, does not appear to have been a visitor to Prynnsberg.

For the duration of the Anglo-Boer-War, 1899 to 1902, Charles

Newberry as an owner to Prynnsberg, with his family, moved back to Surrey, England.

With military connections such as Lord Milner, it is not surprising that Prynnsberg remained unharmed during the Anglo-Boer-War. The estate sits amongst a myriad of Boer farms, destroyed by the Lords Kitchener and Milner's British Scorched Earth Policy, during the Anglo-Boer-War.

Due to neglect and failure in the inheritance line, Prynnsberg entered into administration. The estate and its contents sold at auction in 1996. Prynnsberg lost much of the family heirlooms and portraits. Luckily, before the general sale took place, a man Ed Smith, purchased over three-hundred cultural artefacts and relocated them to a museum in San Diego.

Prynnsberg became the property of the present owner Rick Melvill. He restored Prynnsberg back to some of its olden-day charms.

My friends, Graham and Jenny Newberry, is today the proud owners of the River Bank Guest House in Matlock, Derbyshire. The guest-house lodges within an ancient Victorian building with old worldly trimmings and embellishments.

Kate, the daughter of Graham and Jennie, is the proud owner of Café in the Park. A century-old Victorian timber building embraces the Café in the Park, situated in Hall Leys Park, one of the oldest parks in Matlock. And, most amazingly, my wife Melanie, has been managing Café in the Park, along with Kate, for the last decade; and, if I may say, very successfully.

History has a way of interconnecting incidents and families over centuries. The Newberry's life rests comfortably within the heritage of their ancestors as remnants of Victorian times. Once again, if I may mention, very similar and with exceptional entrepreneurial proficiency.

My Cronje ancestors are central to South African history, inclusive of the Great Trek, British Occupation and the Anglo-

Boer-War. And here I am writing my biography; filled with facts and fiction of the British Imperial Era, the Anglo-Boer-War and Afrikaner Great Trek Expedition.

Who says history is boring and unrelated to present-day life? I just love all the intricacies of life over centuries. I celebrate the relevance along with my new-found British friends; the extended Newberry family.

The Diamond and Gold Rush

African tribal rulers had treaty relationships with the British in the Cape Colony. These African statesmen were less impressed with the Boers. The Boers enslaved their children, stole their cattle, and destroyed their property. The Cape British authorities did not approve of the Boers' actions either. For many years, the Africans and Boers lived with a deep suspicion of each other's presence. This animosity further entrenched the segregation of the South African nation.

Not all Boers left with the Great Trek; many remained in the Cape. Some resentful of the British but unwilling to abandon their farms and homesteads. They adapted to the way of life in the Cape Colony and formed an influential Afrikaner political minority. Some even pro-British, an alliance that gave rise to the United Party of the 1940s; they remained loyal to Britain.

A 21-carat diamond was discovered close to the Orange River in 1867, followed by a further 83-carat diamond exposed in March 1869. These findings led to the Kimberley diamond rush. At the end of 1870, and spurred on by wealthy fortune hunters from all over, even abroad, many flocked to the new Diamond Fields. Ownership of land was in dispute, the Griqua and Tlhaping tribes in the Northern Cape lived on the property and claimed the diamond fields as their territory. The Orange Free State Boer Republic asserted rights to the area by the Bloemfontein Convention. The Griqua regarded the British as the lesser of two evils and demanded

British protection against the Boers. An independent arbitrator found for the Griqua against the Orange Free State. The British annexed Griqualand in 1871, proclaimed it as a Crown Colony in 1873 and by 1880 it was incorporated into the British Cape Colony.

In 1871, four *diamond pipes* opened. The town of Kimberley, turned into an open-mine quarry, worked by 2,500 miners and 10,000 hired labourers. The Kimberley diamond industry established in 1880 and new investment along with a myriad of fortune seekers flocked to South Africa.

With the support of the Griqua, Britain successfully expanded its colonial authority. The worth of colonisation for the Griqua did not materialise. In the end, the diamond-rich area benefitted the British. Cecil John Rhodes played a determining role in the British Imperialistic advance in South Africa.

The British Imperialists flourished in the mining of diamonds and gold in South Africa; there can be no doubt for whose benefit. Almost exclusively for the British Empire and capitalists, not the Griqua or the Boers.

Gold was first discovered in 1870 near Polokwane, followed by more significant discoveries at Pilgrim's Rest in 1873, and Barberton in 1885. Austere and extensive mining started in 1887, a mere twelve years before the Anglo-Boer-War.

The results by the end of 1887, were astonishing, it was clear that the Rand mines were incredibly rich in gold. The discovery of gold led to the rapid growth of the new township of Johannesburg with explorers from abroad. The discovery of gold changed South Africa. To the geographic misfortune of the British Cape Colony, the gold deposits were in the Boer Republic of Transvaal,

The interrelated factors that led to the Second Anglo-Boer War of 1899 included British imperialism, the discovery of gold and diamonds and Afrikaner nationalism. The British attempted to annexe the Boer Republics. The Boers retaliated and launched an attack on the British, causing the annexation to fail.

The Kimberley diamond millionaires moved north to new headquarters in Johannesburg, growing into the most substantial capital in Southern Africa. Today Johannesburg is the 10th largest city in Africa. Gold production manifested and reinforced the capitalistic drive behind colonisation. It also enforced the capitalistic drive leading to the Anglo-Boer-War. The fortunes were enormous, given what was on offer, Britain was euphoric in their capitalistic drive.

Anglo American holdings are split equally between the United Kingdom and America. Within South Africa, Anglo-American Inc. holds half of its operations with interests in gold, diamond, platinum and iron ore.

Anglo-American extracted forty million pounds worth of gold before the Anglo-Boer-War. This wealth presented a real motivation to go to war. The gold-fortune does not include the profits after 1902. To this day British-owned Anglo-American gold mines benefit from the gold and diamond reserves of South Africa. Although coal and platinum added to the fortunes, it was the discovery of gold and diamonds that tipped the scale for the capitalists; once again claiming riches under the umbrella of Imperialism.

The empire of De Beers is now one of about six-hundred companies associated with *South Africa Inc.*; the Anglo-American Corporation of South Africa domiciled at 44 Main Street, Johannesburg. The Anglo-American conglomerate controls South African gold mines as well as the De Beers diamond mines and owns half of the capitalisation of the Johannesburg Stock Exchange.

Cecil John Rhodes played a determining role in instigating the Anglo-Boer-War. His plot involving the Jameson Raid to overthrow the Transvaal Boer Republic I explained in great detail earlier

The *Mammon-Itch* grabbed the attention of the British colonial masters. Greed for the ultimate riches and the wealth-grab triggered the Anglo-Boer War. Britain had to occupy the gold fields for the British Empire; so, to war they had to go.

South Africa

The Anglo-Boer-Wars

The Anglo-Boer-War dotted area corresponds to the gold and the diamond-rich regions on this map, from Kimberly in the south to the gold-rich part of the north; the two Boer Republics, Transvaal and Orange Free State. Ever since 1870, it was clear to the British that the diamond and gold reserves in the two Boer Republics were substantial, it served as an enticing development for capitalism. The diamond and gold wealth was the drive behind going to war; it was all for capitalism, greed and money. Capitalism from the start, and once again, brought the imperial expansionists into play. Mineral riches, the motivation that gave rise to further colonisation.

The timing of Britain in the first attempt of annexation made complete sense. It coincided with the gold and diamond discoveries. The initial effort of British occupation in 1877 failed because the Boers opposed the annexation. British failure led to the First Anglo-Boer War 1880-1881. Once again the Boers defeated the British, corroborating the independence of the Boer Republics.

During African colonisation, it was standard European practice. When the local oppressed nations resisted, the colonial masters would deploy an overwhelming task force to quash the uprising.

Britain did not take the defeat lying down. It retaliated with an imperial military force of 550,000 soldiers from all over the British Empire. Britain waged war against 150,000 Boer warriors from the two Boer Republics, Transvaal and Orange Free State. The second Anglo-Boer-War of 1899-1902 ensued and involved South Africans across the ethnic divide. White and black people participated in the war. It was a war between the South African Nation, led by the Afrikaner-Boer nation and the mighty British Empire. The British called it the Boer Wars, the Boers called it the Wars of Independence, and today it is known as the Anglo-Boer-Wars.

The Anglo-Boer-War efforts coincided with the Colonial Secretary, Lord Carnarvon's endeavour to establish a Confederation of Southern African states. The foreseen confederation would be similar to the Canadian Federation of States established in1867. The objective, greater economic integration and progress under the British Empire. The discovery of gold and diamonds suited Carnarvon's imperial aspirations entirely.

The British fought conventional set-piece battles, opposing forces facing each other in hand-to-hand combat. The hundred-and-fifty-thousand Boers met an overwhelming force of more than half-a-million British soldiers; they had no alternative but to resort to guerrilla warfare. The Boers lodged surprise attacks on unsuspected British units. The guerrilla warfare tactics kept the British army at bay. The British underestimated the Boer commandos. They perceived the Boers to be a backwards, incompetent and only a rural enemy.

The British Government was embarrassed by their lack of success; their casualties amounted to more than double that of the Boers. The British suffered many losses at the hands of the Boers. It was the bloodiest, longest, and most expensive war Britain encountered for more than a century. Britain spent more than 200 million pounds on the war effort.

Reports of deaths and casualties of the war are confusing. Aside from the chaos, the following statistics convincingly illustrate the extremity of the war. A BBC report of 24 June 2010 reported that 55,000 British soldiers died along with 12,000 that perished of diseases. The British soldier fatalities were double that of Boer deaths. The number of Brits missing and injured amounted to close on 34,000. In total casualties on the British side amounted to more than a 100 000.

Another source claims that on the Boer's side, close on 23,000 Boer soldiers died while 73,000 were wounded and fell sick. 26,000 Boer women and children as non-combatant deaths, perished in the concentration camps due to malnutrition and disease. They did not record the total number of African deaths in the concentration camps. The estimated black deaths are 13,000 to 20,000. The loss on the white and black South Africans amounted to more than 130 000. Only 23 000 were actual combatant deaths; half of the British fatalities.

Statistics can be confusing, but the figures quoted, amounted to more than 250 000 lives affected and lost in the Anglo-Boer-War; not considering the physical and mental damage to the two nations.

The destruction of the two Boer Republics and the hurt to Boer-Afrikaner moral is infinite. The damage inflicted is extreme and mind-boggling. The death and destruction were excessively evil; war is a messy business. I am not even trying to determine the exact figures. The war was a disaster; it wiped 15% of the Boer nation off the face of the earth. The dwindling numbers of Boer-Afrikaners over half-a-century are significant.

Ultimately, the Anglo-Boer-War losses along with the white-brain-drain and black-on-white hate crimes of the democratisation era reduced the Afrikaner to less than 10% of the South African Nation in 2017. The white Afrikaner should total at least 35% as a proportion of the South African nation in modern times. I write extensively about all of the above in later chapters.

British Concentration Camps

The British were not the first to deploy the concentration camp system. The first was used as a war strategy in 1896, by the Spanish in Cuba, leaving more than 100,000 dead. Three years later in 1899, the United States of America used concentration camps in the Philippines. Up to a quarter of a million civilians died in that war. Even Cecil John Rhodes applied the Concentration Camp system in the North, crushing the Ndebele Shona revolt before the start of the Anglo-Boer-War

The British implemented the South African concentration camp system in the same year 1899; did they learn from the Americans? The Americans were their partners in the gold mining exploration and wealth grabbing! They took a page from Cecil John Rhodes' book.

In all four instances, the concentration camp system was a containing deterrent against a natural enemy that resorted to guerrilla warfare. The native nation fought an overwhelming occupying colonial force. It is clear that countries learn from each other's methods in war. The British had to rescue their failing war effort. Did they learn from the Americans to secure the Anglo-American mineral fortunes? Did the Boers learn from native countries fighting occupying colonial forces?

The colonial occupying forces had to find a way to control the local citizens who they targeted as the enemy of the occupier. The Boers were not original natives of the land before 1652. They lived as a nation for one hundred and fifty years in South Africa. They developed into an established nation and considered the Boer Republics as Afrikaner land. Britain acknowledged this claim by the two Boer Republic conventions. The Boer Republics were practically independent States.

Scorched Earth Policy and British Concentration Camps

"All is fair in love and war, or is it?"

With the aid of *Lord Kitchener's Scorched Earth Policy*, the British overpowered the Boers in the end. Concentration camps not only swayed the war to the benefit of the British but devastated the Boer nation. The war also had embarrassing consequences for the British in the eyes of the world. British oppression of the Boer nation during the Anglo-Boer War included some incredibly evil measures. The Troops of Lord Kitchener captured and incarcerated Boer women and children along with black workers from farms in Concentration Camps. Kitchener had to destroy the farms to isolate the Boer warriors from farm supplies. They burnt down crops and kill all livestock, depleting the food provisions to the Boer fighters.

The *Scorched Earth Policy* was implemented to advance the British war effort and to reduce the heavy casualties suffered by the British at the hand of the Boer-Guerrilla fighters. The conditions in the camps were appalling. Famine and unhygienic conditions in the camps caused the death of thousands of women and children along with thousands of black people in separate camps for blacks. Apart from the destruction and loss of life, the British deported thousands of men to prisoner camps, some of them as young as nine years of age.

The Hitler-Kitchener Connection

Shockingly there are suggestions that Germany learnt lessons from the British camps and applied the lessons in the Nazi concentration camps. Naturally, the Germans added much more cruelty and genocide in the Nazi camps; they just administered the murder camps *crueller*. Adolf Hitler came to power in 1933. He appointed Hermann Wilhelm Göring as commander-in-chief of the Luftwaffe (German Airforce). Göring became the second-most powerful man in Germany. Commencing the Second World War, the British Ambassador to Germany protested to Göring about the ill-treatment of Gypsies and Jews in the German concentration camps. The web blog *AVClub.com* claims that Göring pulled out an encyclopaedia, providing proof of the appalling treatment of Boer people in British concentration camps during the Anglo-Boer-War. The revelation left the British Ambassador at an embarrassed disadvantage. It impressed on him that the British, as part inventors of concentration camps, cannot call the German pot black.

It might just actually be that Germany did copy practices learnt from the British. Too far-fetched? Nope, not if we consider the congruent and cruel characteristics of concentration camps worldwide; they did learn from each other. There might not be waterproof evidence, but the images freely published seem to be proof enough; *AVClub.com* claims that it is the truth. The suspicion hangs in the air like a dark thundercloud.

Emily Hobhouse – British Heroin - Boer Philanthropist

Emily Hobhouse is a British lady and philanthropist, well remembered for campaigning to change the conditions inside the British concentration camps. In January 1902, Emily lobbied to visit concentration camps. Lord Kitchener, disallowed her to attend camps north of Bloemfontein. In January 1902 ten concentration camps were established in the Northern Cape, Free State and Transvaal. Emily Hobhouse visited most of the camps and was appalled at the conditions. By 28 February 1902 a further six camps were established in the Transvaal Boer Republic.

On 17 June 1902, British Prime Minister David Lloyd-George condemned the concentration camps along with the horrors inflicted on women and children. He warned, *"A barrier of dead children's bodies will rise between the British and Boer races in South Africa."* Prophetic words, the Boer nation hated the British as a result of the camps. The concentration camp atrocities were the determining impetus that inspired the Afrikaner's post-war self-determination yearnings. Ultimately the urge transpired in the hated Afrikaner Apartheid regime.

On the 18th of June 1902, Emily Hobhouse's published a damning report on concentration camps. In summary, Emily stated: *"Numbers of Boers crowded into small tents, some sick and some dying; occasionally the dead among the living. Scanty rations dealt out raw; lack of fuel to cook the food and lack of water for drinking or cooking. No water for washing and lack of soap, brushes and other instruments. Personal cleanliness is lacking, no beds and bedding, bodies on the bare earth. Lack of clothing for warmth and in many cases for decency ... "* She suggested the abolishment of the cruel concentration camp system.

Legend of Lizzie van Zyl

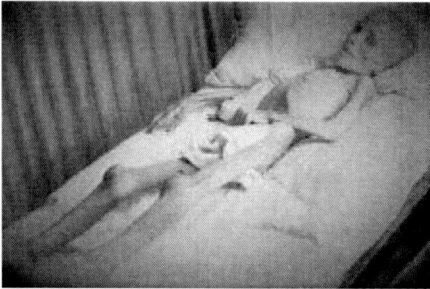

With accreditation to and in compliance with South African History On line: Article by Emily Hobhouse and accompanying image. "Lizzie Van Zyl who died in the Bloemfontein concentration camp, 1902" from South African History Online, www.sahistory.org.za

I quote an event recalled by Emily Hobhouse, as included in the book: *Stemme uit die Verlede* – (Voices from the Past). Hobhouse relayed the facts of young Lizzie van Zyl. She was for all practical purposes left to die in the Bloemfontein concentration camp: *"She was a frail, weak little child in desperate need of good care. But, because her mother was one of the undesirables she was maltreated; her father neither surrendered nor betrayed his people. Lizzie placed on the lowest rations and left to perish of hunger, after a month in the camp, transferred to the new small hospital; her treatment was not only harsh but deadly crude. The English sent a doctor and nurses to her who did not understand her language; she could not speak English. They labelled her an idiot even though the girl was mentally fit and reasonable. One day she dejectedly started calling for her mother, a Mrs Botha attended and consoled her; telling the child that she would soon see her mother again. Brusquely interrupted, one of the nurses told her not to interfere with the child as she was a nuisance."* Lizzie died in the concentration camp as a result of neglect and starvation. Interesting, in later chapters, I relate to President P W Botha's mother incarcerated in the concentration camps. Is it possible that she was the Mrs Botha trying to console Lizzie? One can but wonder.

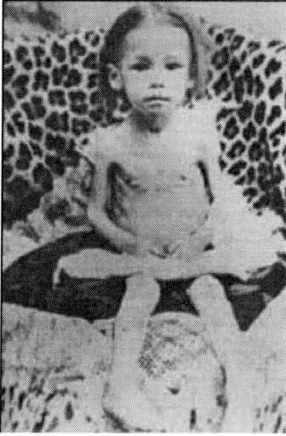

With accreditation and compliance with www.pinterest.co.uk "Boer child in a British Concentration Camp, Anglo-Boer War"

https://www.pinterest.co.uk/pin/423338433698135104/

Set on breaking the morale of the Boer nation, Lord Kitchener made some atrocious suggestions to John Broderick, British Secretary of State for War. Broderick replied to Kitchener: *"Your idea of sending the Boer women to St Helena Island and telling their husbands that they would never return, seems difficult to work out. We cannot permanently keep 16,000 males and females in ring fences, and they are not a marketable commodity in other lands."* This comment seems very crude and inhumane; *marketable and commodity?* Are they talking about people? One comes to the conclusion that the Boer people were treated worse than animals.

On 26 July 1902, Emily Hobhouse once again complained to Broderick on refusing her inclusion to the Ladies Commission; she reiterated that the refusal was only down to the British authorities. On 27 July, John Broderick responded saying: *"The only consideration for ladies to visit the Concentration Camps, will be for particular work. Any suspicion of partiality to the system or the reverse would exclude them."* The War Department apparently did not want their atrocities investigated by people sympathetic to the maltreated Boer people; they obscured the crimes committed in the camps.

Because of her empathy with the concentration camp victims, the British deported Emily Hobhouse from the war zone; her compassion did not sit well with the British.

She wrote to the two British commanders in charge of the camps. First, she wrote to Lord Kitchener: *"I hope that in future you will exercise greater width of judgement in the discharge of your high office. To carry out orders such as these is a degradation both to the office and the manhood of your soldiers. I feel ashamed to own you as a fellow-countryman."*

To Lord Milner, she wrote the following: *"Your brutal orders have been carried out, and thus I hope you will be satisfied. Your narrow incompetency to see the real issues of this great struggle is leading you to such acts as this and many others, straining your name and the reputation of England."* She concluded that; *"the concentration camps are the most efficient method of barbarism and serve as murder camps."*

In addition to the concentration camp atrocities, further reports on British carnages came to light. A firing squad executed Cornelius Broeksma after he was found guilty of breaking the oath of neutrality; he incited others to do the same. After the execution, a fundraising campaign started in Holland for his family printing a postcard with a picture of Broeksma. They offered the card for sale, with the following message: *"Cornelius Broeksma, hero and martyr, shot by the English on 30th September 1901, because he refused to be silent about the cruel suffering in the women's camps."* At that stage, the officially recorded camp population of the white camps was 109,418. The deaths for September 1902 totalled 2,411. To put a man before a firing squad because he campaigned against the concentration camp atrocities seems to be cruel and inhumane.

On 31st May, the British and Boers signed the Peace Treaty of Vereeniging. Afterwards, the inhabitants of the concentration camps were released. Boers claimed the surviving family members. Others left on their own to return to their burnt-down houses and farms. Close on twenty-eight-thousand persons died in the camps inclusive of more than sixteen thousand men, mainly those too old to be in battle. More than four-thousand women and twenty-two-thousand children under sixteen died in the camps.

Kitchener apologists claim that the Scorched Earth Policy happened *a long time ago*. Alternatively, they argue that Kitchener's crimes were *acceptable for the times*. The international community condemned Kitchener's concentration camps via The Hague Convention of 1907. Three British prime ministers criticised Kitchener for his brutality; Lloyd George, Winston Churchill, and Henry Campbell-Bannerman. The Afrikaner Nation erected a Women's Monument in Bloemfontein, Orange Free State to commemorate the deaths of Boer women and children. Interesting, I just wonder, are the black people also remembered? Pragmatically, I doubt that.

I visited the monument and was astonished at the artefacts on display and the images portrayed. The impression I got from the presentations was that the conditions and treatment were inhumanely evil, cruel and atrocious. The Anglo-Boer War became a huge international embarrassment to the British. War failures, the concentration camps and heavy losses forced the British to rethink its tactics in modern warfare. To honour Kitchener as a war hero is dogmatic, obnoxious and offensive; it would be like praising Adolf Hitler as a war hero.

Astonishingly war and conflict produce heroes, murderers and cowards. Martin Mc Guinness, an IRA fighter in Northern Ireland, died in March 2017 He was a liberation fighter of the 1970s that had a hand in the death of many Irish and British people. He died a statesman honoured for his role in bringing peace to Northern Ireland. Whether someone is a war criminal, a hero or a traitor, it will always be confusing when looking at the bigger picture over time. Kitchener and Milner do not qualify as heroes to so many South Africans, black and white people. Both British commanders will forever be war criminals in the eyes of Afrikaners.

Britain honoured Kitchener, decorating him with eight medals, for his war crimes. The following contains the acclamation. *"1ˢᵗ Earl Kitchener, KG, KP, GCB, OM, GCSI, GCMG, GCIE, PC, was a senior British Army officer and colonial administrator who won fame for his imperial campaigns and later played a central role in the early part of the First World War, he died halfway through it."*

Kitchener and Milner, heroes in the eyes of the British, forever war criminals in the view of the Boer-Afrikaner nation. Later I researched the liberation of Namibia. Lothar von Trotha, a German commander, almost exterminated two Namibian tribes. On his return, he was decorated by the German government for services to Germany. What can one say; it is all in the eye of the beholder.

The Peace Treaty: The Union of South Africa

The Anglo-Boer War destroyed the Boer Republics Transvaal and Orange Free State. During the peace treaty of Vereeniging, the British agreed to lenient terms. One can only assume Kitchener's Scorched Earth Policy warranted lax measures within the peace treaty. Britain gained formal control of the two Boer Republics, Transvaal and Orange Free State. The British gave substantial restorative concessions to the defeated Boers. They also committed to rebuilding the Boer Republics. The British established the Union of South Africa as the new governing authority. The two British Colonies, Cape and Natal, along with the Boer Republics, Transvaal and Orange Free State, merged into one Union of South Africa. The colonial rule came to an end, and an elected Union government emerged as the new regime to South Africa.

The Boer Nation survived the Anglo-Boer War but lost the fight for self-determination as well as the ownership of diamond and gold wealth. Anglo American to this day remains a company in British and American ownership.

The Cronje Generals and the Anglo-Boer War

My Cronje namesake ancestors featured prominently in the history of the Afrikaner. They migrated from France in the late 17th century and again relocated with the 1838 *Great Trek*, moving north away from the British Colonists. Some of my ancestors also fought in the Anglo-Boer War as Generals.

Towards the end of the war, the de Wet and Cronje families experienced a family split. Two brothers remembered as traitors and two as heroes. All four were generals and significant contributors to the Boer battles. They fought valiantly for the Boers. Piet Cronje and Christiaan de Wet were heroes, fighters to the bitter end for the Boers. Andries Cronje and Piet de Wet are loathed as traitors, turned Scout Commanders for the British. Afrikaner history remembers the conflict as *brother against brother, a brother break-up and rift*. In the words of Eugene Marais, a well-known Afrikaans poet; *"The hatred is there, as wide as God's earth and as deep as the sea. We hate these people from the bottom of our hearts, because they brought dishonour throughout the whole world, to our actual name. It is not possible to forgive much less to forget."*

The two brothers as Scouts Commanders campaigned for the end to bloodshed and termination of the destruction to farms; they wanted peace. The massive loss of life and obliteration concerned them, they turned in opposition to their brothers, starting negotiations for peace with the British High Command. The skirmish reached a point where Christiaan de Wet said *"I should have killed him"*, about his brother Piet.

Piet de Wet gave his fellow Boer generals a six-month ultimatum, to bring the war to an end, in whatever way possible. He also complained to the British about concentration camps and the appalling treatment of women and children. Most of the Boers did not want to end the war, their successes in guerrilla warfare spurred them on. There was also the belief that they could still win the war, they hoped for support from overseas.

President Paul Kruger armed the Transvaal Boer-army, with weaponry; rifles, and ammunition imported from the Deutsche *Waffen und Munitionsfabriken*. There seems to have been some affiliation with Germany, but task force support was never a reality. There was no support for the Boers from Germany. I explain in later chapters the German allegiance to the South African Apartheid regime.

The National Scout leaders claimed that they could not allow the war to destroy their nation, they argued that the Afrikaner nation became second-class citizens. Their farms and livelihoods destroyed, under the British Scorched Earth Policy.

Hindsight always produces new perspectives, taking the facts into account. British forces totalled 550,000 men, fighting against an army of 150,000 Boer fighters, more than a 3 to 1 ratio. The Boers fought the British Empire not only Britain. According to reports, 20,000 Boer bitter-enders continued fighting for almost two more years, against a half a million British Empire task force. As a result, between twenty and thirty- thousand Boer women and children, and up to twenty thousand black people died in the camps. The dogged persistence of the Boer bitter-enders moved the British to introduce the Scorched Earth Policy. The atrocious policy is one of the world's most heinous war crimes in African colonial history. The National Scouts under the command of the British pursued Boer Farms with women, children, and black workers, vulnerable and indefensible.

The Union of South Africa could have been a reality much earlier at a much lower sacrifice, saving more lives and fewer farms, towns and crops destroyed. On the other hand, without the concentration camps, the favourable peace conditions might not have been on the table. In reality, the Boer Republics might not have suffered as extensively if it was not for the Scorched Earth Policy of Lord Kitchener. Hindsight is easy, but when you are in the thick of war, solutions are seldom forthcoming; it will remain a *catch-twenty-two situation.*

Post-war rebuilding and restitution never go well. Even in the 21st century, post-war plans for reconstruction often fall short; like in Iraq and Libya. The situation was no different after the Anglo-Boer War. In the end, it was too high a price for the Boers to endure; they lost the war and their self-determination along with the gold and diamond wealth.

Heroes and Traitors: Grave Truths Involving the Cronje Family

I researched many atrocities that happened during the Anglo-Boer-War. Terrible sufferings inflicted on Boer-Afrikaner families at the hands of the British army. A variety of Afrikaner families experienced heart-wrenching anguishes; too many to cover individually. Treatment of women and children in concentration camps were inhumane. I write the following whopper inclusive of the suffering of my Cronje ancestors. In my descriptions, I endeavour to picture the scene, nature and extent of real carnages that happened.

The Seamus's family names are only illustrative to set the scene; they do not bear reference to any person. But, mercenary soldiers did profit from the war in the form of farm ownership; real examples recorded in historical chronicles.

My mother told me about my father's family-farm *Wolwehoek.* According to Mum, my great-grandfather lived on the farm Wolwehoek. I researched the location and found a Wolwehoek farm close to the present-day Sasolburg in the Orange Free-State. From the Wolwehoek farm to the Springfontein concentration camp site, is a four-hour drive by car. I cannot in truth corroborate that the atrocities happened at *Wolwehoek.* But, it happened on many Boer-owned farms in the Transvaal, and Orange Free State and carnages happened to my ancestors. Truthfully, I base the portrayal on real-life events.

The Cronje family side of the story, from the Springfontein concentration camp onwards, is the truth. I not only confirmed the connection based on genealogical records but as a young boy I lived the death of my grandfather. My great-grandfather died in the concentration camp. My grandfather as a ten-year-old boy in the camp survived and relocated to Boksburg near Johannesburg after the war.

Start of the Boer-Afrikaner Tale:

Seamus is a wealthy Irish farmer, an adult in his late fifties; it is 1930. Seamus, a landowner in the former Orange Free State Boer Republic, now a province of the Union of South Africa. A wealthy and respected man. Seamus served as an elected member of the Free State Provincial Government. Married to Sally, a compatriot that stood by his side all those years. The two of them rebuilt the war-torn farm, *Wolwehoek*. Sally gave birth to their four children. Now, all of them well settled with growing families. The eldest a medical doctor and one a dentist, both practising in the town of Vereeniging where they signed the Anglo-Boer War Peace Treaty. Vereeniging christened as a result of the coal mining company, *Kolen, and Mineralen Vereeniging.* Translated *Vereeniging* that means *union.* The Vereeniging Treaty is ironic, almost a tongue-in-cheek coincidence. It was a unification aimed at merging the English and Afrikaans-speaking peoples into one nation; an objective impossible and futile. The Afrikaans and English speaking whites were enemies.

But to get back to Seamus, one of his sons was planting maize crops on a farm close to *Wolwehoek*, translated Wolves Corner. The youngest boy was Seamus's right-hand man on his farm; he would be taking over *Wolwehoek* when his father Seamus retires.

Seamus's wealth-gain started way back in 1902, twenty-eight years ago, at the end of the Anglo-Boer War. Seamus was a British

Empire soldier serving in Lord Kitchener's *Scorched Earth* troop. In effect, he was a mercenary soldier from the British Empire.

Britain, as the final resort in the war effort, decided to destroy the supply lines to the Boer Commandos fighting the British; the stores held the Boer guerrilla fighters in the field. Kitchener harmed the Boer nation's morale; he detained Boer women and children from destroyed farms in concentration camps.

Seamus was one of Lord Kitchener's troop commanders. He remembered the day they burnt down the farm of *Wolwehoek*. The farm belonged to the two Cronje brothers, fighting as Boer generals in the Anglo-Boer War. Seamus learnt of them in the walks among the British troops; they were formidable Boer Commanders with fearsome reputations.

Seamus was a soldier paid to do a job in the war. All was fair, and he executed his duty diligently. Targeting *Wolwehoek* was deliberate, the British realised the emotional damage to the Boer Command Generals. Hurt the leaders of the fight against the British, and you win the war.

Seamus's troop burnt everything to the ground, no buildings and no crops spared, then they slaughtered the animals. The old grandfather of the family was in his seventies, an old man and father to his two Boer General sons. His daughters in law, with their children ranging from a newborn baby to teenagers, lived on the farm, twelve of them in total. They stood devastated in the winter cold, the cruel destruction of their livelihood carried out in front of their eyes. No empathy shown, they were the enemies of Britain.

After the devastation, the British moved the Cronje families to the nearest concentration camp, *Springfontein*. The old man on foot, there was no space for him on the waggon. The carriage and horses, Seamus and his men confiscated from the farm *Wolwehoek*. They took all valuable possessions as war loot.

After the Peace Treaty of Vereeniging, Seamus decided not to return to Ireland but to settle in the Orange Free State. Seamus's military pay as a mercenary soldier from the British Empire served him well. He saved every penny, no living expenses. Seamus was a kept soldier. He accrued wealth while fighting.

Seamus bought the destroyed farm, *Wolwehoek* with his saved-up soldier pay; he did well for himself. The farm was cheap as chips, nothing of value to sell. The farmstead burnt to the ground and no animal stock or crops on the land.

The Boer family had no choice, sell and move to the British-owned Anglo-American gold mines, their only chance of survival. They were the defeated Boer farmers. No British relief for them to rebuild their farm as promised in the rebuilding of the Boer Republics. Instead, the new owner of *Wolwehoek* was the victorious British mercenary soldier, the enemy Seamus. He was also the Scorched Earth Troop Commander that burnt their farm to the ground. The war rendered the Boer families as second-class citizens, their livelihood in ruins. Seven of the twelve children and their grandfather died in the *Springfontein* concentration camp.

The British captured General Piet Cronje, the staunch bitter-ender and co-owner of *Wolwehoek*. They deported him as a prisoner of war to St. Helena Island, along with his wife. The surviving women and the Scout General Andries Cronje, along with their children moved to Boksburg. The two Cronje families became fierce enemies. The one, the family of a bitter-end-fighter, a war hero. The other the family of a traitor in the eyes of the Boer-Afrikaner nation.

End of the Boer-Afrikaner Tale.

Back to real life and this is the sad truth, not a story. My great-grandfather died in the *Springfontein* concentration camp. Was his father the old man marched on foot from the farm to Springfontein concentration camp? I don't know but who cares?

My grandfather's name was Andries Stephanus Cronje. He was the ten-year-old boy that survived the concentration camp whose father died in the camp. After the war, my grandfather moved with his family and settled in the mining town of Boksburg. The Boksburg part is real; I was born into the Cronje family that lived in Boksburg. As an adult, my grandfather worked in the Anglo-American gold mines in Boksburg. Andries Cronje's son, Johan Cronje is my father born in 1918. Andries, my grandfather, died in the early 1950s of lung cancer as an ex-gold miner. I was in my pre-teens. I remember his suffering. My grandfather struggled to breathe with lungs devastated by the dust in the Anglo-American gold mines.

I related the story to illustrate the atrocities of the Anglo Boer War. Incidents that happened to the Cronje family, happened to many Afrikaner-Boer families?

Another real-life Afrikaner tale is a genuine story of Susan Nel, no fiction, every detail, the gospel truth. And once again, a heart-wrenching story that played off in the concentration camps.

Susan Nel: A Concentration Camp Miracle

Francois Smith illustrates a further example, exemplifying the conditions and crimes of the concentration camps in his book: *Kamphoer*, written in Afrikaans. I transcribe the story to demonstrate the treatment that Boer people suffered, and also to create some perspective on the role of the Scouts in the War.

There were some heroes but also scoundrels. I was shocked to my core when reading the novel. It opened a new perspective on concentration camp atrocities, and even an alternative outlook on the role Scouts played in the Anglo-Boer War.

My transcription begins:

In real life described in the story was Susan Nel, a young innocent Boer girl aged 18 from the town Winburg in the Orange Free State. Susan, along with her mother and younger brother was incarcerated in the Bloemfontein British concentration camp. Her entire family, father, mother and brother killed; the mother and brother in the camp and father while fighting the British. Their farm and all possessions, destroyed by Lord Kitchener's Scorched Earth troops, supported by the Scouts. The Scouts were fighting their Afrikaner people on the side of the British enemy.

It was New Year's Eve festivities in the concentration camp with loud celebrations. Susan's friend Alice Drew was gravely ill. Susan left Alice's side to find some medical assistance. Walking through the endless lines of tents to the medical station, Susan was grabbed and overpowered by a member of the Scouts. The Joiner dragged her by her ankles into the British Officer's tent, shouting "*camp whore.*"

That was a blatant lie; she was an innocent girl that he hardly knew. The Joiner was apparently seeking the favour of the British Commanders. He was also looking for some self-indulgence and sexual gratification as a bonus. The Scout physically and cunningly delivered one of his people to the British enemy. He was *a fucking traitor, a measly coward.*

All three, the two British Officers and the Joiner raped her and abused her so severely that she was certified dead by the British Camp Doctor. The cause of death was appallingly, and cowardly noted as dysentery, a common disorder due to the terrible conditions in the camp.

Miraculously she was either pushed or fell off the waggon that transported the dead to the burial site. A black medicine man *(witch doctor)*, Tsitsele found her and carried her to a cave where he and a black Sotho woman Mamela, nursed her for months back to life. They used witch doctor medicine, wedging crushed and moistened leaf-paste between her legs, on her body and around her head. Physically and mentally broken, Susan was at the mercy of two black Samaritans. The black couple counselled and nursed Susan back to sanity by singing, dancing and telling tribal tales.

When she recovered, Susan made her way to Cape Town, away from the war zone. With help from Tsitsele and a Samaritan photographer, Percy they transferred Susan to Cape Town. The

British contracted the photographer Percy to take war pictures. Susan adopted her friend's British surname Drew, to escape capture by the British. After Susan's effort to find medical help failed, her friend Alice Drew died in the concentration camp. Overpowered and raped, Susan could not find medical help for Alice.

Percy, the photographer, introduced Susan to Margarethe Koopmans de Wet, a kind woman supporting the incarcerated Boers in the concentration camps. Margarethe made it possible for Susan to go to the Netherlands where she trained to be a psychiatric nurse.

Ironically, Susan treated soldiers recovering from post-traumatic stress disorder *(PTSD),* then classified as Shell shock. Susan worked with psychiatrists researching alternative and primitive treatment methods for *PTSD.* The methods were similar to those used by Tsitsele and Mamela in treating Susan.

During her ordeal, Susan bit off a piece of the ear of one of the British Officers, upon which the Officer knocked her over her head with a bottle of liquor, inflicting a deep gouge in her forehead. The scar on her forehead and disfigured ear of the British Officer, enabled Susan to recognise and re-acquaint with the self-same British Officer that raped her. She met up with the rogue Officer back in Devon, England while she worked at a post-war treatment hospital.

To her shock, she nursed a patient, the real British Officer who raped her. During the process of therapy, he recognised her. Susan took his hand and placed it on her forehead, where he scarred her with the bottle of liquor. She also touched his ear with the gaping scar, where she bit off part of his ear.

When the staff came to his bed the following morning, he was found dead. His death was unexplained. She did not kill him, someone else did, or his conscience drove him to commit suicide. Bed sheets were forced into his mouth and wrapped around his head.

End of the Kamphoer (Camp Whore) transcription.

The face of war is ugly, and the soldiers fighting the war might be heroes, but some turned into animals, the worst you can imagine. Some of them were Scouts, British and Boer deserters. Not all fighters are honourable; Scouts Bitter-Enders and Brits. There were the bad apples that tainted the forces. It is understandable that the Scouts were hated as voiced in the extract by Eugene Marais, and quoted earlier.

Perspectives on the Scorched Earth Policy

The British supportive *SA-Newscast bulletin* described the concentration camps as; *"a full-scale war on the Boer women and children; employing the concentration camp holocaust to force the Boers into submission."*

The *Cape Argus of 21 June 1900*, described the destitution of Boer women and children: *"Within 10 miles we (the English) burned not less than six farm homesteads. Between 30 and 40 homes were burnt and destroyed between Bloemfontein and Boshoff; many others were also burned down. Their houses destroyed, women and children left in the bitter South African winter."*

Breyten Breytenbach, an Afrikaans poet, gave his version of events in the *Danie Theron* publication: *"The destruction done diabolically. Even Mrs Prinsloo, a 22-year young lady was not spared, she gave birth to a baby only 24 hours before. British soldiers, amongst whom a so-called English doctor, forced their way into her room. After making a pretence of examining her, they drove her out of the house. With the aid of her sister, she managed to don a few articles of clothing and left home. Her mother brought a blanket to protect her from the cold; the soldiers jerked the blanket out of her mother's hands. After having looted whatever they wanted to, they set the house on fire."*

Conclusive Comments: The Afrikaner Nation

British colonialism and the Anglo-Boer-War had devastating effects on the Afrikaner nation. Yes, Europe had a hand in the building but also the destruction of Africa. Throughout colonisation and the aftermath of war, the Afrikaner Nation was either under siege or undermined. The Boer enemies were many from all corners of tribal South Africa to the British colonial masters. The rude treatment inflicted by the British was not forgotten nor forgiven by the Afrikaner.

The black African also did not forgive the colonisers and occupiers for the crimes of occupation and oppression; they were the original natives of the land. When colonists entered Africa, the atrocities true to Apartheid came to Africa. The Dutch, British or the Boer-Afrikaner nation, never considered the natives for political inclusion; they were the disenfranchised people. As a result of the exclusion, even today in 2017, the *Rhodes Must Fall (RMF)* and *Black First Land First (BFLF)* activists want to decolonise South Africa. They want to strip the country of white people, perceived to be the remnants of the colonial era; the dreaded *third force* from the West.

The concentration camps described as *murder camps* will forever be a war crime; it intensely fired Afrikaner nationalism. The Afrikaner mindset, fervently fixated on self-determination, at whatever cost; free from oppression and governance by the British and the people of colour.

Boers and black people lived in distrust and even fear of each other. But it must be remembered that the conflict, headed by the Boers, occupied black native land during the *Great Trek*; they colonised black native land to the North.

Thinking back on the two Cronje Boer generals the question arises in my mind; were my forebears the children of Piet or Andries Cronje? One the hero one the perceived traitor? I don't know. My grandfather was Andries Cronje, does that make me a descendant of a Scout and traitor? It is not of real consequence. My father's elder brother had their grandfathers' name Arnoldus Petrus Cronje. Was he the grandfather that died in the concentration camp?

What does it matter, who says history is dull? I used the real-life encounters written as a collection of what happened to Boer families. Also to bring home atrocities that transpired in those days. The Anglo-Boer War and concentration camps left a lasting and hateful impression on the Boer-Afrikaner nation; a hatred towards the British. With such a gruesome legacy, the Afrikaner nation was set on never to be governed by anyone but themselves.

Evaluating the historical events, it is axiomatic that the Afrikaner was a people hurt and aggrieved at the end of the Anglo-Boer War. The Afrikaner nation focused on getting rid of their ancient foes, the British and even the African natives.

They were delusional to the extent that they believed in self-governance for the Afrikaners, and the rest of the world be damned. That and notwithstanding the reality that the Afrikaners constitute an absolute minority of the total South African population. Considering the bigger picture and facts as we know it today, the Afrikaner nation was delusional.

In the next chapter, the Apartheid government, introduced to South Africa by the Afrikaner National Party, will come under the spotlight; Apartheid from the beginning to the end.

Chapter 3

Apartheid from Beginning to the End

The Afrikaner Nation's Perception of Afrikaner Land

Previously we confirmed that the Khoikhoi had a long free reign of existence at the Cape before the Dutch arrived in 1652. The Afrikaner nation developed with the Dutch and French as root genetic material. German migrants settled in the Cape Colony and integrated with the Afrikaner because of religious & ethnic similarities. Over time the Afrikaner grew as the only European nation to Africa. A multitude of ethnicities, like the Malaysians and the natives of Africa, people of colour, augmented the Afrikaner nation. After 1806, Afrikaners were supplemented by the British settlers. The British colonisation and the Anglo-Boer-War not only harmed but inspired Afrikaner nationalism.

Planting a nation-state and growing it is equivalent to planting a tree. The seed gets introduced to fertile soil within a supportive environment, and it germinates. It will grow over centuries, becoming the prominent feature of the forest; to the point when it claims the plantation as its own. European nations planted the Afrikaner-nation-seed in Africa. The seed developed and expanded to the point where the Afrikaner claimed South Africa as its own. Symbolic to the tree, the Afrikaner declared its territory, not to be ignored nor to be denied.

The Boer-Afrikaner nation established themselves as a nation-state over a period of one-hundred-and-fifty years before the British colonised the Cape. One could comprehend, that the Boer-Afrikaner nation, at that stage, was robbed of self-determination by British colonisation. In the Afrikaner mind, they were the actual people governing South Africa; even though the Dutch lost control over the Cape to the British.

By 1795, before British colonisation, the links between the Boers and the Dutch East Indian company became indistinct. The Boers continued to speak Afrikaans, and progressively became independent from the Dutch; they turned into a sovereign nation.

Ever since Europeans set foot in Africa, the people of colour were never in contention for political rights or even human rights for that matter. Being the final stage of European settlement, the Afrikaner as a white minority, governed the country; even though the majority were black natives. Was the Afrikaner in effect the *tail wagging the dog*?

In fact, this is not as far-fetched as it may sound. The Afrikaner was in effect the last nation in the line of governance. The Afrikaner took control and governed the country as if it had always been Afrikaner land. Objectively this seems delusional; the whites are the absolute minority.

Not bearing in mind the two Boer Republics, Transvaal and Orange Free State, the Afrikaner government, effectively, only took control in 1948. Only white people were registered as voters and allowed to elect the government. Why did the Afrikaner Nation extenuate oppression into a constitutionalised system of Apartheid, a cruel dispensation? Tribal Africa did not match the political arrangement of the West. Africans still lived under tribal and kingship rule. Things happened, and there seems to be no rational explanation; just a culmination of events over a period of three and a half centuries. Gradually the people of colour became politically aware and on par with their white European counterparts; they became less tribal and more influenced by western politics.

Recently someone told me her life was not one of choice. Things just happened, and she went through life following the cultural course. When she was born, it was not her choice. The societal design pre-empted school, university and work. That seems to be the case for many of us. We are slaves of our environment, and we follow a social design within our upbringing. Somebody recently mentioned the wise words *shit happens*, and most of the times you can do nothing about it. You just have to go with the flow; follow suit.

I recently spoke to my brother in law; I asked him how they find life within South Africa. He replied *"Well, most of the people just get on with life and we get along with each other within our circle of society. But, then there is the minority vocal portion of society that continuously voices their concern through demonstrations and protests, even destructive activities, disrupting day-to-day life."*

For the majority of people, life is what it is. Even when conditions are adverse, they get on with it, believing that their hands are to no great extent tied. The Dutch have a saying: *'God's water over God's acres';* meaning *let life be*. Over time people just get on with it. The past and present perceptions shape the future.

The Anglo-Boer-War reduced the Afrikaners to second-rate citizens. Ever since the British occupation of 1806 onto the 1838-*Great Trek*, the Boers perceived the British as invaders of the Cape. The British were their enemies trying to anglicise the Cape. They endeavoured to destroy the Afrikaner language and culture, interfering with their ways of life.

This sense of invasion and oppression over thirty-two years gave rise to the *Great Trek*. The Boers moved away from the British. In the mind of the Afrikaner, the British were not their friends; they wanted to rid themselves of British rule. The Afrikaner became obsessed, even delusional, with self-rule.

The Boer interaction with native Africans, especially the Xhosa and Zulu nations were not peaceful. The Boers invaded the land of African natives and enslaved some of them. People of colour were oppressed, first by the Dutch and then the Brits and ultimately by the Boers; all of it enforced on the African natives. That brought about an uneasy co-existence between Afrikaners and the black citizens. They lived in distrust and even fear of each other.

Whether the Afrikaner was delusional or not must be a consideration. Politics progresses incrementally. The whole reality of the political scene is never available in one single take.

Since 1652, exposed to European ways of life, it is only natural that the people of colour changed their tribal ways to the developed European and western ways. Things happened over time with many interfering influences, growing and amending the political scene. People of colour became politically aware of western values. Ultimately they would claim their share of political inclusion based on the life of the west.

News bulletins of present-day ex-colonies frequently reach the international news media. With few exceptions when reporters interview the locals, they are fully conversant in English; even though it will be with a robust dialectal tone. Their manner is also very westernised. The Anglo-Saxon way is ingrained to such an extent that they might as well be westerners.

The moment colonialism terminated in 1910, the nationalism of the Afrikaner and the people of colour saw the dawning of the Afrikaner National Party along with the establishment of the African National Council; it was the dawn of a multicultural nation claiming its political rights.

The development of Apartheid requires consideration of the Afrikaner psyche, their mindset. The Afrikaner nation was a nation scarred by oppression, war and concentration camp atrocities. Influences that caused Afrikaner nationalism to blossom in the postwar era was the 15% extermination of the Boer nation in the Anglo-Boer War. The remaining Afrikaners were discontented and even hateful towards the British.

The scarring provided the real impetus and finality to self-governance and the formation of the National Party. The only self-rule for the Afrikaner was the Boer Republics. They lost their sovereignty after the Anglo-Boer War.

The next attempt to self-determination was the National party, established in 1912, ten years after the Anglo-Boer-War ended. Afrikaner Rule only came to full fruition in 1948, when the National Party took over the government.

After the Anglo-Boer-War, the situation was desperate. Thousands of poor white Afrikaners flocked to urban areas in search of employment in the British controlled Anglo-American mines and predominantly British owned industries. The so-called *Bitter Enders* and those who surrendered, the *scout capitulators*, remained bitter enemies. The post-war governments, inclusive of the Afrikaner Apartheid government, inherited a segregated South African Nation. Uniting the Afrikaans and English-speaking whites was the objective of the Union of South Africa; the unification did not consider people of colour.

Politics excluded black tribal South Africa. They had no political rights; even their human rights were ignored and impaired. A distorted and destroyed post-war environment was the feeding ground of Afrikaner nationalism. The Afrikaner found their political *home* within the National Party and Afrikaner Apartheid.

Parallel to the white uprising the African National Congress (ANC), a black political revolution against oppression, established in January 1912. They also claimed their political rights; commencing a century-long struggle to be recognised and to live free. The powers that people of colour fought for was western values, equal to the white people as descendants of the colonists.

The conclusion to reform South Africa into a Union was significant in the post-war era. The white English and Afrikaans people were enemies. The unification objective was to merge them into one nation; an intention immediately opposed by the followers of General Hertzog considered the leader among Afrikaner nationalists.

The people of colour through the ANC did not accept their exclusion from the land's political system. I commented earlier on the irony of signing the peace deal at Vereeniging, translated it signifies unification; that was the objective of the Union of South Africa. The dilemma, however, was that unification would only be the start of the struggle and segregation between Hertzog's Afrikaner nationalism and General Jan Smuts' British loyalism. The ANC was not part of the unification. The divisions re-iterated the South African nation as a segregated society, in so many ways.

My Perspectives on a Segregated South Africa

I was born in the Union of South Africa; the Union was the last bastion of Imperialism and British rule. My socio-political environment excluded the entire Black, Coloured and Asian population. In the 1970s, the heydeys of Apartheid, I did not have much interest in politics. I was in my early thirties. My interests were sport, outdoor life and family life. With four children, I suppose I was arrogant and ignorant; just getting on with life. Arrogant, because I believed, we the white people were doing nothing wrong. The rest of the world was wrong and only meddled in our affairs. Ignorant, because I did not fully understand concepts like democracy, human rights and citizenship. These thoughts, the Apartheid Government preferred the peoples of South Africa not to consider; especially not the people of colour. In dictatorial regimes, like Apartheid, this kind of political knowledge and concepts, will not be part of the educational curriculum.

The government wanted to steer clear from any cognizance relating to full democracy. Segregation and separate development, eventually transformed into dreaded Apartheid. Apartheid vilified as keeping people *apart* and imparting *hatred* between people from differing ethnic groups; added together it becomes *Aparthate*.

I was happy with my life, under the impression that we were somewhat lovely to our black servants, we liked them, and they loved us. They did good work, and we paid them. The socio-political environment was satisfactory to me. I did not perceive a problem. The Apartheid Government dictated my life. I had no reason to question society and politics. When I became cognitively and politically aware, Apartheid was the political dispensation. I was groomed and raised within Apartheid; it was the apparently natural to me. I realise now, the fact that it was the norm, does not mean that it should have been.

My conversation with my brother in law makes me think that I was part of the majority. It might just be, that the majority perception was prominent among the white population. It was comfortable. What is wrong with enjoying life, for as long as it lasts?

In my mid-thirties I studied international politics, I needed to understand what gave rise to Apartheid. How did the Afrikaner ever come to the atrocious political policy of Apartheid? I will forthwith focus on the mindset and delusion of the Afrikaner that constitutionalised Apartheid.

Afrikaner v British Imperialism: A Two-fold Delusion?

A nation wants to believe in the government, the powers that be. The party that over time perfected the science of *spin*. Sell the government's policy to the people with promises and excuses that will satisfy them. We believed the Apartheid Government. This Apartheid-spin sounds ridiculous and poses the question whether the white South Africans were delusional.

The satirizer within moves me to compare Afrikaner arrogance to that of the British. Shall we compare it to a patriotic equilibrium?

Verse 2 of God Save the Queen: The British Anthem

"O Lord, our God, arise,
Scatter her enemies
And make them fall;
Confound their politics,
Frustrate their knavish tricks,
On Thee our hopes, we fix, God save us all!"

John Bull composed the British anthem in 1619. Coincidently, it is also the century of British Imperialism. Isn't the above trend also the essential characteristics of patriotism, nationalism and imperialism in the early 17th century? Imperialism was in its prime. This verse personifies the urge for success in land-grab and wealth exploitation by British Imperialists.

Isn't that precisely what the Afrikaner Boer Nation did? Isn't the mindset of the 17th century Brit as delusional as that of the *1838 Great Trek Afrikaner?* This expansionist urge was an international endeavour of the Western world.

Colonialism established the United States of America, Canada, Australia and New Zealand as white man's land; land taken from the indigenous and many people of colour. If the Afrikaner is delusional, then these white occupations were also the outcome of delusionary imperialism in the colonial-era. They turned these countries into white man's land; formerly the land of the natives, the people of colour.

Afrikaner Nationalism and Black Africans

The Afrikaner knew one man one vote would result in a black majority government. Atrociously, Afrikaner nationalism marginalised non-white ethnic groups and estranged them; segregation intensified as Afrikaner-Apartheid prolonged.

The novelist Alan Paton commented on Afrikaner nationalism: *"It is one of the dark mysteries of Afrikaner nationalist psychology. An Afrikaner nationalist can observe the highest standards of awards for his kind but can see an entirely different standard towards others; and especially if they are not white. Afrikaners obsessed with fears about their survival did not care about the damage and the hurt that Apartheid inflicted upon others in a far weaker position."*

Afrikaner Nationalism and English speaking South Africans

Due to colonialism and capitalism, English-speaking South Africans remained dominant on capital investment and involvement within mining and industry. Their per capita income was more than double that of Afrikaners. Level of education was also superior, and they held a richer cultural dichotomy compared to the Afrikaner. After 1948, English speaking South Africans found themselves in the political no man's land.

The son of the South African governor-general, Patrick Duncan wrote: *"English South Africans are today in the power of their adversaries. They are the only English group of any size in the world today that is, and will remain for some time, be ruled by a subordinated minority. English speaking South Africans are beginning to know what the vast majority of all (black) South Africans have always known; what it is to be second-class citizens in the land of one's birth."*

Irrespective of what English speaking South Africans or black people thought of the Afrikaner, the Afrikaners as descendants of *Boers* were fired up and set on governing themselves and the country

The Birth of Apartheid: The National Party

The National Party became the government of South Africa in 1948, with Dr D F Malan as Prime Minister. Was this the birth of Afrikaner Apartheid? In effect, the aim since the *1838 Great Trek* was to get rid of the British and attain self-governance for the Afrikaner. The 1948 National Party Government intended to establish the South African Republic and above all to promote Afrikaner nationalism. In the Afrikaner's eyes, the control of the British needed to go, and the exclusion of non-whites must be enforced and enshrined in the Constitution.

But we established that the National Party goes way back to 1914-15; a party founded on the hurt felt by the Afrikaner as a legacy of the Boer wars. Almost a knee-jerk reaction to British oppression. The Afrikaner hated the British, and the Black majority made self-governance impossible for the Afrikaner.

The Founding of the National Party (1910-1914)

I covered the Anglo-Boer War and the Union of South Africa of 1910 earlier. The unification objective was to unify the English and Afrikaans-speaking peoples of South Africa. The Union was a British dominion and had to answer to Britain. Louis Botha was the first Prime Minister after unification and leader to the South African Party (SAP).

The SAP was an amalgam of Afrikaner parties that won the election. The neighbouring co-operation between Afrikaans and English-speaking South Africans was paramount to unification. General J B M Hertzog, was the founder of the National Party in opposition to the SAP. He was a member of the Union Government; a fierce nationalist and aggressively persuaded towards Afrikaner nationalism. He did not support the English-Afrikaans *neighbouring cooperation* objective.

Naturally, this was offensive to English-speaking people and supporters of the British Empire. They wanted Hertzog removed from the Union Government. Hertzog supporters opposed Louis Botha's policies of national unity and had the support of politicians in the Orange Free State and the Cape Province. They preferred English and Afrikaans to develop in segregated social streams.

The Afrikaner supporters of Hertzog insisted on his inclusion in the government. The Transvaal members supported Botha and kept Hertzog out of the cabinet. In the act of revolt, Hertzog formed the National Party, a movement that eventually led to the establishment of the 1948 Apartheid government.

Hertzog formulated the fundamental policies of the National Party (NP), based on Christian beliefs and the Afrikaner culture. The NP wanted an independent South Africa, with freedom from Britain; but no political rights for non-whites.

The NP also insisted on equality of English and Dutch. Dutch being the root language to Afrikaans. Most of Hertzog's supporters were Afrikaans speaking people; they craved Afrikaner nationalism. The National Parties of the Orange Free State and the Transvaal established in 1914. The Cape National Party followed in June 1915.

The National Party strengthens (1914-1923)

It seems like the NP supported Germany in opposition to Britain during World War I. They objected to the invasion of German South-West Africa (SWA) in 1914. However, the government still resolved to invade South-West Africa (Namibia) in support of Britain.

The disenfranchisement of non-white people became government policy shortly after the unification of South Africa. The government finally confirmed the disenfranchisement of people of colour in 1922, when the governing SAP accepted the *Stallard*-Report under Jan Smuts as Prime Minister. The report stated that *"It should be recognised in principle, that natives (non-white men, women and children) should only be within municipal areas in so far and for as long as the white population requires their presence."* The report resonated the Apartheid sentiment imposed with the support of Britain and voiced by Cecil John Rhodes. The report also stated that *"If the native (black) is to be a permanent element in municipal areas there can be no justification for basing his exclusion from the franchise on the pure ground of colour."* Naturally, this was to the dissatisfaction of non-white South Africans. Black Africans already suffered under the burden of economic depression and disenfranchisement.

The Stallard Report gave rise to the passing of the Natives Urban Areas Act number 21 of 1923. Segregation happened long before the 1948-Apartheid-NP government came to power. The Union as a dominion of Britain never intended any political rights for non-whites. The colonisers and oppressors from the Dutch, Boers and Britain, established segregation and subjugation of non-whites over a colonial and union period of three centuries.

Gradually the original natives to the land grew accustomed to western world values. Understandably the demonstration of European values resulted in their empowerment and political awareness. They expected equal treatment under the laws of the country. The inequalities induced by the government led to unrest in the labour market.

The PACT Government (1924-1938)

The Rand Rebellion of 1922, resulted from labour unrest in British-dominated industries. The rebellion boosted the popularity of the NP among white people. The NP and Labour Party merged to form the PACT government in April 1923. The PACT defeated the SAP in the 1924 general election. The PACT entrenched segregation in the labour market and introduced job-reservation. Job-reservation excluded non-white workers from senior and highly-paid positions. Surely this is a form of continued enslavement. Job-reservation fired labour unrest among people of colour within the British industries?

The move from British to Afrikaans brought about changes. Afrikaans became an official language, and the four colour flag became the South African national flag, incorporating the flags of the former two Boer Republics. Was this an anti-British symbolic statement?

The Balfour Declaration

The Balfour Declaration of 1926 hailed the end of the British Empire and the birth of the British Common Wealth. The Declaration changed the imperial political dispensation and introduced the autonomy of British Empire dominions. The Declaration stipulated that: *"The dominions within the British Empire, i.e. South Africa, Australia, Canada and New Zealand, are free communities, with equal status. They would be in no way subordinate to one another or Britain, in any aspect of their domestic or external affairs. Though, they remain united by a common allegiance to the Crown."*

The Balfour declaration seems to have ended the Afrikaans-English unification. The focus shifted onto the black-white nation divide. Hertzog became Prime Minister of the PACT. In response to the more significant autonomy under the Balfour Declaration, Hertzog restricted the political rights of non-whites by apportioning demarcated areas for the different ethnic groups. The change formalised the already ghettoised society of South Africa. The measures curtailed the movement for non-whites outside their allocated areas.

The constitutional changes made PACT more acceptable to British Industrialists. It meant that British Industries and Mines could pay lower wages to the mass black labourers and exclude them from senior and higher paid positions. The changes resulted in enormous growth within the British owned industries. The characteristics of capitalism, as the drive behind colonialism, triumphed once again. The changes resulted in the actual progression and continuation of the remnants of British capitalism that drove colonialism. Even though colonialism ended with Unification, capitalistic overtones persevered. Naturally, PACT kept the white voters on their side. Five years later in 1929, they were re-elected. The PACT Cabinet was made up of mainly Afrikaans speaking NP members. They supported republican independence and Afrikaner nationalism. In 1934 the NP and Labour Party merged to form the United Party, a party with continued allegiance and support to Britain.

The United Party elected General Jan Smuts as Prime Minister in September 1939. South Africa joined the British Alliance in World-War-Two against Germany. Hertzog once again opposed support for Britain. He chose to remain neutral in the war effort causing a split in the United Party. Afrikaner opposition under the NP once again resonated the 35% German proportion and affiliation.

Hertzog supporters became progressively disgruntled with Jan Smuts and the United Party. Dr D F Malan supported by the Cape NP refused to continue with the United Party. He remained an independent and formed the *Herstigde, (Re-established) National*

Party (HNP). The split between the United and National Party drove the German - British support partition to a new height. In the general elections of 1948, Dr Malan became the first Prime Minister of the Afrikaner Apartheid Government, the HNP.

In my early thirties, I attended one of the *Herstigde (Purified) National Party's (HNP)* meetings in Nelspruit, a town in the Mpumalanga province of South Africa. Jaap Marias was the HNP's leader at that stage. Upon his arrival, the meeting rose to their feet, saluting him with the typical Nazi salute. The followers raised their fists in the air, chanting *"Jaap Marais, Jaap Marais, Jaap Marais."* The familiar Nazi salute convinced me that there was a severe allegiance to Nazism. I questioned the morals of the HNP movement; red lights flared up. I did not favour Nazism. I attended out of curiosity but left in disgust. They might as well have chanted, *Sieg Heil.*

At this stage of my life, I was not interested in political matters. Soon my political apathy would change. I started studying International Politics.

NP Ascendancy and Apartheid (1939 to 1958)

The United Party took South Africa into World War II in support of Britain. The disruption of war estranged Afrikaners away from the United Party towards the NP. By 1948, there was mounting frustration among Afrikaners with wartime constraints aggravated by rising living costs. The Second World War was, in the eyes of Afrikaners between Germany and Britain. They did not support the government in their war effort. In fact, 35% of the root DNA of the Afrikaner was of German origin.

In the election of May 1948, DF Malan's HNP changed the Party's name back to the National Party (NP) and won the election by a majority of only five seats and just 40% of the electorate voting. In his inauguration speech, Malan said: *"Today South Africa belongs to us once more. South Africa is our own for the first time since Union, and can God grant that it will always remain our own."* Malan did not have the white-black struggle and Apartheid in mind. Using the phrase *remain our own*, Malan was referring to Afrikaner supremacy and nationalism. He was effectively referring to the rivalry between the Afrikaner and the English-speaking peoples of South Africa. The National Party promised a secure political future for only white Afrikaner people. One of the first decisions made by the NP was to take the Republic of South Africa out of the British Common Wealth; thereby severing ties with Britain.

The National Party mobilised the Afrikaner in an appeal to Afrikaans culture, their beliefs, prejudices and moral convictions. The aim was to assert a sense of shared past resentment of British rule and replace it with hopes for the Afrikaner Nation's future. After the 1948 National Party victory, the government bureaucracy changed, giving preference to Afrikaners. Hertzog's Afrikaner nationalism dream came to full fruition; after centuries of oppression Afrikaner freedom from the British achieved. The Afrikaner established a Nationalist Party and Government. The culmination of a desire dating back to 1838 when the Afrikaner, with the Great Trek, moved away from British colonialism.

Did colonisation and oppression inspire within the Afrikaner, the drive to Afrikaner-Apartheid? Paramount for Afrikaner survival, away from Britain and without black political involvement? Probably; that was the cause and drive behind Apartheid and Afrikaner nationalism. The features of Apartheid and Afrikaner nationalism were part of the socio-political make-up of the Afrikaner. This political preference existed long before the 1948 Apartheid Government came to power.

The 1948 election removed all symbols of historic British allegiance. The NP-government abolished British citizenship. The South African national anthem replaced *God Save the Queen*. A real victory for Afrikaner nationalism; British affiliation finally discarded.

The Ultimate Drive of the National Party (1958 to 1989)

The National Party elected Dr H. F. Verwoerd as Prime Minister in 1958. Verwoerd concentrated all powers onto the white minority. Later in this chapter, I write about Verwoerd's allegiance to Germany. Verwoerd's social-political undertones were racial classification and racial sex laws. He apportioned group areas for each ethnic community. Segregated schools, universities, public facilities and sports facilities became the norm. Job-reservation applied rigorously remained intact; favouring whites. British industries employment offer intensified, and the natural influx of black labour to industries and mines brought people of colour ever closer to towns and cities. Jobs in the so-called black *homelands* was non-existent.

Establishing *homelands* for blacks with legal obstacles, excluded non-whites from access to political rights in any common area. British protectorates and African tribal authorities were part and parcel of the British Empire, but the British guardianship disappeared with the Balfour Declaration. South Africa, within its various political divides, was left to its own devices. It seems like, by implementing the Balfour Declaration, Britain washed its hands off the responsibilities relating to Empire commitments; especially to protectorates for people of colour.

Black political awareness and the ill-treatment of blacks led to protests by the African National Congress, and Industrial and Commercial Workers Union of Africa. Protests became commonplace against the NP's policies in the 1950s and 1960s; black Africans burnt passbooks in protest.

In 1960, the Pan-Africanist Congress lodged a peaceful anti-pass law protest in Sharpeville. The police opened fire on the protesters, killing seventy of them and wounding about one-hundred-and-ninety others. The white minority government continued with segregation. The Rivonia trial and later trials resulted in liberation movement leaders persecuted. Two of which were Nelson Mandela and Walter Sisulu, one incarcerated, one living in exile.

Harold McMillan delivered his famous *winds of change* speech to the Apartheid Parliament at Cape Town in 1960 when he stated: *"The wind of change is blowing through this continent. Whether we like it or not, this growth of national consciousness is a political fact. As a fellow member of the Commonwealth, it is our, Britain's, earnest desire to give South Africa our support and encouragement. But I hope you won't mind my saying outright that there are some aspects of your policies which make it impossible for us to do this without being false to our deep convictions about the political destinies of free men to which in our territories we are trying to give effect."* The *free men* Mc Millan referred to were black people. The same African people Britain oppressed and never acknowledged for political rights.

Britain has moved on from colonial oppression, but the Afrikaner government did not. If the NP followed MacMillan's advice, South Africa probably would be better off. But the dogged persistence of Afrikaner-Apartheid protagonists continued. McMillan might as well have philosophically inscribed on the political billboard: '*MENE, MENE, TEKEL, PARSIN*', meaning, *"God has numbered the days of your kingdom, the kingdom of Apartheid."*

The South African government should have responded by starting early restitution and political change. But, under Verwoerd's leadership, stopping the Apartheid movement was impossible. Britain became the leading opponent and campaigner against Apartheid. The international community isolated South Africa with sanctions and trade embargoes. The British focus transferred onto a new goal, to bring the Afrikaner-Apartheid government to a fall.

Western capitalism was the driving force behind colonialism. They made free and profitable use of the Apartheid system. Oppressing and exploiting cheap black labour. Now, the turn-around was evident; the tables turned to the liberation of the people of colour.

The same Western capitalists that used cheap African labour for centuries became the anti-Apartheid protagonists. They changed from oppressors and exploiters to the liberalizing campaigners.

Anti-Apartheid protagonists like British politician Peter Hain played a significant role in bringing Apartheid to a fall. I discuss Hain's involvement in following chapters. The British government honoured Hain with a Lordship for his services in bringing Apartheid to an end; a Lordship for his services to liberate the people of colour? After centuries of British exploitation? Britain seems hypocritical. It is amazing how governments can turn into political chameleons when it suits their political standing.

The liberation struggle became a real thorn in the side of the Apartheid government. The government needed intensified measures of maintaining command and control. Apartheid had to retain the status quo and along with it, white minority rule. The National State Security Management System (NSSMS) became the mechanism to enforce and maintain Afrikaner-Apartheid. I deal extensively with the NSSMS in later chapters.

The Apartheid National Party Unravels (1985-1991)

Police stations and government installations became the target of the liberation struggle. Consequently, the Apartheid regime announced an indefinite state of emergency in 1985. Desmond Tutu, an anti-Apartheid activist, addressed the United Nations in 1986, appealing for further sanctions against South Africa. Britain became the leading party in opposition of Apartheid South Africa. Amazingly, it was the same Britain as imperialists that promised no interference under the Balfour declaration.

In 1987, consecutive strikes and riots resulted during the 10th anniversary of the Soweto uprising. In 1989, F. W. de Klerk became State President bringing change to Verwoerd's extreme Apartheid. Even though he was a conservative, he realised the futility of defending Apartheid. The National Party entered into negotiations with representatives of the non-white community, leading to the relaxation of Apartheid restrictions in 1990. The African National Congress (ANC) along with other liberation movements became legal. The Apartheid government released Nelson Mandela and other political prisoners from prison.

The Convention for a Democratic South Africa (CODESA)

In 1991, the CODESA was established as a multiracial forum, set up by the ANC, IFP and National Party. The aim was a transition to a multiracial democracy based on a classless system. In March 1992, the white electorate in a referendum endorsed constitutional reform resulting in the vote for political change. The referendum poll was open to white voters only. There were violent protests and clashes between the IFP and ANC supporters. Zulu Chief Mangosuthu Buthelezi represented the Inkatha Freedom Party in the negotiations. Buthelezi opposed CODESA. He supported the idea of a Federal Republic to protect ethnic rights and his Zulu nation's political power base. However, the African National Council (ANC) was in favour of a system of national unity. In the run-up to the election Buthelezi withdrew from CODESA. IFP and ANC supporters engaged in political violence and demonstrations. Before the first democratic elections, Buthelezi reconsidered. He did the last minute turn-around to include the IFP on the ballot papers.

Post-Apartheid South Africa and the New National Party

The interim constitution of 1993, ended more than three centuries of white-minority rule in South Africa. A thirty-two member black majority-multiparty transitional government council came to power. The first Republican multiracial election put the ANC in control with an overwhelming victory. Nelson Mandela became president, and in 1994, South Africa once again became a member of the Commonwealth. South Africa relinquished its last hold in Namibia; the enclave of Walvis Bay. De Klerk and the

National Party quit the government of national unity and became part of the official opposition as the New National Party.

Apartheid and the Western Governments

Britain did not favour the Apartheid election outcome of 1948, but the Attlee government nevertheless offered South Africa access to intelligence secrets from Britain and the United States. They considered it not in Britain's interest to lose the stability of a Western capitalist regime in South Africa. Communism was a perceived threat as reiterated in the following excerpt *"The priority for Western governments was to prevent South Africa, with its minerals and strategic location, from falling under Communist influence."*

British Labour government under Clement Attlee considered the anti-communist aspect more critical than its revulsion for Apartheid. The British foreign secretary, Herbert Morrison, in 1951, also supported a white government for South Africa. He considered independence for African colonies as ludicrous. He argued that black regimes will be: *"Like giving a child a latch-key, a bank account and a shotgun."* Considering the actions of President Jacob Zuma in 2017, Morrison was a clairvoyant. Zuma used the *latch-key, bank account and shotgun* to run South Africa into the ground as a failed state with a junk status credit rating. Today in 2017, the ANC government prefer South Africa's leading traders to be from the East, predominantly China and Russia; not any more from the West. I doubt whether the West is comfortable with the situation.

It was helpful for the Western World to turn a blind eye to the wrongs of Apartheid. They had racist views of their own. American segregation was prevalent in 1945. Capitalism, stability and economic preference, favoured wealth gain above integrated societies. Even today, America is paying the price of discrimination in the form of racial tension.

It became a high motivation for the West to oppose the South African Apartheid government once the world's political attitude changed. The situation that tipped the scale was the establishment of the British Commonwealth as a follow-on to the Balfour Declaration and the defeat of Nazi Germany in 1945. The face of the Nazi Concentration Camps with Fascism and Racism shocked the world. The opposition to racial ideologies led to a push for racial integration, topping the political agenda. India's independence in 1947, increased the pressure to grant subordinated ethnic groups their freedom.

The United Nations became an efficient platform for the developing world to vent their anger. Centuries of Western domination fired the revolt among oppressed peoples of colour. Apartheid South Africa soon became the focus of international anti-racist wrath. Western capitalistic support and tolerance of Apartheid disappeared after World War II. Capitalism lost its preferential stance in the job market. The capitalists turned to support liberation struggles, away from their capitalistic past. Over time Britain became proficient in shifting attention away from its past wrong-doings. They transformed into champions of freedom; attention diverted away from British imperialistic, enslaving and colonising practices.

Congruently, after passing the slave trade abolishment laws, the British colonial authorities became the *protectors and liberators* of slaves. They persecuted the Boers when they mistreated their slaves in the early nineteenth century. Did Apartheid become the scapegoat, hung out to dry for the conscience of the West's wrongdoings during the slave trade and Imperialism?

The West and capitalism remained silent to the atrocity of Apartheid, as long as Western capitalism could benefit. The Western powers even used Apartheid South Africa to oppose communism in Southern Africa through RENAMO. They preferred to turn a blind eye for as long as capitalism could profit? I write in later chapters on RENAMO as an anti-liberation movement but also about liberation organisations.

Not to negate the obvious and in the final instance, Apartheid has to answer for its atrocious disregard of political and human rights for non-whites during the Apartheid era. A responsibility not to be ignored or denied. Apartheid was wrong in the Imperialist period and as continued during the National Party's thirty-year regime; Apartheid had to go.

German Support for Apartheid South Africa

The alliance between the far right movements of South Africa and fascist movements like German-Nazism represent an uncomfortable reality. During the Anglo-Boer-War Germany supplied the Boers in the Transvaal Boer Republic with guns and ammunition. The Afrikaner opposed aggression against Germany during the First- and Second World War. Evidence of a liaison between the Afrikaner nation and Germany appears in historical annals supported by research documentation. Nazism during the Holocaust is a worldwide and uneasy awareness. Not surprisingly, some German Foreign Policy documents confirm the South African alliance. What follows might account for some distressing reading for white Afrikaners from the Apartheid era.

Berlin's Involvement in the Mandela Trial

Bonn aimed to support Apartheid because it considered South Africa a robust pro-western coalition. South Africa provided German companies with lucrative business opportunities. Germany remained Apartheid's most loyal supporter. West German companies supplied South Africa with helicopters to carry out surveillance of protests during Mandela's imprisonment. The support incorporated techniques to identify activists, many of whom were from Mandela's political entourage.

South African Minister Oswald Pirow – A Hitler Fan

Germany's support for South Africa goes way back, before the 1948 victory of the Afrikaner Apartheid government. German-South African relations developed during the *Third Reich* in 1933. The South African Justice and Defence Minister Oswald Pirow, was of German ancestry. He was a Hitler fan and even favoured Nazi anti-Semitic laws applied to the South African Jewish population. Pirow promoted the exchange of Afrikaner students and professors with Germany. He also supported the training of Apartheid politicians in Germany. Hendrik Verwoerd, the 1958 President of South Africa, and *Father of Apartheid* studied in Germany. Verwoerd studied at the Universities of Hamburg, Berlin and Leipzig. Verwoerd affected the cruellest Apartheid legislation that eventually destroyed the NP government.

Bonn and Pretoria engaged in negotiations for a cultural agreement in 1955, related to benefits for South Africa's significant German minority. Trade with South Africa was booming. In the late 1950s, Germany was the third-largest supplier of the South African Industry.

Support from Germany with the Mandela Prosecution

Germany supported the Apartheid authorities during the Rivonia Trial with the aim to undermine the growing resistance and liberation struggle of among other the ANC. The West German authorities provided South Africa with *Chargé d'Affaires* documents relating to the banning of the *Kommunistische Partei Deutschlands* (KPD) in Germany. The materials provided would help with arguments against the ANC defendants. The report suggested that studying the KPD trial would provide valuable insights for the Apartheid government.

Germany: Apartheid's Direct Financier

While the West distanced themselves from the Apartheid regime, Germany maintained a close relationship. German companies expanded trade and investments, approving export credit guarantees for German deliveries. Birgit Morgenrath wrote a book on West German business relations with South Africa, recalling that Germany supported South Africa in becoming a nuclear power. He accused Siemens of having supplied South Africa with equipment for uranium enrichment. West German banks made loans to the Apartheid regime, finally becoming the world's most influential financier of Apartheid.

Comments on the Afrikaner Nationalist Party

Afrikaner Apartheid and delusions materialised as Afrikaner nationalism, born from British occupation from 1806 to 1902. Afrikaner Nationalism turned into a delusional psychosis and conviction of self-determination; never to be governed by anyone but the Afrikaner themselves. Scarred by war and concentration camps, the Afrikaner pursued Afrikaner nationalism and self-determination.

While the West, after World-War-Two, moved on from oppression and the subjugation in the imperialistic era, South Africa doggedly continued with Apartheid. Conflict with black African tribes since 1838 convinced the Afrikaner nation that they do not want to share political power with non-whites. Historically, ever since the occupation in 1652, non-whites never enjoyed political rights, under either the Dutch, British or Boer governments.

Exposing Africa's natives, people of colour, to western values, changed Africa's political scene; the people of colour wanted the political rights of the West. People of colour developed the need for political recognition and inclusion. The white Apartheid Government had their reasons for having Apartheid as a constitutional dispensation. They were only governing on behalf of white people, predominantly the Afrikaner nation. Naturally, this was to the detriment of non-white people. That is why the Afrikaner had to capitulate during democratisation. The government of a country needs to govern for the mutual benefit of the entire nation, not for the preferred few.

Maybe the Apartheid Government should have followed the example of former British Colonies, like Australia. The white-dominated rule materialised as the outcome of genocide and extermination. The genocide of the native population might not have been an admirable example for South Africa to follow. The extermination of the Tasmanian Aborigines is a perfect model for colonialism elsewhere in the new-age western world. White settlers killed between three to fifteen-thousand Aborigines in 1908. The settlers regarded the natives as vermin. In a genocidal attempt, the colonists hunted the Aborigines as a form of sport. Did this swing the demographic balance away from Aborigines towards white people; favour the white settlers? The Australian example is only one of many genocidal exercises practised by immigrants from the western world during imperialism. It allowed the survival of white majority-ruled governments throughout the post-colonial West.

These ex-colonial countries have non-white citizens, but a non-white majority will never govern them because the non-white population is in the minority. A white minority is precisely the root of the white Apartheid government's problem. The native people are the people of colour, and they are the majority.

Are the non-white members of the ex-colonised countries, like America, first-class citizens? The world newscast tells me, NO! So the cruel reality is that South Africa based the voting ban on skin colour. Even the white British, perceived to be the arch enemies of the Afrikaner in the Anglo-Boer-War and living in South Africa, had full political rights. Africa will forever be the playground and battlefield of the Capitalistic West and the Communistic East. I research this reality extensively in later chapters.

There is no question in my mind the atrocious Apartheid policies had to go. It is such a pity that the democratisation process of South Africa did not start with the Balfour Declaration; as manifested in Canada, Australia and New Zealand.

The Afrikaner did itself no favours by stubbornly persisted on segregation of ethnicities within a unitary state. But, it needs emphasising that they only extrapolated what the European Imperialists brought to Africa.

In the next chapter, I consider the derogative treatment of people of colour under Apartheid.

Part Two:

LIVING IN APARTHEID SOUTH AFRICA

Apartheid is a familiar concept the world over. Even though internationally the blame and origin of Apartheid relates to the Afrikaner-Boer nation, the truth is that Imperialism introduced Apartheid to Africa.

The 1948 racialist National Party, constitutionalised apartheid that became known and hated worldwide. The first Apartheid legislation was passed by the British. Even the Dutch maintained a societal system of segregation.

The ugly face of Afrikaner Apartheid meant separate and substandard public services. South African blacks did not have political or even fundamental human rights under colonialism and slavery. Their citizenship tarnished turning them into sub-human beings. Hendrik Verwoerd as President during the Apartheid years verbally reverberated the Cecil John Rhodes' Apartheid ideas. Verwoerd turned South Africa into a Police State. Tribally-based Bantustans separated blacks from whites and abolished their political rights; even negated their land ownership.

The African National Council (ANC) fought for the best part of a century to democratise South Africa under Nelson Mandela. Mandela, also nicknamed Madiba, suffered a twenty-seven-year incarceration. A multitude of political activists lived in exile or suffered imprisonment. I took eighty years since the establishment of the ANC, for the National Party to consent to reform in the

1980s. Apartheid dismantled in 1990 when the then president F. W. de Klerk released Mandela from prison.

In Part Two I will consider living conditions for people of colour under Apartheid. I will also discuss my own experiences along with my life as a Civil Defence Officer for twenty-two-years.

Part Two consists of the following chapters

4. *People of Colour; Suffering under Apartheid* *100*
5. *Are Africans Less Intelligent than Europeans? Why?* *136*
6. *My Career in Civil Defence; Protecting People* *153*

CHAPTER 4

PEOPLE OF COLOUR; SUFFERING UNDER APARTHEID

Political Structures Changed after Colonisation

The cultural clashes between black Africans and white Europeans presented some challenging disputes. Imperial expansion and colonialism resulted in deep-seated grievances and even hatred. Understanding the non-white perspective on the Apartheid system; it is essential to comprehend the differences between white and black cultures. Also one needs to evaluate how black perceptions changed as a result of imperialism.

Africa before white settlement maintained a system of pluralism and flexibility, with accommodating ethnicities readily accepting outsiders. They admitted whites on condition that they respect the rule of the paramount chief. Precolonial African tribes varied in nature. They were either stateless, state-administered or a monarchical kingdom. They were self-governing units instituted on collectivism as autonomous units. All members participated, directly or indirectly, in matters of the tribe.

Tribal Africans do allow for private ownership, they owned cattle and work implements independently as private possessions. However, tribalism did not allow for privately owned land. Therefore, territory commonly held, did not support a market economy or land aristocracy. Due to an abundance of land, dissatisfied individuals could relocate and establish a new settlement elsewhere; no land transactions needed.

The tribal chiefs governed the tribe with one or more councillors based on consensus. If not in agreement, the tribe would assemble, and majority ruling would apply. The Chief did not act dictatorially; he would hear all demands and male adults were free to criticise him.

Some tribes were stateless and had no central authority or class system. The tribe could depose a chief that abused power. Pre-colonial Africa was not designed to be all-powerful; there were signs of a loose confederation.

When British colonies emerged, the secondary regime rule came into play. The indigenous system was consumed and oppressed by the imperial powers. Some political institutions still exist in Africa today, in a re-arranged tribal and rural landscape manner. Only Botswana retained some domestic systems, with a rigid centralised government. But, this does not represent the archaically political environment of Africa.

The colonial employed tribal chiefs were virtual administrators serving as buffers between the tribal community and imperial powers. They were leaders moderated to salaried officials, answerable to white magistrates. Traditional political structures worked ably in smaller-scale societies but were less active in larger communities. Ultimately African tribal structures were based on chieftaincy and royalty and could be problematic where ethnic antagonisms erupted. Under colonialism, tribal communities transformed into a system corrupted by an oppressive white regime; African culture evolved and changed, because of colonialism. Tribal Rule structures diminished into urbanised societies, and western political systems took control. However, tribal and pagan cultures practised oppressive, reactionary tendencies only slightly less grave than that of the racist colonial culture.

Precolonial African cultures used to be dynamic, today they are merely historical manifestations. The South African occupation and European colonisation, along with the Great Trek of the Afrikaner Boer nation to the North, introduced conflict between Brit, Boer and Africans. The Great Trek led to the establishment of the two Boer Republics, Transvaal and Orange Free State that opposed the British in the Anglo-Boer-War. This conglomerate of occupations, colonisation and Great Trek, harmed the people of colour extensively. Stripped of political- and even human rights without exception. Segregated societies established throughout Africa.

Informal segregation of non-whites took hold when the first Europeans arrived in Africa. Dutch colonists and the ethnically diverse slave population lived separated. This state of social life gave effect to a formalised system of racial stratification; a social condition developed under the Dutch Empire in the 18th century. Various Cape legislation continued the discrimination against Africans. The policies of the Boer republics also excluded non-whites from everyday politics. The Apartheid government constitutionalised the centuries-old segregation when the National Party came to power in 1948. According to current demographic classification introduced by colonialism and Apartheid, South Africa has four primary groupings, African, Asian, Coloured, and White. The imported peoples, as a result of colonial migration, are the Whites and Asians. The Apartheid laws grouped Coloureds, Asians and Africans as non-whites.

The root genetics of Coloureds is the Khoikhoi ethnic tribe, original to the Cape before colonisation. The Coloureds of modern times have their origin in multi-racial marriages from differing ethnicities. Apartheid classified children from parents with different ethnicities as Coloureds; similar I suppose to Eurasians. The Western Cape Province, with Cape Town as the capital city, is the natural habitat of Coloureds.

When considering African people, there are nine ethnicities. They are along with the Khoikhoi-coloureds, the original natives of Africa, all people of colour. The nine primary African ethnic groups in South Africa include the Zulu, Xhosa, Basotho (South Sotho); Africans speak a variety of Bantu languages.

The Population Registration Act of 1950 ultimately classified all South Africans into the four racial groups, the criteria being; *"appearance, known ancestry, socio-economic status, and cultural lifestyle."*

The history of segregation and discrimination against people of colour efficiently dates back to 1652, when the first Europeans set foot in Africa for the first time. Gradually over centuries discrimination became law and finally constitutionalised as Apartheid by the National Party from 1948 up to democratisation in 1994.

Land Ownership Dispute

Land ownership after Imperialism remains a contentious issue. When the Europeans came into contact with the people of colour, the disparity in land ownership culture, between black and white people were prevalent. The black tribal collective land ownership allowed the Boers during the *Great Trek* to settle on land freely. The Boers, on the other hand, had a culture inclusive of private land ownership. For instance in Griqualand, Boers arrived in Griqua town after the colonisation of Natal by the British. The Boers acquired land from the Griqua, buying it in exchange for horses, liquor, firearms and ammunition. However, the British under the banner of a British *protectorate* colonised Griqualand upon the discovery of diamonds. Britain did not buy the land, they just colonised it, and then they extracted the diamond riches for the sole benefit of imperialist Britain. I explained the Griqualand colonisation earlier. Blacks claim that the whites stole their land. Is it true in respect of imperialism? Britain did not buy Griqualand. Britain just took the land with all its diamonds.

In modern times black people like the *Black First Land First (BFLF)*, often accuse whites that they stole land from their black ancestors. Based on black tribal culture, relating to land as common property for all, irrespective of ethnicity, this theft claim does not wash.

Furthermore, there is clear evidence that the Boers traded land for valuables. One must assume that the deals were consensual.

The SA Communist Party support white land ownership stating that: "*South Africa belongs to the people living on the sub-continent.*"

Or maybe they say one thing and practice something different. The black claims of property theft, especially after centuries of white ownership, is grossly delusional and a manifestation of arrogance and ignorance.

Robert Mugabe for instance recently made the statement to a white audience claiming: *"Zimbabwe will never be yours."* How ignorant and arrogant can a black President of a country be?

White Zimbabweans in the 1950s produced unprecedented prosperity for Zimbabwe. Like South Africa in the 1950's under the white rule; Pound for Pound, the currencies correlated with Britain. Today £1 equals 485 Zimbabwean $. With productivity plunging and the country became more and more dependent on imports. Hyperinflation peaked at 89.7 sextillion percent for Zimbabwe by 2009. Like South Africa, Zimbabwe is a failed state. What does Robert Mugabe want? A Zimbabwe that belongs to an impoverished, backwards black nation? Or would it not be better for everybody to have a Zimbabwe that belongs to a multi-cultural prosperous and proud society, free from racism and despotism? In any case, before the Rhodesian man migrated to Zimbabwe it belonged to nobody.

It is the above disparities and cultural clashes that gave rise and persist among blacks and whites, posing the question; what is morally right and what is wrong? I dealt with citizenship in chapter one and confirmed that the land on earth belongs to man, irrespective of ethnicity. Only once man lay claim and introduce laws on migration does he have a right to the land. When did Mugabe claim Zimbabwe? In this chapter, I will investigate what the people of colour perceive to be wrong with Apartheid.

How do Non-Whites Perceive Segregation cum Apartheid

My next survey focuses on an understanding of how the non-whites and oppressed people of South Africa viewed Apartheid. The outcome might elucidate a grasp, clarification and origin of the contemporary psychosis of mistrust and fear that grips the modern South African nation. Throughout my life, I interacted with so-called non-whites, they were different, nine official languages and a myriad of ethnic tribes. I will elucidate the segregated and Apartheid effect on people of colour by reflecting on my life experiences and also transcribing some published encounters.

My Young Life with Coloured People in the Western Cape

My namesake Cronje ancestors fled from France as French Huguenots. In 1678, they settled in *Wamakerskloof* in the Wolseley District of the Western Cape. Pre-teens, our family visited our grandfather's wine-producing farm in Tulbagh. The estate called *Vrolikheid (happiness)* is situated close to where Pierre and Estienne *Cronier (Cronjé)* settled. *Vrolikheid*, my grandfather's farm shaped many facets of my character and understanding during my youth.

Grandfather Carsten had a team of coloured workers on the farm as non-whites. They were called coloureds with light-brown-skins and often blue or green eyes. Grandfather referred to them as the *Volk*, translated I suppose *folk*. They are witty and intelligent. A master-and-slave relationship developed over centuries as a continuation of colonisation. The Dutch started societal segregation followed by the British and finally constitutionalised by the Boer-Afrikaner Nation. In modern times relationships and integration have changed due to democratisation; relations almost normalised. But, segregation is still prevalent within the South African nation.

On the farm Vrolikheid, coloured workers lived in lodgings on the winemaking farm. They depended on the farmer for their livelihood. My grandfather would provide for all their needs; accommodation, food and clothing. On some farms, they even attended the evening prayer meeting, conducted by the farmer. That was not the tradition on my grandfather's farm, *Vrolikheid*.

The *Volk*, coloured workers, earned a weekly wage, along with their daily quota of wine. Three servings a day in an empty fish-tin, as part of their regular ration. The fish-tin-top removed and the tin rinsed. The goblet became blackened over time. It had a measure of two hundred and fifty millilitres. Along with the goblet-tot, a takeaway of two half-jacks of wine was provided by the farmer. One before siesta break and one at *tjaila-time*; end of the daytime. The half-jacks measured three hundred and seventy-five millilitre each. The total consumption per day amounted to almost one and a half litres in the day. That will turn anyone into an alcoholic. One-and-a-half litres should be your minimum fluid intake per day, but not all in the form of wine.

Elevated to the position of *wine steward*, I became a person of interest to the *punters*. They entrusted me to serve the daily quota of wine. I abetted their day-to-day and boozy pleasure. The decadence of the moment, the Bacchus's blessing. The pouring pitcher was a proper oak wine barrel. It hung from a wire-handgrip with circular metal hoops and copper rivets. On the top rounding sits a wooden stopper, encased in a hessian cloth to seal the contents from the perishing outside air. Knock the stopper, this way and then that way with a wooden mallet; it will loosen. Once the stopper heaves from its airtight seat, pouring could begin. Just thinking of it, the smell of the wine cellar still lingers in my nostrils. I had to pour the wine into the fish-tin-goblet, the improvised-wine-beaker. The meniscus had to bulge upwards, at the top-goblet-rim, a nick from overflowing. A hollow meniscus at the rim was unacceptable and will produce a grimace of disdain from brash eyes in judgement.

Once decanted and endorsed with a grimace of pleasure, a sombre ceremony commenced. With eager quivering hands, the goblet will rise to anxious waiting lips, careful not to waste a single droplet. They swallowed the Bacchus benediction as if an angel pissed on their tongues. The alcohol ravished their taste buds in one single hallucinogenic moment of pleasure. Their lips would curl outwards, and they would savour the heavenly moment with profound celebration and the smacking of moist lips. A wriggling quiver of their thin, sinewy bodies concluded the ceremony. "*Thank you, Master."* They would show their appreciation with a smile as broad as the horizon. The satisfaction is written all over their wrinkled faces. They were inebriated and happy, ready for the hot day's work in the vineyards.

The small decanting hand-held-cask, I refilled from twenty-gallon wine barrels. Equipped with a funnel and mallet, I had to lose-tap the stopper of the big wine barrel. A tap from the left then again from the right, till the stopper loosened. Then I released the stopper from its seating and funnel-filled the handheld decanter to the rim. Grandfather would load two empty twenty-gallon wine barrels on the horse-drawn cart. There would still be a full one in the cellar. We would head to the stately Drostdy-Hof wine cellar, halfway to the town of Tulbagh, re-filling forty gallons.

We would park the horse-drawn carriage, called *a trippy*, with the barrels, next to large wine tanks. They looked like silos, towering metres into the blue skies with their long thick decanter hoses. The attendant would loosen the stopper on the two casks; then he would fill the vats. As the barrels filled up, the *trippy* would sag and creak under the weight. Drinking was a serious business on the wine producing farm, *Vrolikheid.*

Due to the intense midday heat, work started at five am, with breakfast break at nine. *Siesta* break was between eleven am and three pm. Mid-day summer was too hot to work in the sun. Coloured workers will only work for a wine farmer that serves wine rations.

The white farmer's wives protested against this practice. They wanted the provision of wine to workers to stop. Women, as carers, are more in touch with their noble and kind souls. Men, the hunters, focus on getting things done, dealing with the pragmatic. To the white male farmer's perception, they treated their coloured *Volk* well. Even the coloureds themselves accepted the relationship as *usual.* They showed complete allegiance to the master in all manners of life. It was a pseudo-feudal relationship. I never considered the connection as *acceptable and normal.*

Even maintaining order on the farm was the Master's prerogative, little to no interference from the Police. Weekends the coloured workers would go to town. As a result of their alcohol addiction, they would drink beyond limits. On returning home, they would be inebriated, rowdy and fighting among themselves; bent on being destructive. It was standard practice for my grandfather to intervene with a whip and restore the order. According to the coloured workers, the treatment was reasonable and the Master's prerogative. The general acceptance of this false relationship *(allegiance),* I perceived as delusional.

During colonisation and onwards, Coloured workers would adopt the farmer's family name as their own, abandoning their tribal culture. Names like *Apple van der Merwe and Blom (Flower) Beukes* were given to children of coloured parents. The worker adopted the lifestyle of the white man. But, they were still tribal Khoikhoi, Coloureds in light brown skins. The characteristics of colonisation persisted, it demolished the culture of the natives. They were given European names and subdued to the will of the settlers' Western values.

Non-white children, in a conducted survey, were asked the question; *"Who is the most powerful in life?"* the response frequently was; *"the white man."* An apparent symptom of colonisation and cultural change.

Culturally, the Khoikhoi and the San (Bushmen) speak Khoisan languages. They are the languages of Africa that have click consonants. Most have no written record, but when printed the characters are obscure. The Ju'hoan language, one of the Khoisan languages, has 48 click consonants and nearly as many non-click sounds. Authentic ancestral Khoikhoi denominations would be; Kharkoen and Hoaaran. The names naturally had meanings. Aixallaies meant Afrikaner. Han-Khau-an said descendant from the Beersheba tribe and Habeas-Khartoum meant *Velskoendraers;* Afrikaans for *leather-skin-shoe-wearers.*

Some authentic Khoisan today still live in the Kalahari Desert; primarily in Namibia and Botswana. Khoisan languages are considered endangered, fading or extinct. Earlier I described how the Khoikhoi fled from Dutch oppression into the desert. The remaining Khoikhoi integrated with the Cape population as Coloureds. They speak Afrikaans, no Khoisan languages, and living in western culture. The true Khoikhoi in the Western Cape is for all practical purposes extinct.

"I am not a Ka fir; you do not talk to me like that."

I grew up in the present Gauteng, among the Africans, they are black in skin colour and members of the black northern African tribes. They are different from the Cape Coloureds. I became accustomed to the Gauteng African's manner of speaking. But, the coloureds communicated on similar phrasing with whites. Their first language was and still is Afrikaans. The black people of the north had tribal languages, the likes of Zulu and Xhosa.

The Africans had to learn Afrikaans or English as a second language to connect within a multi-racial society. Black people's communication is loaded with animation and compromising sentence constructions. If you talk in the animated black African manner of speaking with the coloured workers, they will scorn: *"I am not a ka-fir, you do not talk to me like that."* Grandfather would confirm; *"show respect, they are coloureds, not ka-firs."*

I thought they were just non-whites? Wow, I learnt quickly!

The coloureds also had an intimidating way of initiating newcomers to their farm-world. Lessons I had to learn while working on the farm during school holidays. The coloureds harvested grapes in bushel baskets with two handles at the top. Carrying the basket shoulder high to the horse-drawn cart, the coloured worker would hand the basket up to me to empty the grape content into the horse-drawn cart. Cunningly, on the first take of the basket, the coloured worker would deliberately drop his shoulder, lowering the basket. Off-balance I dived head first into the basket full of grapes. I fell from the cart, basket and all to the ground; crown buried ear deep into the soggy grapes. There were laughs all around, including Grandfather. I was humiliated and initiated. After that we became friends, my status accepted equal to the coloureds. I was a farm worker. I carried bushel baskets and harvested grapes shoulder to shoulder with the coloureds. For my six weeks, holiday work on the farm, grandfather will give me the enormous pay of ten shillings. He was a tight-fisted old man.

I had to address the more elderly coloureds as Outa or Ou-Aia respectfully; they were the equal of grandpa and grandma. You might find this an intriguing social relationship. Effectively they were Grandfather's *slaves*. They deserved respect from white youngsters. It was part of the package.

This strange relationship developed almost organically on farms within an Apartheid society. Within urban and city environments this relationship would most probably not happen. All-in-all, none of the inter-ethnic group associations, reflect an integrated South African Rainbow Nation. Because of inequalities, the nation remains segregated.

The memories I recall, date back to the 1950's and will most probably have evolved. Today the situation probably levelled out some of the differences. But, in the early years of Apartheid, relationships across the colour-line was strained and not integrated.

Fanie and Jabulani: Young Lives - Black and White

I got my inspiration for this story from a freedom song, by Lochner de Kock and Richard Van Der Westhuyzen. The song *Fanie and Jabulani* take me back in time, evoking old memories. It serves as an allegory to the problems young boys on both sides of the skin-colour line experienced during the Apartheid years.

Real-life experiences, I lived through as a young boy, figure in the story. The farm, big tree, bees, all the imagery of my life as a young white boy.

Start of my Parable

I am the 5-year-old Fanie.

A white son of the farmer living on the farm. The farm has lots of cattle, vineyards and orchards. My brothers and sister are off to school. I am not school-age yet. It is early morn, and mother sent me outside to play with Jabulani. His Dad is a big black Zulu man. Jabulani doesn't go to school. I do not understand why he is older than my eldest brother. Apartheid says he does not have to go to school. Jabulani's Dad is black. I like playing with Jabulani, his name says; laugh big, *jabula gakulu*. I am waiting under the big old Eucalyptus tree, at the back of the house on the river bank. It's the break of dawn, and the sun paints the sky orange-red. Jabulani is late. He lives in the worker's village down by the river. He has to sweep the yard and tend to the chickens before we can play.

The coloured people work on the farm, some with my Mum, some with my Dad. Dad and the coloured men left with the tractor and trailer. It's only me and Mum and the women of colour at home. They are working in and around the house tending the sheep, chickens, and the vegetable garden. There is also that naughty billy goat. He thumped me in my tummy. I keep an eye on him. He is shrewd and nasty.

The farm is big with lots of families, been that way for three generations, since Grandpa and Great-grandpa's time. The enormous Eucalyptus tree is full of flowers, and that bee is busy-busy, buzzing and collecting nectar and pollen. We're going to pay that bee, with his honey a visit today. I can hear the wind talking to the old tree moving the leaves and rustling its branches. Dad said the wind brings stories from far-far away and whispers it to the wise old tree. Dad said if I listen and use my imagination the tree will tell me a story. *Imagination*, it is a big word. Dad said it is like dreaming, just keep your eyes open. I believe him, but Jabulani does not.

"The tree has no ears," Jabulani says. *"The wind just pushes the tree and moves it around, and when the wind gets angry with the tree, it will break the tree's branches. That's when the tree won't listen to the wind,"* he said.

So, the tree has ears, it just won't hear, like Mum always tells me off: *"You do not listen, Fanie."* That is when I do not pick my clothes up from the floor.

We often lie on our backs Jabulani and me, side by side. We can see the blue sky, high up through the leaves, opening and closing, opening and closing, like a curtain of leaves. I closed my eyes. I know Dad said *open eyes*, but maybe, just maybe. I wait, and I think, and I listen, and I dream. No-go, the tree still doesn't tell me stories, not yet. It will someday tell me a story, I know.

"Sago-bona, I see you Fanie" Jabulani greeted me in Zulu from the corner of the house. Kunjane, how are you Jabulani? I shouted back, delighted to see him. We are going to get some honey today, aren't we Jabulani? Yes?

I greeted him with my all-round-my-head smile and jumped to my feet. If my ears were not in the way, my smile would be all over my head; Mum often tells me.

"Yebo, yes", Jabulani said; *"I have the potato sack and matches, we'll make smoke. That will chase that bee away. Then we will take his honey."*

I am scared of the bees, but Jabulani is brave. He promised he would teach me how to pinch the bee's, honey. I did not tell Mum, she would not let me go. But I trust Jabulani. He showed me lots of things in the bush. He knows how to kill a bush-dove with his catapult. He calls it his *catti*. He made it himself using old car tube, a tree branch, and a patch of leather from an old shoe. We barbecued a dove the other day on the open fire, without salt. It wasn't nice, but Jabulani loved it. Maybe he was starving. I had a big breakfast. Mum says breakfast is important, never to miss.

We set off barefoot on a lazy jog. The wind ruffled our hair. But, not to worry, the ant heap will be there with the bees coming and going; making the honey. The bees were waiting for us. They met us halfway. The closer we got the more they buzzed. They tried to chase us away, humming, buzzing, round and around our heads.

"Hhlala lapa, stay here, Fanie," Jabulani warned me while he lit the potato bag. There was smoke, lots of smoke. Jabulani waved the smoking bag around, and the bees calmed down. Jabulani slowly walked towards the anthill. The termites left long ago. The bees had taken their nest. I followed a few steps away. The bees got angry again. Jabulani broke a piece of the ant hill to get inside. The bees were all around us, swarming, swishing, and stinging. The first find was young-bee. Jabulani took a bite of the brood of young bee and handed it to me. The bee larvae were still breeding in the honeycomb. I took a bite, the juicy white goodness trickled down our chins and made white streaks onto our tummies. My taste buds started to dance. We don't wear shirts on the farm. Jabulani wears an animal skin loincloth, like his Zulu ancestors. I wear khaki shorts.

I wanted to run. Jabulani was as calm as a cucumber. He just said: *"Gahle, Gahle Fanie, wait, hold on, haikona balega, slow down, don't run young boy, the bees will chase you."*

I had to be brave. Do not be a sissy, Dad always tells me. *Big boys don't cry!*

So I stayed, and one bee zapped me. It burnt like hell. *Big boys don't cry*, I whispered to myself. Jabulani's hand came out of the ant heap with a second piece. A beautiful piece of honeycomb, white-waxed it oozed with runny honey. *Ouch*, another bee-sting in my neck. That hurt and *ouch* another one on my cheek. The bees were angry; we had to get out of there.

"Boya, boya futi umfana, tina balega, come Fanie young boy get over here, we have to run," Jabulani shouted. We ran, honeycomb in Jabulani's hand. I had the young bee in mine. The smoking potato bag dropped next to the ant hill. Still smoking to keep the bees at

bay. We ran for the safety of the river. I don't think we outran the bees; they are fast. They must have lost interest, or the smoking rag calmed them down.

When we got to the river, the clothes flew in all directions. We placed the honey and young bee on a rock. We darted for the cooling, soothing water and doused our burning stings. *Don't bother with swimming trunks on the farm. Your birth suits are your bathing suits*, Dad says. Dripping wet, we wriggled our bodies and basked in the sun to dry, counting our bee stings. Jabulani removed the bee barbs from my skin with his *Best* pocket knife. Just scrape the barb off, don't squeeze the venom bubble, it will send all the poison into your skin. Then I helped him to remove the spikes on his black skin. They looked like tiny snowflakes on black marble. Proud as peacocks we bragged, daring and chuffed with our honey-booty and the young bee as a bonus.

Arms cuddled our knees, cupping our ears. Our arses hovered over the dirt. *'Mum's going to have my backside tonight, bath time, big-time, for sure,'* I thought.

We had to take another dip in the river, washed the sticky fingers and cheeks. The young bee made white streaks down our cheeks, chins and all over our chests and tummies. We were well fed, bellies bulging, thanks to the bees.

Bath-time Mum told me off, big-time, and she scolded Dad. She said he must have a word with Jabulani: *"Jabulani should know better."* Mum said. Dad just chuckled, he knows growing up on the farm. It is a third-generation family farm. His forebears all played with the coloured boys. Dad knew all too well. It was as if Dad showed me the ropes himself. It's like a walkabout in the outback. Dad trusted Jabulani.

Fanie: I am 12 years old

Seven years had passed, things changed, and I went to secondary school in town. Jabulani worked the lands with my Dad. He turned into a big strong Zulu, but, no more laughter. We did not play any more. We just *greeted "Sago-bona Fanie, I see you Fanie." And I,* Kunjane, how are you, Jabulani? We both responded, *"lungile, lungile, we're okay."* Jabulani was the only Zulu on the farm. The other workers were coloureds; even his Mum was a woman of colour. Childhood days were gone, I entered teenage years. My peer group became all-white, no faces of colour. Apartheid meant no integration at school. They played soccer, and we played rugby.

Dad talked about the Rivonia Trial, Mandela and the terrorists, the *Toy-Toy* demonstrations and the burning townships. There were tear gas and shootings. *"We will have to make peace,"* Dad said. *"This cannot go on. The world is against us and change will have to come. The news is full of liberation, the government will have to free Mandela, and democratic elections are on the cards."* Dad rambled on. He did not want Apartheid, hated it, so did I.

Jabulani regularly visited the coloured township and his black and coloured friends, the liberation fighters. Dad said he joined the ANC Youth League. Dad thought Jabulani was a freedom fighter with Umkhonto we Sizwe, the military wing of the ANC. Jabulani moved to Johannesburg.

Why? Who is he fighting? Who is the enemy? We are his friends. He is my best friend, my childhood mentor, my buddy for life. We heard it on the news; Sharpeville, the shootings, and the killings.

Jabulani came back home. His black body draped in a coffin. They buried him next to our honey spot, the ant heap on the rocky ridge overlooking the farm. I remembered the fun, the treats of honey. Our young-bee haven, our river swims and catapult hunts. Our childhood playground, our soul-sharing oasis, shelter and retreat. All gone, all wasted.

Fanie - I've grown up, I am 25 years old

I returned to the big old eucalyptus tree and the farm. It is the Post-Apartheid years. We have a black majority ANC government. The sun had gone down, the sky turned grey and mottled, and the world is grim. The ANC government took our farm after three generations; gone to democratisation and non-white farmers. The farm gate, leaning askew and warped against the crooked gatepost. Aghast, open to the new South Africa. The old farmhouse in ruin, burnt to the ground. No animals to roam the land. No promise of a harvest this year. The big old tree is all that's left.

And the tree finally told me a story, a picture story about our farm. About Jabulani, our wasted young lives. A desolate reminder of the beauty that had been. Jabulani, the Zulu man that died. And me Fanie, the white man that remained. We lost everything because of Apartheid. It all seems unreal, like a long time ago and far far away. The big old tree shadows the memory of Jabulani and my youth. Now Jabulani lies in a grave in the grass. Just a heap with the lone cross and the carved epitaph: RIP Jabulani - Nkosi Sekelel Afrika - God bless Africa.

End of the Parable Fanie and Jabulani.

I Am Sad: A Poem on Apartheid

Another appropriate reminder from my youth is a poem, I wrote it long ago. My childhood friend Norman, the Zulu gardener. Was he our garden slave? We spent our childhood years in the backyard of our family home in the present Gauteng Province. Norman was the elder, in many ways of life, he was my mentor. I was the Boss's, white son. Fortunately, my dad did the right thing by Norman. He taught him to drive a heavy goods vehicle. The big truck became Norman's adult livelihood. Norman had a good job.

The start of the poem: I am sad:

I am sad, the stones
The black African migrants
But there were the diamonds
I am glad, Norman, my youth friend, family gardener
Taught me my second language, young days, Zulu
The black Zulu teenager, my youth confident
I was skin white; he was skin-black

Entangled in racial discrimination, the State dictate
Forced apart, forcefully impaired
We did not matter, too young to concern, culturally cursed

I am glad. Norman bought cheap offal, intestines
We stripped it clean, by hand
Wind-dried on the barbed wire fence
Foraged wild spinach, Normans *Marog*
Cooked the stew, Norman's *Sheba*
Stewed Corn porridge, Norman's *Puto-Pap*
We huddled low down, no chairs, knees cupping our ears,
Bare feet, arses hovering above the dirt
Ate with bare hands from the black-burnt-paint-tin-pot
Hand-scooped *Puto-Pap*, mould into mouth size clumps
Dipped into the *Sheba*, finger licking good
Manna from heaven

I am sad, poverty, Ebola and Coca-Cola
I am sad, capitalism and colonialism
The stinking rich, the absolute impoverished
Mammon the dragon, capitalistic jargon
My Dad taught Norman to drive, to earn a living
His eighteen-wheeler truck, big, bold and boisterous
Norman the proud grown-up man, he came to visit
Parked his eighteen-wheeler up front, filled the street
Proudly, his black frame packs the space, the high-up cab

I am glad, Mandela and de Klerk killed Apartheid
Mandela was not mad, de Klerk was a reasonable man
Some were diamonds; some were stone.
End of the poem: I am sad.

Apartheid in my Youth: Rebecca our House Maid.

Apartheid featured prominently while growing up. Fondly I reminisce about the people of colour that literally and figuratively coloured my young life. It was wrong but beautiful, pleasant memories. Growing up, we always had an in-house servant, Rebecca. She would live in a room in the back garden next to the garage and coal-storage-room. Next to her room was an outside toilet, no bathroom. She washed in a zinc tub in her room. She was a South-Sotho woman originating from the Ficksburg area; one of the so-called Bantu *homelands*. She was an ignorant woman, but an experienced housemaid. The maid term became *meid*, pronounced like *mate* in Afrikaans. It became an offensive term in the same sense as *kafir*. Over time these were considered derogative and bigoted words.

Employed as a housemaid and holding a passbook, Rebecca could stay in for employment. Effectively she was our house slave. Mother had to work night-shift as a nursing sister. Rebecca had to take care of us four children while mother would be sleeping in the daytime. Uneducated, she had to sit us down at the kitchen table and supervise us doing our homework. She was the four children's formal and full-time guardian and mentor.

Rebecca had her metal food plate and cup. Her stuff kept separate from the kitchen crockery. At mealtime, Rebecca would receive her food from mum in the scullery on the outdoor veranda. We called it the *stoep*. She had her meal outside while we sat at the dining table. Her only function was to clean the house and tend to us children. She never sat on any chair inside the house. It was the ugly face of Apartheid.

Ironically, Rebecca was Mum's oldest and closest friend; if that can at all be plausible. The two would discuss a myriad of topics. From the neighbours, the kids and anything that happened in the neighbourhood. The discussion would not include political issues. The Apartheid political dispensation accepted by both as the given.

That was what it was. Apartheid was standard. The position that *it should not be this way* was not part of any of the two women's frames of mind.

Discussions restricted to the kids in the neighbourhood being naughty and stealing fruit, formed some topics of their interaction. Even another housemaid's boyfriend arrested by the police, staying the night without a *dompass* would become part of the discussion. What I found intriguing, was that even Rebecca would see this type of detention as the standard. Also, though it was wrong and discriminatory, it did not appear to bother her.

The general mothering issues formed to a great extent common ground for discussions. But, no close-up personal gossip. Like the white man next door having an affair with the local hairdresser. That would be a white taboo issue. Mum would not discuss white scandal with her black maid. It would be too close to the bone. There was the unspoken class difference. Apartheid had to be kept intact.

Superstition among Africans

Rebecca was superstitious. She was afraid of the *Tokoloshe*. In her tribal and cultural mind, he was a supernatural spiritual being. That is why she would support her bed on top of several layers of bricks. Then the *Tokoloshe* can pass under her bed, without harming her. Black cultures were notably gullible, and superstition was part of the black people's beliefs. Especially the older generation would still believe in the witch doctor.

I vaguely remember the mysterious old black men roaming the suburbs. They were draped in animal skin and carrying bones and stones in their loincloth. They wore a headband of hairy animal skin. You could hear them before you see them. They draped bands with objects round their ankles. It made a tingling and rustling sound as they walk.

Mum would warn us off: *"Do not to go near them, they are from the devil,"* she said. As kids, we were curious and observed from a *safe* distance. The black people would gather on the sidewalk in a circle with the witch doctor in the centre. The witch doctor would mumble in an unfamiliar voice and throw the bones and stones on the ground. The bones and stones fell in a pattern on the tarmac. He would keep on mumbling passing his hands over the rocks and bones, pointing and gesturing. There would be enthusiastic and loud animations with the onlookers joining in. Money changed hands. The audience would disperse after the consultation. The witch doctor would be on his way to his next consultation.

Colonisation had a determining influence on the traditions of native African people. They surrendered their indigenous and ancestral traditions for the Western way of life. European missionaries brought a change to the African tribal scene. Nowadays evangelistic churches have more massive black than white congregations.

Until Mum's dying day, she stayed in contact with Rebecca; even after Rebecca retired back to Ficksburg. Mum would pay Rebecca's train fare so she could come and visit. They would have endless talks, catching up on old times. Rebecca was indeed mum's lifelong friend and confident. Sad they were not friends in the fullest sense; their friendship marred by Apartheid. Even on her visits, Rebecca lived in the servant's quarters. Not in the guest room and she just reverted to her status as a housemaid. Mum was an Apartheid protagonist and for that matter a racist but she was kind to Rebecca, almost endearing. Mum was still white, and Rebecca was black. So segregated they must live; the cultural curse of Apartheid remained intact.

Sometimes, before mum passed away, we were talking about the old times. I commented: *'Mum, as a young man Apartheid was wrong. I could have had a colourful young love life. I missed out big-time due to the skin colour issue. I had only white girlfriends.'*

Mum did not take kindly to my comment, she responded with a disgusted snort, accompanied by a ferocious dismissal.

Alas, when South Africa democratised she was already cursed, she lived her entire life under the spell of Apartheid. Too late, the evil of Apartheid deeply ingrained. She would not change in her late eighties. Mum believed in Apartheid. She was part of the generation that created it. How could it be expected of her to overturn her life-long ambitions; her beliefs and convictions? I voice all the above comments with great empathy and respect. Rest her soul; she died a racist, a super Mum. I still love her, dearly.

"There are no Ka firs around; I will carry my case."

Then I grew up and interacted with non-whites in the workplace as an adult. In the early 1980's, it became a *fashion* to acknowledge black executives within society. Companies like Anglo-American would promote black people to senior positions; maybe this was window-dressing. The dawning of liberation and democratisation brought changes. It remains an enigma when the changes in attitude started?

Anglo-American was one of the capitalists that exploited black labour under Apartheid. Well, one should at least give Anglo-American credit for the measures of restitution. They were a significant part of the capitalistic pack that exploited non-whites and used Apartheid for wealth gain.

As part of my career environment, I filled a senior position in my career institution with the Civil Defence Association of South Africa. During conferences, we invited dignitaries to deliver papers on a variety of topics. At one of these meetings, we asked a black personality from the Anglo-American Corporation to address the conference. Tasked to welcome and introduce him to the conference, I met him at his big American car.

A handshake and a word of welcome and he moved round to the open trunk, looking around commenting: *"Seeing there are no Ka firs around, I will carry my case."* All of us in the welcoming party had a good laugh, he grabbed a leather case, and we were off to the conference venue.

In his address, he humorously explained his career progress within Anglo-American. He referred to his first job as a chauffeur to one of the big bosses. They would stay at hotels. The Director would apologise, for being unable to welcome him to the dinner table and superior rooms. He said he always refused with pleasure. The servings in the dining room were finicky and small. His room was comfortable, like home. He would instead go round to the back kitchen door and get a decent plate of African food. An excellent piece of meat with maize meal porridge and an enormous serving of Sheba-gravy.

During the transitional democratisation era, humour was a reconciliation tool. It diffused the uneasiness of segregation and discrimination.

I had a colleague from the neighbouring local authority in Stellenbosch, Western Cape. He was a black Civil Defence Officer, appointed during the late 1980's; it was the years preceding the death of Apartheid. Was this also window dressing? At conferences and due to the ingrained culture of Apartheid, the attendees were blazing white, only one black person. He stood out like a sore thumb. He was darker than dark, almost purple-black. Endeavouring to lighten the mood he remarked: *"My Mum left me in the oven, (meaning at birth), too long, so I came out a bit dark."*

Poison Ndlovu and some Swazi Women

The names always amaze me. *Poison*, probably not an African tribal name. Typical colonisation, change their names and culture; westernise them. Earlier I referred to the funny names given the Coloureds in the Western Cape. The surname, Ndlovu is a common tribal name, more acceptable than the borrowed and fake colonial names.

Swaziland was an ex-British Protectorate during the Imperial era. During a recent visit to Swaziland, I found the Swazis to be a friendly people. More often than not, they will have typical English names like Joyce or Margaret; the legacy of the British Protectorate era. The truth is, they all have tribal names as well as their English names. I insisted that they tell me their Swazi names with significant meanings. I met Nolwiza during our safari holiday in the game park of Milwane, Swaziland. I asked her the meaning of her Swazi name. She explained her parents wanted her to be knowledgeable. Nolwiza means lots of knowledge. Another girl, also at Milwane, was called Senani, she translated her name says *no problem*. When she was born, her father wanted a boy. But, he settled for, *no problem*, she was a girl. The Swaziland visit side-tracked me. I drifted a bit. Let's get back to Poison.

I married early, at the age of twenty-two. Appointed as Storekeeper, thanks to *job reservation for whites*; I filled a middle management position within the Barberton Local Government. Barberton is a small town in the Mpumalanga province of South Africa. Poison Ndlovu, a black man, in his early fifties, was my assistant. He had been working for the municipality for twenty years doing the same thing, store keeping. He knew the store inside-out. The learner was me, the newly appointed white Storekeeper. I asked him: Poison, you see this job so well, you should be the Storekeeper and me the assistant.

"No Boss, my job is outside, your job is the office," Poison explained in his humble way. The boss is white, and the assistant is black. Boss, translated *baas* in Afrikaans. Master and servant was the relationship. That is what it was; Apartheid accepted as the norm.

Faith Nthuli, the woman who raised my Children

Faith Nthuli was our first house servant during my early married years. Once again the enigma of an English first name. Faith was the same generation as my wife and me; only a year or two difference in age. She had the same educational qualifications as my then wife and I. Not the same schooling. Apartheid education for blacks was not of the same standard, as I will explain later. But still, she passed the final year of secondary school. On par with my wife and me. As whites, we could apply for highly paid jobs. But being black, Faith could only be a housemaid or tea-girl, low paid jobs. She had little to no prospect of career growth.

Faith raised the four children of our family. Homework tutoring, childhood guidance, she did it all. She even accompanied the family on holidays to Mozambique. We invited her to our home as an equal. But she never accepted. She always reverted to a subservient position. Faith had two kids a boy and a girl. They were the same age as our eldest two. We seldom saw them. They were in the care of her mum, their grandma, in the black township, outside of town. When on holiday in Mozambique, I said to Faith: There is no Apartheid here. When we go to a restaurant, you join us at the table. She did not feel comfortable to do that. She had a takeaway in the car outside. Apartheid is ingrained to such an extent that she did not feel pleased joining the family.

Later in life, I changed jobs and relocated to Potchefstroom in the North-West Province. We ensured that Faith would have a good job. I recommended her to the newly appointed Magistrate family; they employed her. We called at Barberton from time to time and visited Faith. We were all happy seeing each other. We enjoyed exchanging news about the kids, the family and whatever interests we shared. Just like my mother, we kept in touch with our servants. They were our dear friends.

Adrian and Ou-Jan – A Namakwa Fanie and Jabulani.

My mom's younger sister married a white farmer from Namaqualand. His name was Adrian. Namakwa land is a semi-desert region in the North-Western Cape, where remnants of the Khoisan still lives. They are less westernised than in the Western Cape urbanised areas. Adrian had a childhood friend, a coloured boy that lived on the family farm. He was a descendant from the

Khoisan with the name Jan; a typical Dutch name gave him by the farmer, Adrian's dad or the school he attended as a young lad. My Grandfather, the father of Adrian's wife, was also Jan. Naturally, one of Adrian's sons should have the Grandfather's name. That was when Adrian's coloured friend's name had to change to *Ou-Jan (Old Jan)*.

Adrian and Ou-Jan grew up in a mirror image of *Fanie and Jabulani*. Ou-Jan lived with Adrian's family all his life. He was employed by Adrian when he turned into a grown man. Adrian became the Master and Ou-Jan, the servant. The isolated farming environment was much less hostile and more organic. Adrian and Ou-Jan remained *friends* for life. Both died on the farm in their old age.

I can remember my family visiting Adrian's farm when I was a young boy. Adrian and Ou-Jan were inseparable. They walked the farm, working, discussing farm matters as if they were business partners. The only difference was, Adrian was the Boss, and Ou-Jan was the servant. They developed a relationship that worked on the farm. It would never have worked in a white segregated township. There would be segregation and discrimination, the full effect of Apartheid.

Michelle Faul a Coloured Woman - Life during Apartheid.

Michelle's story is an authentic illustration of non-white life under Apartheid. She was a non-white according to the South African Apartheid policies. The derogative treatment that non-whites received, I will always find difficult to comprehend. Michelle's story gave me first-hand insight into what life was for a non-white, in Apartheid South Africa. I will relate a condensed transcription of her version of events:

Michele's story starts

Michelle described that her mother was furious, the gas station in rural, racist South Africa took her money to fill the car. But they would not allow her to use the toilets. The toilets were for whites only. It was the 1960s Apartheid, the law of the land. So her mum ordered Michelle and her two sisters to urinate next to the fuel pumps. They obeyed Michelle recalled, crying and traumatised. Michelle remembers she could not go. She explains that her widowed mother, Ethel Pillay, was visiting family in South Africa. There was racism in Rhodesia. But, Michelle clarified that it was not the institutionalised South African legal code, turning blacks into a subhuman people. Michelle recalls that hotels only catered to Whites. So they had to drive nonstop. Carrying piles of food and drinks, because her mother refused to go to the back door of shops. They only served whites inside the stores.

Michelle remembers that they did not say *blacks and whites.* Black people were called *Africans.* Michelle's family were *Coloured,* and whites were called *Europeans.* She also recalls the crazy system of deciding your race inspecting the moons of your fingernails and the stock of your hair. If the pen pushed into your hair slid through, you could be considered white. Michelle also remembered that Chinese were classified as Coloured with straight hair while Japanese were white because they were trading with South Africa. Michelle explains that the variations within the family will result in separating children from their parents. It was possible to find siblings ranging in shades from deepest black to fair with blond hair. Michelle remembers that even one of her mother's sisters *played white.* Walking past her mother, she pretended not to know her. She explained to Michelle: *"That is what she had to do to make a better life for herself and her children, decent health care, school attendance, and you could live where you wanted."*

Michelle recalls that the only black professionals were teachers, like her mother, nurses and doctors. They could only serve blacks. Michelle moved to England when her mother fell in love with a white man. His mother strenuously objected to the marriage. She remembers that for years, he was estranged from his mother until Michelle's mum forced him to reconcile. She also recalls seeing whites doing menial work in England commenting to her mother: *"But those are Europeans picking up dustbins!"*

When Michelle obtained a British passport, she could go to white hotels, restaurants, movie theatres, places reserved for whites, but not the beaches reserved for whites. Michelle's mother explained to her that they did not teach racism, it is something that; *"Children were intoxicated, unconsciously, it automatically became a part of you."*

End of Michele's story

Relating Micelle's story, even after I lived through those years, is shocking. It still sends shrivels down my spine. Apartheid preached and condoned even from the pulpit of the Dutch Reformed Church; the official church of the Afrikaner. It was almost a *tool* in the hands of wrongdoers. First, the Dutch then the British Missionaries and later the Afrikaner Preachers in the Apartheid era. They all used religion as an avenue inducing cultural change. They dominated and subverted people to the will of the oppressor. Whatever happened in the non-white political world, the non-whites had no say. Their movement controlled and restricted. Their place of residence decided for them. They could not own land. If they did, they lost it to the white settlers.

Life of a young black boy in South Africa

I reflect on how a young black boy from a rural village experienced life, to understand the presence of non-whites in the so-called Bantustans as apportioned homelands. How he would live in the family unit in the homelands, allocated for blacks by the white Apartheid Government. He would live a life of tribal traditions, foreign to western cultures. There would be mostly women, old people and children in the community. Adult men *worked* on farms, mines or in the industries within the *white man's land*. They lived away from their family home. The mother and grandparents would raise him. In some cases, even the mother would live in servants' quarters, in the back garden of the white employer. This arrangement will be at the discretion of her white madam. The non-white mother will also have a *dompass* legalising her moving away from the so-called homeland and permitted to live in the white neighbourhood. The arrangement is similar to Rebecca, our housemaid in my youth.

At a young age, the black youngster might be herding sheep and calves in the field. While away with the herd, he would hunt birds or fishing. He would forage for wild honey, fruit and edible roots. If he had free time, he would play with other black boys. If the adult men were in the village, the boys would hear stories of historical battles and warriors. In the absence of adult men, the women would pass on legend and fables, with moral lessons entwined.

The young black boy would learn through observation and by physically doing things. He would not undergo instructive learning and schooling. His education was not compulsory as was the case for his white counterpart. He would learn from cultural practices, rituals and tribal stuff. These would be passed on from the ancestors. In the rural homelands, few white people would be around. White visitors would be tourists or government officials. No white boys would be part of his playgroup; unless the black family lives on a white farm, as farm labourers. On the farms, the white- and black boys did play together. Often they would become close friends. Almost a neutral bubble in the Apartheid environment. On farms, the situation was much more organic; like *Fanie and Jabulani* in their young years. It also illustrates the awkwardness. The divide that enters the relationship in later years posed real adversity.

As the black boy grew older and ventured away from the village, he would meet white people. He will then face full prejudices of the white people and segregation. If the black boy had been fortunate enough to attend school, he would get an English- or Afrikaans name. It would be the only name used at school. If the school was British, he would learn about British ideas and culture. If it was an Apartheid governed class, he would learn in Afrikaans. No part of the curriculum would cover his African culture. Apartheid educational policy structured to reduce him to a third class citizen. There was no intention to elevate him to be an educated and intelligent young man in Western culture. If the young black boy lived in urbanised areas, he would live in townships apportioned for blacks only. He would eat or drink at black establishments. He would use only black hospitals, public toilets, doctors, and schools. He would not own land or vote in his country, nor would he marry interracially.

At the age of sixteen, the now young man would have to apply for a passbook, containing all personal information designed at controlling him. The authorities would fingerprint him. Working in a *white area*, required of him to have his passbook endorsed. Failing to comply he could be arrested and detained without trial for months at a time. If he opposed Apartheid, he would be a political prisoner. White people might be sympathetic to his oppression. But, the majority of the whites chose to preserve the status quo and remain in control.

Surviving the 1960's to 1980's, unscathed, the black man would consider himself lucky. If he survived the 1990/91 repeal of the Apartheid laws, it would most probably please him. He might witness Nelson Mandela, released from prison. Even see him become President of South Africa. How would he ultimately feel? Presumably, he would be happy. But, he might feel outraged at the treatment of the past. Hopefully, he would be optimistic about the future. Not aggrieved to the point that he craves retribution and retaliation.

Moving from a tribal- to a western cultured life, proved to be a severe hurdle to black people. There was a continued flux between westernised- and tribal culture. The phasing over from the one to the other proved to be difficult with grave pitfalls introduced by Apartheid.

Over time, the tribal culture of African traditions deteriorated, and the Western values came into play. European status and the political endowment are not what the Apartheid government envisaged for black Africans.

Me a White Young Boy in Apartheid South Africa

I grew up a white boy in a mining town Springs to an Afrikaans family; close to Johannesburg. As a pre-teenager, I lived a privileged life and upbringing. I had access to the best schools, most excellent doctors, choicest food and excellent accommodation.

I was aware of the class difference. *The rightful lowly* place for non-whites ingrained in me from birth. We formed a close-knit relationship with our black servants. But, Apartheid prevailed as the norm. I avoided socialisation, other than giving instructions and accepting servitude from them. I respected a Government Official's right to detain a non-white. In my mind, the black man should not transgress race regulations of the government. I was free to move anywhere in South Africa without restraint. I was supportive of the Apartheid regime. Often aggrieved and puzzled by the anti-Apartheid protests of the 1960's and 70's. I was possibly concerned and upset when the UN in 1974, expelled South Africa.

Conscripted to serve in the Citizen's Army for three years, I considered it my duty to serve my country to defend South Africa. I lived in South Africa, a happy white man, and in a well-paid position. My logical development and next progress were university studies. I commenced my studies in my mid-thirties. When CODESA formed, I finished a Masters' Degree, studying International Politics and majoring in Public Management. I was born and bred a Westerner. I did not have to phase over to a new and foreign culture. Not like the young black African boy.

Education for Non-White People under Apartheid

Dr D F Malan as the first Prime Minister of the Apartheid government retired in 1953. In 1954 advocate J G Strijdom became his successor. After the sudden death of Strijdom in 1958, Hendrik Frensch Verwoerd became President of South Africa. He is accredited as the mastermind behind socially engineering and implementing the racial policies of Apartheid. During an address to Parliament, he explained the system of Apartheid education: *"I just want to remind the Honourable Members of Parliament that if the (black) native in South Africa is being taught to expect that he will lead his adult life under the policy of equal rights, he is making a terrible mistake. The native must not be subject to a school system which draws him away from his community and misleads him by showing him the green pastures of European society in which he is not allowed to graze."*

Verwoerd did not consider the black African equal to the European. One wonders whether the old misconceptions of the 17th century still ruled Verwoerd's mind. I find it difficult to comprehend Verwoerd's and the *obsessive Apartheid-Afrikaner's* mindset. It is clear that they wanted the African to remain tribal. Almost like an animal in a game reserve, Africans within a *homeland / Bantustan*. I find this disgraceful. The attitude makes me ashamed to be the descendant of the Afrikaner tribe.

But, to be fair I did not, like so many Afrikaners, share those derogative convictions. In the same way, I do not and will not ever accept decolonisation and reverse discrimination. The initiatives presently propagated by black conscious movements like the RMF and BFLF. They condone black-on-white hate crimes in the process of de-whiting South Africa.

The Apartheid protagonists did not accept the reality. Africans developed and became *civilised* with western values. The fixated perceptual differences were precisely the discernment. It set the scene for racial discontent and strife; in modern times coined as segregation and ethnonationalism. Black emancipation gave rise to conflicting expectations not sustainable within Apartheid South Africa.

Verwoerd engrained the delusion of separate development for blacks and whites. He embarked on entrenching Apartheid in the country's education policy. In 1959, universities segregated, followed in 1963 by a separate school system for Coloureds. Asian schools developed in 1964 and education for whites became law in 1967. Two years later the Sharpeville massacre took place.

Scholars attended a state school, designated for their particular *ethnic group*. It was illegal for a school to admit a pupil from the *wrong population group*. There were gross inequalities between the four schooling systems relating to teacher qualifications, teacher-to-pupil ratios, buildings, equipment, facilities, books, and stationery. The discriminatory outcomes reflected in the proportions and levels of skills as well as the worth of certificates awarded.

Is it coincidental that Civil Defence became law alongside the dreaded NSSMS- security system within seven years after the segregation of education? Seven years of discontent among non-white scholars festered hatred and evolved in the Sharpeville massacre, protests and demonstrations. Segregation and Apartheid infuriated the people of colour in South Africa. The state of emergency corresponded with resistance and the militarization of liberation struggles against Apartheid.

The following discrepancies were paramount in education: White schools were far better off than any of the others. Asian and Coloured schools were better off than those for Africans. Schooling was compulsory for Whites, Asians and Coloureds but not for Africans. The Apartheid government used education to enforce the Apartheid delusions. Schools were one of the system's starkest Apartheid instruments. Structurally education maintained and implemented the central principle of Apartheid. There were nineteen education departments, each designated to an exclusive ethnic group with its school infrastructure.

Curriculum development during Apartheid was centrally controlled and manipulated. Examination criteria and procedures were instrumental in promoting and structuring the Apartheid political objectives. It allowed teachers little latitude to determine standards and to interpret the work of their students. The prime Apartheid objective was to subjugate the black African people at a very early age; school going age.

Comments: Life of Non-Whites in Apartheid South Africa

The imperialists and colonists were exploiting and subjugating Africans for centuries before they realised their wrong-doings. In the third decade of my life, I also came under the authentic impression of the mistakes of the Apartheid saga. Through studies, my eyes opened to oppression and liberation struggles. Worldwide and early on, house slaves were the poor whites exploited by the wealthy. Later the colour of house aids as slaves changed to people of colour. They were imported to do forced labour and then to do work that the white workers did not want to do. Even today the bulk of British taxi drivers and bus drivers are from ex-colonial countries like India and Pakistan. The contemporary difference being, they became people from Eastern Europe. Workers are exploited by paying lower wages and inducing subservient employment conditions.

Slavery over the centuries manifested in a variety of formats showing ugly faces. I am not referring to freedom of movement and personal choice. I am talking about people trafficked and forced into labour along with exploitation at low wages and unsavoury work conditions; similar to the dark ages of slavery. Sweatshops also feature in modern times as labour exploitation. Is this a hybrid of colonisation by capitalism? In Africa, it was more comfortable from the moment imperialism ensued, the natives of Africa were available from the very dawn of colonialism. Underdeveloped and inferior in technology, modest and defenceless.

My life as influenced within the Apartheid bubble allowed me to make unreserved use of my privileges. Schooling, swift career progress, family life. It was as standard as breakfast and sex. I did not have to earn it. In my formative years the Apartheid government proffered priveledges to me; just because I was a white man in South Africa. The symptoms of the Apartheid atrocity were standard for the entire South African nation. Every European migrated or African-born participated in the proffered privileges. Is it wrong to enjoy your environment at the expense of others? Entrepreneurial inclination avails the opportunity, if not exploited, the entire concept of betterment and growth would go to waste. Even in the most democratic and advanced countries, it is near impossible for the individual voter to change the political course of a nation single-handed.

Apartheid should never be ignored or cognitively disposed of. The testaments of non-white people like Michele Faul shout to the world out there. Why did it take centuries, to unravel discrimination? Why did the world need freedom struggles and civil war to end colonisation and Apartheid?

Apartheid education was designed to steal non-white children's youth and to mar their future. The disparity will forever be an atrocity. It scarred the non-white population of South Africa, for centuries past and for generations to come.

It was the prime reason why African intelligence materialised as a backlog compared to Europeans. The Apartheid government prolonged this unfair separation of blacks from a creative environment. I deal with the phenomenon of black intelligence in later chapters.

Apartheid annihilated Black tribal culture and traditions, families devastated and a black nation urbanised with dire and lasting consequences. It is understandable that non-whites are aggrieved and angry. Unfortunately, there are those set on retribution. They resort to killing people, destroying lives and enter into the delusion of decolonisation.

Retaliation is a futile continuation of injustices; sadly it is induced by vengeance. Two wrongs never make a right. Gandhi proclaimed: *"An eye for an eye leaves the whole world blind."* We have to learn from past atrocities and create a better world and future for our children. We should never repeat the mistakes of the past.

I can only reverberate Michele Fauls' words: *"When that evil Apartheid system finally crushed, we all were in awe of Mandela's insistence on reconciliation and not retribution. It is a tribute to him that today, as he ordained, I and others forgive but do not forget."*

I would agree with Michelle if only Mandela's legacy lasted. Presently the Communist-inspired ANC government turn a blind eye to the murder of Mandela's legacy. They murder white farmers under the delusion of decolonisation.

In the following chapter, I will indulge in the reasons why Africans were so vulnerable and susceptible to subjugation by the West. Were they less intelligent than the Europeans?

Chapter 5

Are Africans Less Intelligent than Europeans? Why?

Want Peace? Prepare for War

Si Vis Pacem Para Bellum, The expression in Latin proposes: *"If you want peace, prepare for war."* From that, I assume, that if you want peace in your country, you have to practice to engage in battle against possible occupying forces. The flip side is as real. If you're going to conquer and or defend, prepare to participate in the intelligence of war. Build your intellect around survival, defence and attack. That will be the capacity that Europe acquired, but, that Africa apparently lacked in the colonial era. So naturally, my question is: *Why did Africa so effortlessly succumb to the European conquerors in the colonial period?*

A vast difference in the levels of development existed among the so-called first- and third-world countries relating to military intelligence and power. My study will focus on Europe and Africa. The African continent comprised mostly of third-world nations while Europe, in general, maintained a high level of intelligence, development and technological growth.

I understand that there is remarkable third world knowledge developed over the ages. Some that in modern times cannot be fully understood or fathomed. I also respect that Africa probably possesses expertise relating to, for instance, survival in nature. The Bushmen, for example, have survival skills in life that perhaps surpass that of European people, not used to living in the wild. But when I consider the concept of intelligence, I refer to the ability to deal with aspects of attack and defence in the colonial era of expansionism.

The invasion of Africa by Europe required excellent transport, technology, weaponry and communication skills; along with survival in the process to overcome African nations. Why the contrast in development between Africa and Europe? Was Africa less intelligent than Europe? I hesitate to address the sensitive matter of intelligence. It might kick off waves of rage and protest.

Knowledge and intelligence are related but differing concepts. Education is the collection of skills and information through experience and exposure to creative intelligence. Cleverness is the ability to apply the knowledge acquired. I am not succumbing to ostrich behaviour, hiding my head in the sand. Any moderately minded person needs to consider the intellect disparity. When dealing with attack and defence in the 15th to 20th century, intelligence difference played a determining role. European colonisers succeeded in developing *first world* pockets within the countries they colonised, like South Africa. But, Southern Africa is still predominantly a third-world sub-continent. Europe did not uniformly upgrade the entire Southern African sub-continent to a first world standard.

False Perceptions that led to Racism

Europeans created a racist ideology during world exploration in the fifteenth century. Imperialism led to cruelty in the slave trade. Racist beliefs justified oppression and subjugation. Africans were not considered equal to Europeans Accepted as sub-human, uncivilised, and inferior; they were commodities to be owned, traded and exploited for profit. Racism was central to the slave trade. The British equated blackness with death and evil. When European explorers came across black people, they assumed that blacks were some form of evil monster. From this perception, and from tales, arose a stereotype. Africans were *cruel people, prone to excessive sexual behaviour, lazy, untrustworthy and even cannibalistic.*

In the early 17th century David Humein claimed Africans are naturally inferior to the whites. He stated that Africans and

137

Europeans developed independently and thus differed. According to Humein blacks were not part of the genetic makeup of Europeans. Many, scientists like Sir Thomas Herbert in 1634, considered Africans as descendants of apes. The evolution theory of Charles Darwin allayed these perspectives. He declared all humans belong to the same species, Homo-Sapiens, all humans share a common ancestry. The *Rhodesiensis* man compares synonymous to the *Neanderthal* strain. However, they do infer differences, but the root genetics are similar.

When considering Verwoerd's reasoning of the 1950s while he implemented Apartheid rule, one wonders if equality did come to full fruition. Verwoerd and the Apartheid government did not consider black people to be equal to Europeans.

The abolishment of the slave trade gradually turned the fallacy of genetic differences between Europeans and Africans around. Notwithstanding all of the theories surrounding black intelligence, the British in the colonial era considered themselves to be smarter and mightier than African people. Europeans believed that the African countries are exploitable. The British public supported this authoritative perception. Racism was usual to the British nation. Over centuries, Africans within the British Empire was on the receiving end of racism. It was this *Imperial racism* that found its roots in Southern Africa. It became the dreaded *Apartheid* of the Afrikaner government after the 1948 National Party take-over.

Compared to Europeans African people, genetically, have similar ability to learn. They might not have had the European quality environmental exposure. By the time European Imperialism came to Africa, Africans had lacked nurturing in the quality of industrialisation, defence and attack.

Intelligence exposed Africa; it had lesser nurturing than their European counterparts.

Intelligence of African People: Idang Alibi from Nigeria

To get some perspective on what a black man might think on the subject of black intelligence, I researched an article by a Nigerian, Idang Alibi. He commented on Dr James Watson's perspectives on black intelligence.

Watson, a Nobel Prize winner for his research in unscrambling the intricacies and human genetics of the human DNA. Watson was involved in a row when he implied that black people are less intelligent than their European counterparts. Watson re-opened the fiery debate about race policies. He suggested that the West's approach towards African countries are wrongly based on the assumption that black people are on par with their white counterparts. Watson in discussion with *The Sunday Times* claimed that he was not impressed by the prospect of Africa as a result of his findings. According to Watson, there is a natural desire to accept all human beings as equal. But, the perceptions of people working with black workers, dispute the equality. Naturally, the implication that blacks are less intelligent than the European counterparts is offensive to people of colour.

In August 2010, Idang Alibi stated in The Daily Trust Abuja: *"I Agree with Dr Watson who says that there is a difference. African people are less intelligent than their European counterparts."* Alibi in his modest opinion, states that what Watson profess seem to be the self-evident truth; African people are less intelligent. Alibi continues by saying: *"We blacks do not show any intelligence organising society for the benefit of our population. I am so ashamed of this and sometimes feel that I ought to have belonged to another race."*

Alibi refer to his country Nigeria, being a prime example of the inferiority of the black race, unable to organise credible and efficient elections. He asks why African elections do not produce politicians that can govern his country professionally. Why can't they provide well-organised services for the people, systems that will run industries and service homes? In spite of abundant reserves,

Nigeria is unable to tap into the available natural resources and equate the value to services and growth to the country as a whole. Alibi states that Nigeria does not have what the Western world accept as the standard. Alibi blame the failures on poor leadership. He asks: *"Why Blacks must always suffer poor leadership, is that not a manifestation of intelligence?"*

Amusing, when the African National Congress's, President of South Africa, Jacob Zuma faces the spotlight, Alibi's convictions rings true. Time Magazine' front page cover in February 2017, had a full cover portrayal of Zuma with the following caption: *"Jacob Zuma, a Fraud who can't read or count, has five wives, 20 children and he shagged his best friend's daughter."* I deal with the corruption of the ANC government later when I evaluate a quarter-century of rule under the ANC ruling party.

Alibi makes a damning statement when he says; *"Smart politicians accumulate wealth for their people, but among the blacks, the practice is to steal from their country. They would confiscate state funds and syphon the funds to other people's countries."* He asks: *"Is it intelligence to take billions and hide it in wealthy western nations?"*

Alibi's claims on the corruption is a particularly damning and mocking accusation. In the slave era, African tribal chiefs sold their country folk to the west for personal gain. Now they steal from their countries to enrich themselves and stash away their loot in western countries. Alibi continues by stating: *"Where blacks live among other ethnicities, the blacks tend to be the poorest, they are least educated, the least achieving, and the most violent race. When compiling indices of underdevelopment, black people and countries will be the lowest ranked."*

Alibi claims that Africa should be a relatively affluent continent based on available mineral reserves. Alibi, however, is astounded at the insignificant achievements by his country. He expressed the opinion that every race takes the Nigerians for granted. Alibi perceives Nigeria to be weak and foolish. Alibi takes the view that

black people should consider Watson's report as a wake-up call. He further states that a man of intelligence should recognise genuine criticism, and endeavour to improve. Not abuse Watson for voicing the obvious.

Nigeria's Oil Corruption

Alibi's words of 2010, seems to have been prophetic! In April 2017, seven years after Alibi questioned the intelligence of Africa, corruption once again comes under the spotlight. This time fraud involved the Dutch Shell Oil Company's oil exploration and refinery in Nigeria. Oil supposedly accounts for 75% of the Nigerian economy. However, it is unknown what the actual production is due to theft of hundreds of barrels of oil daily.

On 10 April 2017, the *Financial Times* reported *Shell's* crime with investments in Nigerian oil assets. Allegedly, *Shell* in conjunction with *ENI* of Italy delivered a windfall for Nigeria's then *petroleum minister, Mr Dan Etete.* The corruption triggered bribery investigations in Nigeria, Italy and the Netherlands. Anti-corruption campaigners highlighted the case as an example of how Nigerian rulers collude with multinational companies to plunder the country's oil riches. The conspiracy happens at the expense of ordinary citizens.

President Buhari of Nigeria, before the 2017 corruption, took personal control of the oil ministry. The *BBC World Service Inquiry Programme* talked to Buhari as early as 21 October 2015. The BBC asked of Buhari: *"Can you resolve this mind-boggling level of corruption in your country's oil industry; can you succeed?"* Well, the answer in April 2017 is: *NO!*

The perspective put forward by Alibi does not date back to the colonial era. It is views expressed in 2010. The intelligence referred to, do not relate to defence and attack, but governance of a country. The corruption equates to the prosperous and continued existence of a nation. Everybody is entitled to his or her opinion, but it is worthwhile to look at more research and findings on the topic of black intelligence.

Christopher Jencks and Meredith Phillips

The research findings of Watson commented on by Alibi, are confirmed by that of Jencks and Phillips. Jencks and Phillips conclude that the intelligence of blacks in America scores lower than that of white Americans. Vocabulary, reading, mathematics and scholastic aptitude were tested to obtain the scores. The assessment revealed that the gap appears before children enter kindergarten and persist into adulthood.

Since 1970, they found that blacks still score below American whites. In some tests, the black American scores proved to be below more than 85 percent of whites. Jencks and Phillips state that the test score gap does not reflect an inevitable fact of nature. They blame environmental exposure and nurturing for the difference in intelligence. They point out that genetics do not have the final determining effect on intelligence in the modern world. Jencks and Phillips admit that enormous effort by both blacks and whites is necessary. They project that it would require more than one generation, to close and even eliminate the gap. The difference in intelligence was established over centuries and is due to blacks not exposed to creative environments. This backlog is repairable, but it will take time.

J. Philippe Rushton: Black Intelligence

Rushton is a professor of psychology at the University of Western Ontario and the author of *Race, Evolution, and Behaviour: A Life History Perspective*. Rushton's research and findings acknowledged some impressive results. To start off, Rushton equates African IQ to be thirty percent lower than that of Europeans. Rushton's research reasons that one way of thinking on African IQ is to correlate intelligence with *mental age*. By this, he implies mental maturity compared to chronological age. An average IQ of 100 is considered to be the mental age of a European 16-year-old. Sixteen-year-old African-Americans, according to Rushton, have a mental age of approximately fourteen, ranging from eleven to sixteen year-olds.

Richard Lynn: Differing Intelligence among Peoples

On 7 June 2006, Richard Lynn published a report on the differences in intelligence among people of the world. He quoted a French scientist Alfred Binet who in 1905 conducted the first intelligence tests. Binet attributed the lowest IQ's to the Sub-Saharan Africans seventy and the Australian Aborigines sixty-two. Europe's advanced intelligence Binet ascribe to the many separate states that engaged in war frequently resulting in an interstate ambition to have the best military intelligence. Europe's science development was discouraged in some countries, while it flourished in others. In Spain, the Roman Catholic Church opposed scientific and mathematical inquiry. Therefore, Spain contributed less to developments. According to Lynn, Europe was eager to gain new science and technology on military products to improve their war efforts. The demand for war technology provided an impetus for advanced military intelligence. From the 16th century onwards, war intelligence was financed and culminated in government policy.

Among the Sub-Saharan, Africans Lynn confirms the average IQ is 70. Afro-Americans according to Lynn, have 25 percent European genes, and they live in an affluent society run by Europeans, this gives rise to their increased IQ's. Their living environment provides them with intelligent environmental advantages conducive to healthy nurturing. Lynn contributes the low IQ of sub-Saharan Africans to their failure to advance in civilisation. He also confirms that Sub-Saharan Africa, during colonisation was in a transitional stage between hunter-gatherer and agricultural societies. They had no written language or number systems. Lynn describes the behavioural characteristics of black Africans as impulsive, intolerant of sustained work effort, live for the present, and have reduced self-control.

Gavin Evans: Analysis - Black Brain, White Brain

The book published by Gavin Evans: an *Analysis: Black Brain - White Brain: The new wave of racist science, March 2015*, reveals impressive results. Evans reflects on the recent revival of the old and long-discredited idea, that ethnic origin influences intelligence. Evans questions Nicholas Wade, a journalist with an Oxford degree and former deputy editor at Nature and former science correspondent for the New York Times. Evans states that he should know better than to publish the book, *A Troublesome Inheritance*. In the book, he announces that racial genes made: *"Africans violent, over-trusting tribalism. For similar reasons the Japanese were authoritarian, the English enterprising and the Finns violent and impulsive drunks."*

Evans dismiss Wade's claims: *"As the work of a dangerous crank."* Evans reference several publications on intelligence differences and conclude that: *"In fact, attempts to find intelligence genes have drawn a blank, and it is now accepted that it is governed by a network of thousands of genes."*

Evan's conclusion is substantiated by the leading US-based palaeopathologist Ian Tattersall when he stated: *"Long before humans left Africa, they reached the end of the line as far as the significant evolution of their brains is concerned."* Considering IQ and environment, Evans reference the world's leading IQ theorist, Jim Flynn, on the situation. Flynn is known for the *Flynn-Effect*; declaring that IQ has nothing to do with genetics and all to do with the situation. IQ scores rise or remain static pending the type of situation people live within. According to Flynn, it is absurd to compare the IQs of different populations. He states that when you remove IQ scores from the toolbox of the scientific racists, the rest of their case falls to dust.

Mind-boggling stuff, but I had to ask the question and query some research on black intelligence. Ignorance is much worse than arrogance. Arrogantly we sometimes jump to conclusions without substantiating our ramblings. That is an absurdity. In modern times, genetic intelligence is, accepted as the same among all ethnicities.

It might just be that during four centuries of slavery and colonialism the African people were devoid and robbed of an intellectual environment. The backlog referred to by Jencks, Phillips, Rushton, Lynn and Evans, should have been addressed at an early stage. Instead, the West and Europe decided on exploitation and oppression. The capitalistic drive ignored depravity in favour of wealth accumulation. Money was more important than development and philanthropy.

The reflections on African, or to be blunt black intelligence, as laid out in this chapter, relates to twenty-first-century opinions and studies; not the Africa of the 17th century. It is doubtful whether 17th century Africans were more intelligent than the contemporary African. Probably, British colonists shared Alibi's views way back in the 17th century and endeavoured to introduce an Anglo-Saxon way of life to Africa. Cecil J Rhodes during his famous Oxford speech voiced precisely this discrepancy. If the philanthropic colonist attempts materialised, the world would have benefitted greatly. Instead, modern society pays a high price for its greed and exploitation during Imperialism. My next question: If Africans are less intelligent than Europeans, why did Europe develop more progressively than Africa? Europe had the technology and might to colonise: Why?

Jared Diamond on Acquiring Intelligence

Jared Diamond in his book *Guns, Germs, and Steel: The Fates of Human Societies* explains why Eurasian civilisations have survived and overcome. He confirms that the difference in ability and technology is due to environmental nurturing. Exposure to an intellectual environment procured advanced levels of cleverness. Knowledge of the situation allows people to communicate, survive, defend themselves and resist pandemic diseases. Information advances in commerce and trade are the result of learning from what happens within the more comprehensive environment. Humans apparently enter this world with genetic *hardware*, genetic DNA. Exposure to the environment provides the *software with* the learning and nurturing that enables man to function more efficiently.

An undeniable reality is that there are intelligence differences in DNA within the same ethnic group. But, that would be standard among all races. Bright individuals will always stand out as intellectuals within any community irrespective of ethnicity or skin colour. Does that mean the level of advancement will depend on the attainment of knowledge from a creative environment? That must be the case. Genetics (DNA) will be what you are, a white-skinned European with straight blond hair and blue eyes. Environmental exposure and nurturing will be *who you become*. What knowledge you acquire and what is available to you, textbooks teachers, etc. Once exposed to an environment of highly skilled mathematicians, people in their surroundings will learn mathematics. Man's intellect growth will be directly proportionate to the level of his exposure to knowledge. Nurturing will gain information from his / her environment.

Europeans were intelligent in the performance of abilities to conquer because of their surroundings. They had an edge on Africans who did not have the defensive ability to ward off occupation. The Eurasian countries had a way to accumulate knowledge on warfare, and they based their power on informed cognisance.

Africa survived on intelligence for basic survival in nature. They gathered food and herded animals. Without exposure to knowledge of attack and defence, they were left vulnerable. A country needs skills, techniques and infrastructures to retain its sovereignty, on par with countries that embark on imperial expansion. Great advancement culminates in the power to expand and conquer. The accumulation of information leads to growth in intelligence.

Jared Diamond attributes the advances of the Eurasians to opportunity and necessity. He concludes that culture develops as the result of a chain of events, each made possible by individual preconditions. Jared identifies the areas of development as the essentials for change and growth. These prerequisites he clarifies as follows.

Progression from Hunter-Gatherer to Agrarian Society

Basic survival and existence happen when the nomadic hunter-gatherer provides enough, only for short-term survival. For development and growth to occur, certain conditions must come into play. Access to high-protein vegetation that withstands long-term storage is essential. For instance, climate dry enough for storage. Conquering the said abilities will allow for the preservation of food over extended periods of time. Animals, docile and domesticated, must be accessible. Stored food and domesticated animals, made advanced transport possible. It will also set labour free to develop alternative skills and processes. For example producing weapons and strategies for attack and defence.

Communication and Understanding

When travelling, people come into contact with foreign nations, new frontiers. They need to learn from the visited country and need a common language for understanding. Understanding foreigners are imperative to gain resources and acquire new techniques. To grow the knowledge in new resources requires the *cross-pollination* of advantages and expertise.

Lingua Franca is an ancient common language between speakers of different styles. It represented a bridge language devised to overcome differences in understanding. The Lingua Franca technique of communication developed over time in Europe. It derived from the Italian, French, Greek, Arabic, and Spanish languages. No African languages participated in the Lingua Franca. Or, did they?

African Fanagalo as a Lingua Franca

The British capitalists used cheap African labour in South Africa, especially in the mining sector. They devised a hybrid Lingua Franca, they called *Fanagalo*, meaning, *like this you do it*. Fanagalo is spoken with lots of body animation and gestures to bring the real meaning home. Earlier, I made mention of the coloured farm worker on my Grandfather's farm that told me off because I spoke to him; *like he was a kafir.* I suppose that was the *Fanagalo* I learnt in the present Gauteng among the Zulu people working in the mining industry. I grew up in the gold fields of the Transvaal now Gauteng, learning Fanagalo. I can still communicate reasonably efficiently, only to make myself understandable. No full comprehension is possible.

I will test understanding by asking: *Lo skat mina kuluma, wena hizwe?* Meaning literally; when I talk *(kuluma)*, do you hear *(hizwe)* me? Animatedly, I will use body language, when I mention the word *kuluma*, I will point to my lips, and when I say the phrase *hizwe*, I will touch my earlobe. If the response is: *"Yebo, mina hizwe sterek,"* meaning literally: Yes, I hear strongly. Then we probably have a communicative base of understanding.

Black workers migrating from Mozambique spoke Shangaan. Zimbabweans spoke Shona and Ndebele. A multitude languages exist in South Africa. All migrant workers to the mines are dependent on a shared medium for communication. The African Lingua Franca *vis-à-vis* Fanagalo provided that common medium. The white English and Afrikaans speaking mining shift bosses, as well as the migrant workers, had to learn Fanagalo to complete the communication circuit. Without Fanagalo, work would not be possible in the mines. It would have been like trying to build the *Tower of Babel.* Informed and developed British colonisers with their excelled language skills, found a way to communicate. They put the uneducated black African worker to task by bridging the language barriers with *Fanagalo*.

Developing Alternative Skills

According to Jared, once crops- and livestock propagation give rise to food surpluses, it will create time and opportunity for specialisation, developing alternative skills. Skills obtained not just for physical survival but development and growth. Combining essential durability and alternative techniques and processes, led to co-operation and an increase in knowledge leading to intelligence.

Opportunities created by social- and technological changes and advances contributed to development. Without change, there is no growth. This extraordinary- and procedural event was the impetus that gave rise to industrialisation. Industries produced weapons and equipment for warfare that conquered nations. Due to some individuals becoming more able and intelligent than others, class differences established.

Entrepreneurial and fruitful people became powerful and wealthy. They created power bases, developed strategies of manipulation and control. Power gave rise to bureaucracies that developed into nation-states and empires. The Guilds of the past are examples of the development of trades and skills, boosting the economy and technological progress. Accumulation of power gave rise to the establishment of corporations and companies. The Dutch East Indian Company and Rhodes' British South African Company were such businesses. They were the capitalists that colonised the Cape of Good Hope and Rhodesia, under the umbrella of imperialism.

Movement and Trade

Jared continues by referring to advancement and growth that allowed the developed nation to move to adjacent countries to barter. They might come across new and useful animals, most notably camels, horses and donkeys for use in transport. Large domestic animals offered the significant military and economic advantages of movement. Development in sea fairing transport made oceanic travel possible. Global travel and trade finally gave rise to capitalism, which exploited slavery and colonisation to gain wealth.

Immunity to Diseases

According to Jared, when colonisers moved into new-found territories, the expansionists introduced diseases to the populations they visited. The travellers might have developed resistance to the conditions that they imported. But, the local people might not have resistance to the introduced disease. That led to epidemics that broke out in the countries visited and destroyed the local populace. European colonisation of the Americas resulted in the demise of 95% of the native Americans. The Colonists survived as a result of their immunity to the disease. The *Rinderpest* imported from Somalia disseminated the herds of the Herero Tribe in Namibia. The outbreak had an enormous and derogative effect on the Herero nation. It resulted in the almost total genocide of the Herero. I describe this in Part four.

Border control nowadays is set on restricting and regulating any substance, even infected people, from entering the country. Immunity to diseases among colonists will maintain an advantage over the people of invaded nations with limited protection.

Conclusive Comments on Black Intelligence

African people were less intelligent than their European counterparts, especially during the colonial era. The reason for the black-intellect-backlog was the result of an under-provided intellectual, environmental exposure over centuries. Exposed to a less creative and evolving environment, they had an intelligence deficiency. A non-creative conversational nurturing is the shortcoming to be blamed. Genetically the DNA of all people, black and white, are accepted as equal. Therefore, Africa did not develop on par with Europe to fend-off suppression from invaders. Africa was technologically and militarily weak, merely set on primary and physical survival. Africa was there for the taking, a lesser people vulnerable to the invasion of Europe. Southern Africa was emerging from hunting, herding and some agriculture intellect when the Europeans arrived. Africa never embarked on noticeable trade expeditions across the oceanic divides. Intellectually Africa had a backlog in military abilities, enabling Europe to conquer and colonise.

The Europeans succeeded in building development upon development, accumulating essential and better structures loaded with technology, administrative and overcoming power. When the colonists arrived in Africa, the local African populace was left wanting. I suppose the conclusion is foregone and irrevocable; Africans were less intelligent.

Morally colonisation, imperialism and expansionism, call it whatever you like, to the modern mind, it is unacceptable. But in the 15th century, it was acceptable and unavoidable. In the observation of Cecil John Rhodes, Africa was underdeveloped. Perceived as not real human beings, weak exploitable and available to be disenfranchised. And, what's more, Africa, according to Rhodes, "*would benefit from exposure to the Anglo-Saxon way of life.*"

The real world, historically teaches us that the planet developed exogenously, due to ethnic differences. Countries and nations differed in customs and traditions. Some countries developed ahead of others causing an imbalance in abilities. These abilities can be in the form of attack and defence, or it can be the capacity to survive in nature without advanced structures and techniques. The difference between Europe and Africa is apparent. Africa was underdeveloped when attack and defence counted.

I worked for twenty-two years as a Civil Defence Officer. The South African Nation consisted of multi-cultural ethnicities. Did I serve them equally; irrespective of colour and creed?

In the next chapter, I will consider my career of two decades as a civil defence officer. Civil Defence aims to protect civilians in times of disasters and emergencies. Did I add value to the safety of all South Africans?

CHAPTER 6
MY CAREER IN CIVIL DEFENCE; PROTECTING PEOPLE

My Mindset Starting a Career in Civil Defence

My adversity to Apartheid might be confusing, considering my involvement with Apartheid government's civil defence; an organisation that was established to protect the people of South Africa. But, it protected the white people primarily; a reflection on my years employed as a civil defence officer. I Safeguarded especially the white citizens of the country. It was also the years of military struggle both sides of the colour line, white and non-white. My prime objective in this section is to put my two decades of being a Civil Defence Officer under the spotlight. Why did I, in my early career support Apartheid, and when did I change course and opposed Apartheid.

My mindset entering civil defence is the culmination of all the episodes I described earlier. But let's be real, the racism I explained, was prevalent in my young- and early career life. An isolated and partitioned environment for Afrikaners. Racism prevailed when I entered my career in Civil Defence. The only difference was racism as imparted by the Apartheid regime.

My Apartheid upbringing convinced me that I was doing my bit to safeguard the South African nation; I lived a contented existence. However, the traumata and aftermath of the suffering of the Boer-Afrikaner nation still firmly fixated in my mind, made me comfortable with the Afrikaner living in the Afrikaner-land and governed by an Afrikaner government, without interference and oppression.

I might be presumptuous, but I applied the civil defence directives and standard work practices to the letter, and very successfully. I secured an A-grading, repeatedly for three Local Governments. To me, that was the rule, the average life, based on the Afrikaner history. We were fighting for survival and self-determination. When I commenced my studies in international politics, I realised the wrongs of Apartheid and racism. It dawned on me that I only work for the safety of the white minority; retaining Apartheid rule and opposing the freedom struggle of black and oppressed people. In my revived mind, I realised, Apartheid was wrong.

My turn-around might seem simplistic but, it did not happen overnight, I spent twelve years studying at two different universities. At least, after years of study and contemplation, I came to my senses. I acknowledged my misconceptions and made an effort to do the right thing.

The people of colour were the original natives of Africa. The Apartheid dispensation was a delusion among white South Africans; cultured and brainwashed into acceptance of Apartheid as the norm. To so many white Afrikaners including me; it was as regular as breakfast and sex. The divisions within the South African nation, introduced to Africa by Europe, as far back as the 15th and extrapolated into the 21st century set the scene for discrimination. Ghettoization with all its hatred and fear, over time, became the Afrikaner Apartheid dispensation.

At this point of my reasoning, it should be abundantly clear, oppression and exploitation of people of colour by Europeans were natural and accepted as a Western world prerogative; ever since capitalism introduced slavery and imperialism. In the 15th century, before the first colonial white man set foot in South Africa, the oppression of blacks was routine; segregation and Apartheid were the norms.

After all the deliberations, explaining my mindset, I now only, arrive at the position where I can extrapolate on my coming into the world of a civil defence career. I can now progress to the real deal of civil defence in South Africa. Against a backdrop of all the manifestations discussed thus far, I along with so many white Afrikaners had preconceived delusions affecting our outlook on life.

Civil Defence in the Apartheid Years

The Universal Declaration of Human Rights allocate, among others, the following fundamental human rights to a civilian within society:

- Right to equality
- Right to life, liberty and personal safety
- Freedom from slavery
- Freedom from torture and degrading treatment
- Right to recognition as a person before the Law

Authentic civil defence as a social activity is the fundamental human right of any individual or organised group. Groups and individuals are entitled to lay claim to these rights and also to protect themselves against any threat that jeopardises the rights quoted.

A fully integrated nation will have no problem; an efficient government and country will maintain and respect these rights. The Civil defence activity will work for one-and-all, and any government intervention will be democratically applied accountable to the people. The authentic civil defence was not the objective of the Apartheid government. Civil defence had a white face, a very biased and apartheid-segregated face. The legislated civil defence of the Apartheid government was an instrument to enforce and retain Apartheid, aimed at suppressing any initiative that might threaten the white Apartheid stronghold.

The National party, not elected by non-white people could not be held accountable; it answered only to the white electorate. However, Apartheid got it wrong and should not be part of the country's constitution. Democratisation and political rights for all had to become a reality. It happened in 1994 when the ANC government took political office. But after twenty-two years of

ANC governance, the country is even more off-course than under Afrikaner Apartheid.

Was the Apartheid, government clairvoyant to hang onto an illegitimate government? At least the Apartheid government *cared* better for non-white people. Considering South Africa today the racism of Apartheid seems almost trivial. White-on-black racism and Apartheid changed colour; the ANC regime just reversed to black-on-white racism. The ANC in effect stepped-up discrimination *with genocidal- and de-whiting (de-westernising)* conducts.

If we did not remove racism and segregation from the South African political scene, why did we bother to democratise? The next step might be a civil war where the two factions fight it out in civil conflict and war. It will not help contradicting the past wrongs by inflicting present-day wounds. Apartheid was wrong and will forever be a mistake; but why replace it with more severe discrimination?

Afrikaner Apartheid in the final instance was a desperate attempt to secure Afrikaner sovereignty in the face of a growing black uprising. The blacks revolted against continued subjugation and oppression. The Afrikaner's extreme anxiety resulted in mutative outcrops of cancerous Apartheid security structures. Apartheid Civil Defence and the NSSMS systems were such outcrops.

White Apartheid Civil Defence legislation surfaced almost simultaneously with the National State Security Management System (NSSMS). The NSSMS was a dreaded system institutionalised to govern the country as a dictatorial Junta State. The NSSMS enshrined Apartheid and the status quo for the white minority government. Government civil defence aimed at manipulating information, calming the white nation into a false sense of security. It proclaimed that civil defence is a non-military, non-police activity. If that were true, oppressed peoples would have had no protection, no recourse to liberation from subjugation.

The Apartheid Civil Defence intentions proved to be my biggest objection; the terminology changed continuously with explanations that became laughable. Civil defence protagonists forever tried to explain what civil defence is not; they never succeeded in saying what civil defence authentically is. I rebelled against the manipulative, secretive and undemocratic protection of civilians and for that, I was ostracised and removed from the civil defence infrastructure. Covertly I was blacklisted by the Junta Apartheid Government and Bureaucracy.

To retain an objective approach to the subject-matter at hand, I have to distance myself from murders and decolonisation efforts and concentrate on civil defence as such and practised by the Apartheid government.

The Origin of Civil Defence

To understand the misconceptions of public protection and also the abuse of it, I will shortly explain the subject-matter. Civil defence is nothing new to the world. The Civil Defence that existed before 1977 was insignificant efforts under the Civil Defence Act 39 of 1966 (RSA). The legislation provided for the establishment of a Directorate of Civil Defence in the Public Service. The legislation gave powers to take measures in times of emergency for the protection of the Republic and its inhabitants. The legislation clearly did not cater for the problems encountered with the so-called terrorist onslaught of the 1960/70's or the liberation offensive against the Apartheid government. But it was a new concept to South Africa in the 1970's.

I suppose there might probably be civil defence frauds and hybrids all over the world. In truth, there is only one universally accepted format of civil defence; the South African governmental combination was a false one.

Government Civil Defence

Apartheid civil defence was a human-made creation, not the real organic and general protection of defenceless civilians. Britain probably formalised the original model of formal civil defence in the 1st and 2nd World Wars. War strategies changed over the centuries, aggressors soon learnt that once you harm the Homefront of the enemy, you destroy the morale of the contending forces; the will to fight will diminish. Kill the Homefront, and you starve the warring soldiers. The *Scorched Earth Policy* of Lord Kitchener in the Anglo-Boer-War, forced the Boer nation, into submission. The Boer Homefront consisted mostly of women, children, and the elderly, isolated on farms and not capable of fighting, a vulnerable and soft target. There was little to no civil defence ability on Boer farms.

Governmental and formal civil defence makes use of volunteers from the Homefront to safeguard the civilians, it focuses on the management of information and introducing a state of preparedness. Activities of civil defence include risk assessments, organisational structures, command chains and warning systems. Authentic civil defence represents an organised state of affairs devised to respond to threats.

When the perceived terrorist threat in South Africa escalated with the uprising of liberation struggles, the Apartheid government turned to formal civil defence. Unfortunately, it did not involve the entire nation. The Home front was white South Africans. The threat was the oppressed non-white freedom fighters. The government called them *terrorists*; they were the black natives of the land fighting for liberty and freedom.

Informal Civil Defence

The liberation struggle is the exact configuration of informal civil defence. It is organic and authentic to the generic character of Civil Defence. It is the fundamental entitlement, of any individual or organised group, to protect themselves against the abuse of their human rights. The protection can configure as military, law, order and any method of defence. Apartheid was the threat to the human rights of the non-white population. The liberation movements were the real civil defence organisations. The African National Congress, Pan African Congress and Inkatha Freedom Front surfaced as liberation movements and defended the human rights of people of colour.

My Life as a Civil Defence Officer

I was in civil defence for twenty years of my working life. Initially, my understanding was not congruent with authentic civil defence. By 1977 when the Civil Defence legislation was promulgated I completed eight years of my initial local government employment. Every local government was compelled to establish a Civil Defence Corps (organisation). I was one of the first emergency preparedness officers appointed to make this happen in Barberton, Mpumalanga Province. The government instructed us in their understanding and prospects of civil defence.

Over a period of twenty years, I was head-hunted by two more local governments. I presume I was successful in developing a Civil Defence Corps. My final corps was within the Western Cape Metropolis. Was I successful, or did I fail? Let me explain. I obtained an A grading for each Local Government. But, what kind of success did that represent? I complied with government objectives in civil defence. I protected the white civilians in the white segregated townships. They were all white-skinned South Africans. I served white and coloured communities in my last commission in the Western Cape, but there were no black communities involved. Was there only white South Africans in Barberton, Potchefstroom and the Cape Metropolis? NO! Eighty percent plus of the population was Black, Coloured and Asian. Protection of a nation means the whole society, all colours and ethnicities. Did I qualify for success? NO, not in my mind, I was part of an institution that segregated protection, only favouring white people.

The white Apartheid system threatened life and limb of everything non-white. The little civil defence efforts in communities of colour were just window dressing and never materialised as protection. In my last Civil Defence Corps in the Western Cape, I served predominantly coloured townships, reflecting a more balanced approach.

My understanding fully surfaced later in my life when I came to a full and authentic realisation. I studied International Politics as part of my master's degree in the late 1980's. The title of my dissertation is *The Management and Administration of Civil Defence in South Africa - Master's Degree in Public Administration (MPA), 1992.* The script is available online in my first language, Afrikaans. The *Resume* is available in English. The MPA-Thesis is a standard research document, with no promise of entertaining reading, I will not bore you, the reader with a research report. However, I will endeavour to highlight essential aspects and developments.

The Efficiency of Civil Defence in South Africa

Efficiency in the final instance is crucial. The fact that Civil Defence exists and appears in legislation in fine detail does not mean that it answers to the question of *effectiveness and efficiency. Effectivity* relates to reaching your objective, i.e. driving a nail home in a piece of wood, irrespective of the outcome. *Efficiency* refers to how *cost-effective* you hammer the nail into the timber. Did you abuse the process by driving the nail with a steam hammer, or did you efficiently use a claw-hammer, no damage to the nail or the wood?

Apartheid and Formal Civil Defence

Civil defence, as a legislative strategy, presented the same distortions as with Apartheid education policies. Whites were the best off, and the non-white population were left behind and ignored. Services rendered to non-whites were sub-standard and underdeveloped. Civil defence in South Africa amounted to a failure in efficiency; it did not follow a need-driven approach. The need was only a white minority requirement. Transparency along with the public participation of the entire population was lacking; the understanding of the *need* and the public choice was absent. The whole community was not part of the system. Manipulative Apartheid inclined systems replaced harmonious and integrated nation existence. The phenomenon of entropy, relating to a state of disorder and degeneration, was endemic to formal South African civil defence.

Informal Civil Defence: The Liberation Struggle

The resistance movements and authentic civil defence show an acceptable and high standard of efficiency. After almost a century of liberation struggles, there is substantial evidence of widespread success. The protection of civilians materialised; the process delivered a democratic and representative government. The elected government is a people's choice; all of South Africa's people. Whether this democratic and resulting ANC government is efficient to its rule that is another question. I already explained the bad political behaviour by President Jacob Zuma and atrocious reverse discrimination. What I already touched on, and what I deal with later is disturbing. The corruption of the ANC government I deal with in later chapters.

The National State Security Management System (NSSMS)

A huge stumbling block with the Apartheid government was the National State Security Management System (NSSMS). The system described, like a giant octopus with its tentacles in every nook and cranny of society. Commanding and controlling the community for the benefit of the dictatorial Apartheid government.

The Chief Executive Officer (Town Clerk) was the local Chief of Civil Defence, a perfect scenario for command and control. This hold on power fits the central monitoring and oversight structure of the NSSMS like a glove. The command and control line of authority snaked down from the central government NSSMS to every *nook and cranny*, down to the grass roots level of society in every town and city.

In 1960, the liberation movements changed from passive resistance and demonstrations to violent resistance and guerrilla warfare. Black liberation threatened Apartheid and the continued success of white minority rule. Increased violence and attacks by *Umkhonto we Sizwe*, the military wing of the ANC, moved the Apartheid Government to resort to extreme defensive measures. The situation became intense when demonstrations and attacks on especially police stations throughout South Africa, intensified. The Apartheid government called the National State of Emergency, allowing for extreme measures to safeguard the country; in this instance the white communities. From the 1960s to 1980s, several emergencies were declared, resulting in the incarceration of thousands of political activists along with many fleeing abroad.

Civil defence, introduced by the Apartheid government had a clear message; *establish a Civil Defence Corps within your community and live prepared. The government's military and police will take care of the terrorist onslaught.*

The non-military and non-policing claim were emphasised to coerce the white nation into acceptance; engineered to prevent a fear neurosis and to allow for the pacified acceptance by the white communities.

However, Apartheid civil defence favoured ex-military and ex-police officers as emergency preparedness officers. Many of my colleagues in civil defence were ex-military and ex-police officers. The Apartheid dictatorship had with civil defence, one thing in mind; coercion and incorporation of the private sector and public. To have ex-military and ex-police functionaries within civil defence will help ease the cause of the Apartheid status quo. Ex-military and –police incumbents were *comfortable and aware* of the government's security objectives.

The forerunner of the NSSMS was the *State Security Council (SSC)*, established in 1972. The SSC served as a permanent committee *advising* the Cabinet on intelligence matters. The consultative status of the SSC did not help the urgency of the situation dealing with the revolutionary uprising. Civil defence legislation followed in the wake of the NSSMS in 1974. Once levels of anti-Apartheid activities reached critical proportions, the SSC transformed into the National State Security Management System (NSSMS).

Under State President P.W. Botha, the NSSMS became an active policy-making forum in 1978; decisions not democratically accountable but rubber-stamped by Parliament. The transformation from the SSC to the NSSMS did severe damage to accountability within the government. The NSSMS was decentralised to regional and local control conferences, coordinating all walks of life as a policy-making forum.

The actions of the South African Defence Force (SADF), the South Africa Police (SAP) and Civil Defence Corps were tightly roped in and integrated into the NSSMS system. Civil defence was looped in and coerced as the non-military private sector and national community to enforce the objectives of the NSSMS. The primary aim was propaganda, information management and preparedness of the white Home front. The approach steered away from non-white protection; this direction was not only suspect but grossly discriminatory.

Demise of the NSSMS:
The Truth and Reconciliation Committee (TRC)

The last white State President, F W de Klerk, abolished the NSSMS in 1989. The cabinet once again took direct control of national security, returning the system to be accountable to Parliament. During 1997-1998 the TRC exposed the full ramifications of NSSMS activities. The TRC reported on the former

South African government and its security forces, castigating South Africa's last hard-line Apartheid president P W Botha. Botha was held responsible for gross human rights violations sanctioned by the NSSMS. The report stated: *"By his position as head of state and chairperson of the NSSMS, Botha contributed to and facilitated a climate in which gross violations of human rights did occur, and as such is accountable for such violations. The TRC also found that the NSSMS had contributed to the prevailing culture of impunity by failing to recommend punitive action against those members of the security forces who were involved in gross human rights violations."*

Botha was guilty of contempt because he refused to appear before the Truth and Reconciliation Commission. The TRC held Botha responsible, as President and Chairman of the NSSMS, for gross violations of human rights. As Prime Minister, Botha chaired the NSSMS, making remarks and recommendations that were highly ambiguous and interpreted as authorising the killing of people.

Botha took no action against government agents who carried out atrocities. He also ordered police to blow up the Johannesburg offices of anti-Apartheid groups. By engaging in such activities, his nickname *Great Crocodile*, was deservedly applicable. His legacy reaches far back in history; his father was a *bitter-ender* who fought the British to the last hold of the Anglo-Boer-War. Lord Kitchener interned Botha's mother in the Bloemfontein concentration camp. Botha was a member of the pro-Nazi *Ossewabrandwag* movement in 1938, implying his legacy and affiliation to Germany. Botha's associations resonate the Afrikaner obsession with self-determination, free from black African and British interference; the dream died with him in 2006.

South Africa honoured Botha with a state funeral; this might present bitter irony. He was never held to account for his wrong-doings. He refused to appear before the Truth and Reconciliation Committee. Legendary figures like Kitchener, Martin Mc Guinness, P W Botha and so much more, are sometimes remembered as war criminals. But, they are also in time recognised as political leaders, heroes, traitors and peacemakers alike. They can even switch roles over time due to changing affiliations and circumstances. However, I hesitate to group Kitchener in the same category as Botha. But, what is more, relevant and pressing, I could not refrain from, once again mentioning Lords Kitchener and Milner; they will remain in my mind and so many Afrikaners war criminals.

I was Informally Black Listed by the NSSMS

My findings of political failure in my M-Thesis was a thorn in the side of the Apartheid Government. The Lwandle debacle provided the opportunity to the NSSMS to expel me from their ranks. Earlier I mentioned Lwandle in the Orffer murder dilemma; the *misnomer* where the two murderers were taken and shot. The black shanty town, Lwandle, is situated in-between the white townships of Strand and Somerset-West. Lwandle, relative to Bellville, lies in the opposite direction from Muizenburg.

Lwandle was a so-called *oil-spill* area, where unrest and terrorism loomed. Two white youngsters were killed when they entered the shanty town to purchase alcohol from a *Shibine*, the killings created an *oil spill* in the eyes of the NSSMS's local Joint Management Centre (JMC). A Shibine is a so-called rogue and illegal liquor-outlet, selling alcohol outside legal selling hours. During a regional meeting of the Joint Management Centre, I represented civil defence and the Local Government. The so-called *oil spill* was discussed to find ways to resolve the matter. I addressed the meeting suggesting that we should identify the recognised black community leaders within Lwandle to ascertain what the grievances might be. I was a dreamer, this sounded like democracy, and it did not feature well in the NSSMS. Silence fell over the meeting; they did not want to discuss the matter of free justice. They decided to build more toilets, corrugated shacks with buckets as sewage collecting vessels. There was no water-borne sewage in black Lwandle. It was also agreed to provide more communal water taps in the town.

This type of modus operandi was synonymous with the NSSMS culture. Do not address the real problem by dealing with the causes of unrest; instead, appease the oil spill by dealing with the symptoms that will favour the status quo of Apartheid Rule. I later learnt that the black community vandalised the corrugated toilet shacks. The corrugated sheets were removed, taken to build more shanty houses. I suppose the water taps were useful. The buckets, the black community used as water receptacles from the provided communal taps. But, the strife and unrest persisted within the Lwandle community.

Naturally, I was not prepared to let the matter rest. At the next meeting, I submitted a written document, suggesting we enter into negotiations with the Lwandle community. During negotiations, I proposed we address grievances with the community so solutions could be found and agreed. Democracy was indeed the deal breaker; the NSSMS did not allow for democratic initiatives with non-white populations.

The NSSMS powers did not invite me back to the JMC meetings. In fact from that point in time, I was barred from NSSMS activities. I was not welcome to attend any further meetings. Two strikes and I was out; criticising the government civil defence plus challenging the NSSMS. Isolation gradually filtered through to my career- and the associative environment. The Apartheid Bureaucracy formally blacklisted me.

My Liberation Books Disappeared from my Office

After the *blacklisting*, I realised that I was a *watched and marked* man. I became labelled as an enemy of the system of Apartheid. As part of my studies in International Politics, I obtained several books on civil defence, dictatorial governments and liberation struggle worldwide. I kept the books on my office bookshelf. For no reason but my *marked* status, my books on freedom struggle started to disappear. I realised that I had become an *oil spill* to the Regime. The black-listing and criticising of the Government civil defence, filtrated into my associative career environment. My position became toxic in the Apartheid supportive beaurocracy.

Suspect Activities: Israel Military Reconnaissance Visit

Uriel Davis is an academic and a civil rights activist, serving as Vice Chairman of the Israeli League for Human and Civil Rights. Davis sees Israel as an Apartheid state. He is a lecturer in Peace Studies at the University of Bradford. Davis maintains that Israel is a bad example for South Africa to consult considering Apartheid policies. During my final years in local government, my fellow Civil Defence Officer, with a military background, visited Israel on a recognisance mission. The aim was to learn from Civil Defence in Israel.

This mission flared up an amber light in my mind. Why Israel, with a reputation as an Apartheid Regime? I suddenly realised the real motivation for the purpose. He had to learn from Israel how to retain control of *Apartheid* in the face of the Palestinians on the Israeli doorstep. To this day Israel still succeeds. That is why I consider the visit a *military reconnaissance visit; not Civil Defence*. Well, that is if Civil Defence is a non-military activity?

Suddenly it made perfect sense, congruently to Goering learning from Lord Kitchener's concentration camps in the Anglo-Boer War, Apartheid needed to collude with Israel on the retention of Apartheid. This type of consultation and conspiracy was the culture of top corporate management in the Apartheid years, the years preceding democracy.

Isolation and Jobless after 22 years' Service

In the years, bearing up to the first democratic elections there was a frenzy among top management within local government. Still white and in power, the bureaucracy and remnants of the Apartheid era lobbied for survival. Many of the top incumbents were close to retirement. They needed to survive affirmative action in the transition phase. So, *if we can't fight them, let's join them.*

The to-be-appointed black politicians were not accustomed to the detail-hands-on administration of local government. They had to rely on the present and still-in-power Apartheid bureaucrats to train them. So, suck up and save the white bacon, ride out the last white incumbent years before retirement. Local Government was in the flux of re-organisation in the face of democratisation. It was as if the still Apartheid power-base wanted to re-organise before democracy takes effect. The Apartheid Government amalgamated Local government areas into larger bodies, especially Metropolises. Re-organisation obliterated the autonomy of my Stellenbosch District Council. We became part of the Cape Metropolitan Council.

Stationed in one of the smaller local council areas, I was swallowed up into the bigger Cape Town-based local government. An ideal opportunity for my Metropolitan controlling office in Cape Town to take control. Suddenly I was without staff and alone in a massive room with a conference-size-table complete with all the equipment and data processing systems. My entire staff compliment transferred to Cape Town, leaving me with, basically nothing.

The window-dressing of inviting me to meetings by the Metropolitan officials did not help with my integration into the re-organised structures. Isolated in my satellite office, contained by the still in power Apartheid bureaucracy, I had to be kept at bay, I was too liberal in my thinking, too democratic. The solution; secondment to the LGTC, a training centre. I was formally isolated.

Secondment: Local Government Transitional Centre

During my final year with Local Government, I read for my PhD. The script title once again relating to Civil Defence - A Future Perspective. My superiors within Local Government in the end apparently saw me as an *academic.* My concluding commission within the local government was a secondment to the *Local Government Transitional Council (LGTC) Training Centre*; tasked with procuring training material. The LGTC administered training workshops for the new non-white *bureaucrats* and *politicians*. Once democratisation and the ensuing reconstruction and development take effect, they will take over critical local government positions. The training team strictly controlled on what to procure and administer. I was finally and completely isolated.

Termination: Civil Defence Association of South Africa

DMISA is the present day version of the original Civil Defence Association of South Africa. According to its manifesto, the renamed version, Disaster Management Institute of South Africa (DMISA) aims to advance DMISA and create learning and networking opportunities for its members. DMISA had been in existence for 25 years by 2010. DMISA's primary objective was to liaise and coordinate with the South African National Disaster Management Centre (NDMC) for state security. The NDMC being the replacement and new face of the State Security Council, cum NSSMS.

I was a founder member of the original Civil Defence Association of South Africa established in 1985. At that stage, employed by the Potchefstroom Local Government. The most significant problem the Civil Defence Association had to deal with was describing Civil Defence. DMISA progressed from *defence* as the prime objective to *information management*. DMISA's role became that of data management, proactive citizen preparedness and resource management. All actions related to preparation and threat evaluation along with the restructuring administration during disasters. The changing face of Civil Defence, as seen by DMISA and according to their website, is illustrated in the following schedule over 25 years of name changes:

"–26 April 1985: Founded as the Civil Defence Association of South

Africa. I was a founder member and served over time on the National Council as Councillor and Deputy President.

-1994: Name change to Civil Protection Association of South Africa.

-1996: Name change to Emergency and Disaster Management Association of Southern Africa.

-1998: Name change to Disaster Management Association of Southern Africa.

-2000: Name change to Disaster Management Institute of Southern Africa (DMISA)."

From the name changes, it transpires that DMISA had a severe problem finding its unique niche in the protection/ defence environment. The misinterpretation of what civil defence authentically means, confused the bureaucrats for more than a quarter of a century. There was a culture of forever stating to the world what civil defence is not, instead of affirming what it is. Acknowledging the real character of civil defence was incomprehensible.

If the actual nature of civil defence were respected, it would have compromised the Apartheid's government objective of a minority government. The exclusion of non-white people from the political environment, would not support the exact and genuine character of civil defence. Apparently, this delusion extrapolated into the post-Apartheid era. Civil defence protagonists still do not understand the real nature and meaning of civil defence.

Civil defence, an instrument of liberation available to oppressed people, was never recognised. In truth, liberation struggles were the enemy of the state and formal Apartheid civil defence.

As a founder member, I served on the National Council, but I also chaired the Training Committee of the Association for most of my tenure. Shortly before becoming unemployed I terminated my membership of the Association as well as Deputy President. My published M-Thesis, followed by my subsequent NSSMS *blacklisting*, made my affiliation with the Association untenable. The still white dominated and Apartheid inclined Council, with many ex-military and police incumbents, placed me in an intimidating position. At the final conference, the aggressive attitude of my fellow councillors was a clear manifestation of my isolation. The NSSMS through my work- and associative environment turned me into a marked man. When I resigned, the Association had less than ten non-white members, less than one percent, an association dominated by the white membership.

As previously mentioned, I was reading for my PhD. The vision of a disappearing career and no prospect of progressing with my vocation, after almost a quarter of a century, left me disillusioned. I terminated my studies. I was disappointed fed-up and at the end of my tether. To this day, I regret my decision. I should have opposed the bureaucrats. I did nothing wrong.

I accepted the offer of early retirement, following the path of least resistance. Ousted from local government after twenty-two years and without a career or job.

Information Management under Dictatorial Rule

Civil Defence went wrong in South Africa. The question remains, why? Bruneau's research as quoted below might shed some light on the problem.

I decided to bring the following explanations into play, to understand what goes wrong with information manipulation during periods of conflict. Information management and the difficulties surrounding it, during politically violent situations, are complicated scenarios. Dictatorial conditions have been the subject of investigation and research throughout the world. Thomas C. Bruneau, a distinguished professor of national security, writes extensively on the Brazil case, under Portuguese colonial rule.

Bruneau from the outset come to the following important conclusion: *"Control of information services poses serious problems in non-democratic regimes. An essential element of scrutiny is paramount in which human rights abuses often follow. An inherent tension exists between intelligence and democracy."* Bruneau found that probably the most challenging issue is the control of information services. The monitoring and complexity are typical within the legacies of former, non-democratic regimes. The intelligence or security apparatus is an essential element of control in dictatorial regimes. Apparently, this caused the dilemma with Apartheid South Africa. Human rights abuses were often prevalent and permitted. Democracy requires accountability to the nation; the critical ingredient is transparency.

Established democracies develop mechanisms to deal with information management. New democracies have to create new processes, and Apartheid South Africa suffered this deficiency. The NSSMS proved to be a dangerous predicament. The Communist-inclined ANC government, are also susceptible to this danger. It already promulgated secrecy laws to prevent journalism from reporting on government corruption. Who will be the nastier statesman? President P W Botha or Jacob Zuma?

Shifting Focus: Nation to Junta Police State

I focussed too much on my negative experiences within the *Apartheid Civil Defence*. The artificial shift established a biased perception in my mind. I did not want to associate myself with the delusional approach and was chastised by the authorities as a result. The adverse experience might overshadow my reason.

The real issue was a Civil Defence distorted by the Apartheid government to retain minority control. My rebellious criticism dumped me in opposition to the bureaucracy. My take on Civil Defence was a community founded action not an abduction of a right thing to do wrong. In the first and second world wars, Civil Defence was from the people, by the people and for the people. They safeguarded themselves against a threat of war. Women on the Home front took over farming, food supplies and industry to keep the economy and agricultural in as close to full production as possible.

Civil Defence should be available to every individual or societal group to protect themselves from any abuse and or infliction of their fundamental human rights. Civil Defence cannot be divorced from military and law enforcement actions. That is why the liberation struggles were authentic civil defence. They applied the full spectrum. The Apartheid version was a false hybrid version.

Apartheid and its Civil Defence structures battled with the misconceptions. They did not acknowledge the true nature of Civil Defence. If Apartheid did admit correct Civil Defence, they had to recognise the legitimacy of the struggle and liberation movements. That is why Civil Defence could not be involved with the neighbouring countries refugees fleeing into South Africa. Civil Defence could not be deployed to help the refugees in the camps. The negation of the true nature of Civil Defence is also the reason that the denominations of Civil Defence were distorted to hybrids as reflected in the name changes of the Civil Defence Association of South Africa. The first identification was correct. But, it did not reflect the objective of the Apartheid government.

Bruneau's findings resonate applicable when it comes to assessing the NSSMS and Civil Defence security infrastructures.

Conclusive Comments on my Civil Defence Career

In the first three decades of my existence, I was caught up in the cultural curse of Apartheid. I was born and raised an Afrikaner, a nation scarred by oppression and war and coerced by a nationalism that excluded people of colour.

I entered the literary world of advanced studies, and my eyes opened to the truth of democracy and liberation. My world changed, and I saw people for what they should be; equal and free.

Democratic aspirations and convictions marred my career development. I was too democratic for a still racist and Apartheid public sector. I committed the cardinal sin to applaud the enemy of the Apartheid government, the liberation struggle of the people of colour. I commended the terrorists on their freedom, their struggle and their civil defence successes. But, most unacceptable to the Apartheid government, I heavily criticised the Apartheid government's false Civil Defence.

In a sense, I can sympathise with the two Boer Generals, Piet de Wet and Andries Cronje during the Anglo-Boer War. They as commanders of the National Scouts movement for peace were ostracised and made out as traitors and so-called *hands-uppers*. But, they only took a stand for Afrikaner survival. I say this tongue in cheek. Some scouts fought their people and also attacked their own. There are some seriously bad apples among the warring factions.

If I published my M-Thesis after democratisation, things could have been different. The timing was not in my favour it signalled the end of my career. I was not welcome in the midst of dictatorial Apartheid and still a white bureaucracy. I exposed the failures of legalised civil defence harshly.

But when researching, the only point of departure and arrival is the truth. Research needs to be integral to be sustainable. Maybe I should have done what the majority of the white bureaucracy did, compromise and not rock the boat. Let the storm blow over. See how I can salvage my white bacon within a black dominated public sector in Post-Apartheid South Africa.

Democracy was the issue, black inclusive of white. I could not live with the undemocratic lie. I could not be a conformer to something that I could not intrinsically support. I did try to effect change from the inside but failed miserably. I was not prepared to be part of the restraining and dominating white bureaucratic force. I did not want to be part of an induced and continued Apartheid system. The Afrikaner Apartheid Government blacklisted me.

Today, in the post-Apartheid era, I still hold true to my convictions. Apartheid is and was a terrible dispensation. It is even more valid today than in the white Apartheid years. But, black-on-white Apartheid is even worse, white people are suffering. And the ordinary coloureds and blacks are even worse off than under white Apartheid.

Why-oh-why did we democratise? Maybe, so the Communists can take over, in fact, it seems like they already control South Africa.

In Part Three I will focus on Post-Apartheid and reverse discrimination. I will explain how eight Southern African countries and protectorates liberated from colonialism. I will also evaluate the state of South Africa after twenty-two years of democratisation under a majority black ANC government.

Part Three:

Post-Apartheid, Reverse Discrimination

1926, the British Imperial Conference, chaired by British Prime Minister Arthur Balfour, as Lord President, introduced the autonomy of British Colonies. Conference replaced the British Empire with the British Commonwealth. It affected South Africa and Zimbabwe. South Africa's Prime Minister, General Jan Smuts was one of the campaigners to free the country from the British supremacy and impart Afrikaner self-governance. The Declaration confirmed full independence to ex-colonies with allegiance to the British Crown. The Declaration was ratified in 1926 and became a Statute of Westminster in 1931.

The Balfour Declaration marked the beginning of liberation for British Colonies. South Africa continued as the Union of South Africa and progressively extrapolated imperial oppression of the people of colour vis-à-vis the Africans and non-whites. Segregation and oppression under imperialism, ultimately transformed into Apartheid. Imperialism never adorned any political rights onto the people of colour.

The Portuguese Empire came to an end after World War II. In 1974 a military coup ousted the Portugal regime and brought an end to Portuguese Imperialism. Portugal granted independence to its former colonies Angola and Mozambique.

In part three I will research the liberation of eight countries within Southern Africa. I will also explain what happened after decolonisation, especially in South Africa. I deal with the Post-Apartheid incidents in detail. The increasing *hate crimes and de-whiting*; attempts to purge Africa of the imperial west. Apartheid did not end; it just changed faces and colours from black to white discrimination.

Part Three consists of the following:

7.   *Liberation: Eight Southern African Countries*................... *178*

8.   *Democratisation and Reverse Discrimination*................... *206*

9.   *South Africa Today, Post-Apartheid*.................................. *235*

Chapter 7

Liberation: Eight Southern African Countries

The Ex-Colonial population

Countries Colonized within Southern Africa	Colonial Population Figures in Modern Times		
	Europeans Still in Ex-Colonies		Total Population Millions
	Total Millions	% of Population	
South Africa	4. 60	8. 36%	55. 00
Angola	2. 20	9. 96%	22. 08
Namibia	1. 50	5. 84%	25. 70
Mozambique	0. 83	3. 06%	27. 00
Botswana	0. 68	2. 91%	23. 50
Swaziland	0. 41	3. 11%	13. 20
Zambia	0. 40	2. 68%	14. 95
Zimbabwe	0. 29	1. 91%	15. 05

Statistics are estimates based on recently published papers and reports.

Up to six million Europeans still live in Southern Africa's ex-colonies. During colonization, approximately 60 million people left Europe to populate occupied countries all over the world. The conquered people of the colonies were vulnerable and under-developed. Subjugation was part of the imperialistic expansion of the wealthy and developed western nations. Capitalist greed was the motivation behind imperialism. The West wanted to exploit the mineral resources and abundant cheap to free labour of the countries colonized. There were some moral and altruistic statements of improvement made by the Imperialists. That turned out to be lip service. Imperialism was all for the enrichment of the West.

The migrated Europeans multiplied rapidly within occupied countries. Before World War I, 38% of the total world-population was of European ancestry. Millions returned from colonised countries to Europe. One million Portuguese vacated African colonies during the 1970's liberation under violent decolonisation. Decolonisation often resulted in the loss of life, hostility and the deterioration of infrastructure. In the first decade after democratisation, South Africa lost 15% of its white people as well-qualified professionals; a migration coined as the white brain drain. Well qualified and in the prime of their working lives, people leaving the country for a better life elsewhere. Free of violence and deteriorating infrastructure.

The colonists, in general, were not kind to occupied nations. The subjugated natives were without exception enslaved, oppressed and exploited. Colonial powers had to maintain control by military force that led to mass killings. As a result, when liberation came, the natives revolted and in some cases drove the occupiers out or killed many of them. Violent revolt against Europeans is referred to as decolonisation, and recently de-whiting. The revolution manifests as a rebellion against the West. The western world was perceived to be wrong-doers, they occupied and colonised native African countries.

In this chapter, I describe the decolonisation and liberation process within eight Southern African Countries. I will highlight the violent decolonisation as well as the relatively peaceful liberated colonies.

European masters of colonisation allowed their countrymen to return home upon decolonisation. The only country that did not allow their expats back to Europe was the Netherlands.

South Africa was fighting a Border War

I cannot plead ignorance. I was aware that South Africa was fighting a *border war* for the retention of the minority and Apartheid rule. It was expedient to call it a *border war*. Patriotically it seemed like saying; we are protecting ourselves, our country. Taking into account the Afrikaner's obsession never to be governed by anyone but themselves, it might be seen as a conserving attitude. However, not considering the non-white and disenfranchised people might amount to delusional boldness. The obstinacy is equal to the *courage* of Israel's retention of an oppressive government in the face of the subjugated Palestinian people.

The truth, South Africa was fighting the liberation movements inland and in the countries bordering South Africa. Apartheid was fighting the people that the colonists and Afrikaners oppressed for centuries. My research on the liberation struggles of Southern Africa shocked me. I unearthed gruesome facts, cruelty and terrible actions. Atrocities committed by Apartheid South Africa and the European colonists.

South Africa borders on and land-locks seven different sub-continents: Mozambique, Zimbabwe, Swaziland, Namibia, Botswana, Lesotho and Angola. They are all part of the Southern Africa sub-continent. Without exception, all eight countries, South Africa included, were affected by Europe's imperial expansionism. All eight colonised or put under European protectorates by the colonisers. Native black people originally inhabited all eight countries as indigenous populations. Five centuries ago there were no white faces in Africa.

Countries involved in Liberation Struggles

I researched the historical origin and development of liberation struggles. I aim to evaluate the incidence of occupation along with the ultimate liberation of these countries. I identified two groups of countries.

First, the five countries that experienced the full spectrum of colonisation. Three nations plagued by liberation struggles and even civil wars. The efforts led to decolonisation of Mozambique,

Angola and Zimbabwe. The states spared violent decolonisation at the time of liberation was South Africa and Namibia. However, taking into account the present day de-whiting calls, and renewed decolonisation attempts, by mass democratic movements, South Africa still seems to be in the firing line for violence and decolonisation. I write extensively about this new development later.

Secondly, I researched the three countries as British protectorates. Swaziland, Botswana and Lesotho. They largely escaped the crippling experience of liberation struggles and civil war.

Countries that Experienced Decolonisation

First I will deal with the states subjected to the full force of colonisation. The interfering and ever-present battle between the Capitalist West and Communist East complicated colonisation.

Mozambique

Southern Africa's liberation movements are intricate and entangled. Mozambique was just one piece of the Southern Africa liberation struggle jigsaw. Nonetheless, it had a crucial influence on the course of the region's conflict. The Portuguese were active in the slave trade of Mozambique since 1498. In 1920 when the slave trade took effect, they formally colonised Mozambique to exploit the colony's agricultural reserves.

Portugal empowered private companies with administrative authority and encouraged them to develop sugar and cotton plantations. Relative to other countries Mozambique colonised late. The settlers deployed a forced labour system marked by cruel practices subjugating African labour. Approximately two-thirds of the Portuguese colonists could not read or write resulting in administrative inadequacy. Disparities in practices were widespread.

The colonists had no interest in Mozambique and its people. Their only interest was capital gain and to return to Portugal enriched. The export of cotton underpinned Portugal's textile industry. It formed an essential element of Portugal's export trade in Europe. The Portuguese companies prospered, particularly during World War II. Portugal's neutrality enabled them to trade with both sides of the war.

Native African workers became progressively disgruntled. The workers protested against horrendous living conditions, slave labour and low wages. The police, PIDE *(Polícia Internacional e de Defesa do Estado)* responded by deploying 50,000 troops. They opened fire at Muende and massacred 500 people. The uprising and brute military force resonate to what happened in South Africa during the Anglo-Boer-War.

In 1967 *FRELIMO (Freedom for the Liberation of Mozambique)* supported by Communism formed within Mozambique. They amassed 8,000 natives and migrant workers to liberate Mozambique. FRELIMO'S headquarters was in Dar es Salaam. FRELIMO strengthened support among the indigenous population by establishing collective farms, health clinics and schools. A parcel bomb, delivered to the house Mondlane, killed FRELIMO's leader. PIDE in all probability had a hand in his killing. Samora Marchel took over the leadership. The Portuguese Colonists introduced concentration camps congruent to the Anglo-Boer War Concentration Camps, denying FRELIMO the support of Mozambicans. The camps demolished the supply of food and assistance to FRELIMO. The Portuguese also strengthened the PIDE by calling up local Africans for military service alongside PIDE.

In April 1974, the Portugal government in Europe fell to a right-wing dictatorship. The Portuguese signed a ceasefire with FRELIMO; not willing to continue with expensive imperialism. Mozambique's liberation did not happen without bloodshed. Decolonisation violently drove the colonists from Mozambique. The mass exodus of the colonialists crossed the border to South Africa. I lived in the Mpumalanga Province, bordering Mozambique. The convoys of fleeing colonists crossed the Komatipoort border into South Africa. The government did not mobilise the South African Civil Defence Corps. One would expect the civil defence to become involved to protect life and limb. Apartheid ruled that Civil Defence did not fit the Government's non-military objectives. They did not want civil defence engaged in the liberation struggles of colonial oppression. The majority of the 250,000 Portuguese colonists left Mozambique and returned to Portugal penniless.

The Mozambique economy was dependent on Apartheid South Africa as the primary source of foreign revenue. Mozambique's migrant labour worked in the British-owned Anglo-American mines of South Africa. The West viewed the Mozambique and Zimbabwean governments as *ungodly Marxist threats*. The West supported South Africa to counter any Communist involvement in Southern Africa. South Africa started a long and violent civil war against Communist-supported FRELIMO. South Africa paid a high price fighting this war. When it came to the crunch for democratisation, the West turned on Apartheid South Africa; they hung South Africa out to dry. In world politics, collateral damage is often the price to pay for the *greater good*. In this case, Apartheid South Africa was the price to pay, while the West still to this day supports Apartheid Israel.

With reluctance, President Marchel of Mozambique closed the Nkomati Accord with South Africa. They agreed on a non-aggression pact. The Mozambicans honoured the accord. South Africa through RENAMO undermined both the Mozambique-FRELIMO and the liberated Zimbabwean government. South Africa remained Mozambique's principal trading partner. Mozambique stabilised in recent years and showed substantial progress. By 1993 more than one-and-a-half million Mozambicans, returned from exile in neighbouring countries. The tourism sector recovered showing significant growth.

The Zimbabwean War of Independence

I elaborated on Cecil John Rhodes involvement in South Africa early on. Rhodes played a decisive role in the colonisation of Zimbabwe. After huge successes in the South Africa mining industry, Rhodes set his sight further north. Rhodes sought expansion to the north in pursuit of his Cape to Cairo railway dream.

In1884 he persuaded Britain to establish a protectorate over Bechuanaland. Britain ultimately annexed the then Bechuanaland; today's Botswana. Rhodes had immense influence in the Cape Parliament. He never abandoned his imperial vision of Britain becoming the world ruler under a British Empire.

In 1888 Rhodes targeted Matabeleland and Mashonaland; in present-day Zimbabwe and Zambia. The acquisition he reasoned will compliment his Cape to Cairo, rail-link expanding the British Empire. Rhodes believed the area held untapped gold reserves. He embarked on ways to exploit the mineral wealth of Matabeleland and Mashonaland.

In 1887, King Lobengula ruled the Northern Ndebele people, historically called Matabele. He signed a treaty with the Transvaal Boer Republic. Rhodes got concerned that the Boers were moving in on his imperial dreams for the north. The colonial scramble for Africa was well underway. Rhodes was also aware that the Germans, French and Portuguese had Matabeleland in their sights. He used the threat of Germany and other European imperial powers, to sway the British Government in support of his plans for the North.

John Smith Moffat, Assistant Commissioner to Sir Sidney Shippard in Bechuanaland knew the Matabele Chief Lobengula well; their fathers were friends. After negotiations prompted by Rhodes, they signed the Moffat Treaty of February 1888. Mostly, the Treaty agreed on a relaxed British protection between Lobengula's Matabele land and the British Government. Rhodes was not convinced. He was concerned that the Moffat Treaty was too weak to hold Matabeleland in the face of Dutch and Germans moving into the territory.

Rhodes with the assistance of Rudd formed the British South Africa Company (BSAC) Rhodes crafted the company on the Dutch East India company model. He urgently mobilised his British South African Company (BSAC) to put Matabeleland under British control. BSAC as commercial-political entity aimed at exploiting economic resources to advance British imperialism. In March 1888, shortly after the Moffat Treaty, Rhodes sent his business partner Charles Rudd to get King Lobengula to sign an exclusive mining concession to BSAC. When Rudd arrived at Lobengula's kraal, there were British rivals, ready to pursue a similar objective.

Using Rhodes's authority, Rudd was able to win over the support of the competing British officials. Rudd convinced King Lobengula that the BSAC had more power and influence than any of the other petitioners. Lobengula signed an exclusive mining grant to BSAC. He signed in the hope of British protection against Boer migration onto his lands; also to protect his tribe from their domestic enemies.

The Rudd Concession was not a reasonable agreement. The Concession posed only as a cover for the colonisation of the Ndebele and the Shona. Rhodes managed to get Royal monarchical support for his plans under the British South Africa Company (BSAC). The support gave BSAC full imperial and colonial powers. In effect, it granted Rhodes full administrative authority. It allowed the maintenance of law and order, building of infrastructure and engaging in mining explorations. The Royal charter authorised Rhodes to colonise Matabele and Mashonaland. Rhodes's proposal did not have any financial implications for Britain. It extended the reaches of the British Empire finding favour with the British.

Rhodes's ambitions became a reality, and in his own words he will not be stopped by what he called *"A savage chief with about 8 000 warriors"*. Rhodes immediately planned to populate

Matabeleland and Mashonaland, with white settlers. The Ndebele could not oppose them. Rhodes prepared to take the land of the Matabele and Shonas by force. He even recruited young Brits from influential families in Britain as mercenary soldiers. Rhodes knew, when these young Brits become exposed to danger from African aggression, the British will come to the rescue of their countrymen with overwhelming military strength.

But, Lobengula allowed Rhodes' free access into Matabele and Mashonaland. Rhodes was cautious and reasoned that: *".... if he attacks us, he is doomed. If he does not, his fangs will be drawn. The pressure of civilisation on all his borders will press more and more heavily upon him. And the desired result will be the disappearance of the Matabele as a power. If delayed, the result is yet the more certain."*

Rhodes established what he called a *Pioneer Column*. The men staffing the column rendered their services in return for gold concessions and land. The condition was, they occupy Mashonaland. On 13 September 1890, BSAC's *Pioneer Column* invaded Mashonaland. There was no opposition from Lobengula. The settlement took place in the area of the present day Harare, where they raised the Union Jack, proclaiming it as a British Colony.

The expectation of gold did not materialise; there were no possible gold reserves to explore. Lobengula granted farming land to the settler pioneers. The giving of farmland was not part of the Rudd Concession. However, Lobengula avoided conflict with Britain in return for peace and tranquillity of his people. Rhodes's gold failure harmed him financially.

Clashes with the Ndebele was inevitable. The British settlers attacked the Ndebele. They justified their attacks on the Ndebele arguing the protection of the Shona against the vicious and savage Ndebele warriors. BSAC fought the war with young mercenaries and advanced warring equipment and techniques. Again, the mercenaries fought in exchange for land and gold promises.

The deceit of BSAC frustrated the Ndebele endlessly. Lobengula wrote to Britain; *"Every day I hear from you reports which are nothing but lies. I am tired of hearing nothing but lies. What Impi (task force) of mine have your people seen and where do they come from? I know nothing of them."*

Leander Starr Jameson and his Company of troops, police, employed by Beit and Rhodes' British South Africa Company (BSAC), once again came to Rhodes' assistance. The Rhodes and the British Government joined Jameson with his group of mercenary soldiers; they overpowered the Ndebele. Earlier I wrote about the Jameson Raid on the Transvaal Boer Republic.

Lobengula and the Ndebele lost out to Rhodes and Jameson. In desperation, he destroyed his stronghold and fled with his Impi of fighters. Lobengula died in 1894, of ill health.

Rhodes's Consolidated Goldfields Company funded the war costing £66 000. The occupied land became Southern and Northern Rhodesia; today's, Zimbabwe and Zambia. Rhodesia remained a British colony for more than half-a-century.

Ian Douglas Smith was the Prime Minister of Rhodesia from 1964 to 1979. In 1965 he led the predominantly white Unilateral Declaration of Independence (UDI) government, terminating British imperialism. The independence from Britain introduced a new struggle for the black population. The Ndebele and Shona tribes had a battle against the minority white UDI government. The international community did not recognise the Smith-UDI government.

On 21 November 2017 The Telegraph reported that Zimbabwe's President Robert Mugabe resigned, ending 37 years of despotic rule. He started as a hero of the struggle against white rule. In later days Mugabe was responsible for reducing the country to economic misery. A Facebook post satirises that; "South Africa's prayers for Zuma to go, was answered in Zimbabwe.

The RENAMO Terror – South Africa and Rhodesia

In 1976, Ken Flower, served as the UDI's intelligence chief, under Prime Minister Ian Smith. FRELIMO, supported by Communism, was a grave concern to the West. The West found it essential to counter Communism and supported Apartheid South Africa and Rhodesia UDI, to neutralise FRELIMO. America played a significant role helping the colonial rulers. Fowler established the Mozambique National Resistance Movement (RENAMO) as an anti-Communist liberation movement. South Africa operated beyond its borders with the purpose to quash the communist supported liberation movements. It provided military help to Europe's minority colonial governments. Apartheid South Africa did not want the white minority governments to fail.

By 1976 South Africa's internal struggle against the freedom movements within the country reached extreme proportions. The cross-border war stretched the military abilities of South Africa to its limits. The Apartheid government had its hands full in opposing the black uprising in neighbouring Namibia, Angola, Mozambique, and Rhodesia. Angola and Mozambique became liberated and decolonised.

FRELIMO provided refuge to freedom fighters from Rhodesia and South Africa. Anti-liberation and Western-supported RENAMO had some success with the native Mozambique people oppressed by FRELIMO; they found shelter with RENAMO. RENAMO, on the other hand, exercised intimidation to build its support, they were responsible for some barbarities against civilians and often resorted in banditry and the destruction of infrastructure. RENAMO received continued funding and direction from Apartheid South Africa and the West. They obliterated five hundred of the one thousand two hundred health clinics in Mozambique. Two-thirds of all primary schools were destroyed or closed. Three thousand plus rural shops were demolished or closed, most never re-opened.

The support for RENAMO from the West continued after Zimbabwe became independent. The war against RENAMO cost Mozambique half of its potential GDP at that stage.

Samora Marchel, the leader of FRELIMO, died in an air crash upon returning from Malawi. South African agents interfered with the radio navigation beacon, deliberately interfered with the flight course of the plane. In 1998 the widow of Samora Marchel, Graca, became the third wife of former president Nelson Mandela. The citizens of oppressed countries were often attacked and abused from both sides of the war, colonial powers as well as the liberators.

War and liberation have an ugly face of cruelty, including abuse, rape, destruction and death. Even today in countries like Somalia and Ethiopia this kind of violence prevails. White South Africans are also in the present day subject to the same ill-treatment in the form of black-on-white hate crime and decolonisation efforts.

Recently, Mozambique economy got a boost due to gas and steel developments. I spent a week in Mozambique during January 2016. The South African company SASOL, is active in field drilling programs for oil and liquid petroleum gas (LPG). Also visibly busy in Mozambique is Communist China, building extensive road networks, impressive dams and water reservoirs. If the benefit of these developments is not beneficial to the people of Mozambique, it will once again go to foreign companies and countries. Exploitation transformed into a modern hybrid of colonialism. One would only trust that Mozambique learnt lessons from imperialism.

The two nations colonised but not decolonised are South Africa and Namibia. They experienced relatively spoken peaceful transitions. At the time they seemed free and democratised, this conclusion is not genuine. Namibia suffered severe colonisation evils as later elucidated. Based on present-day atrocities in both countries, *peaceful liberation* might be a pipe dream.

The Effect of the Border War on South Africa

By late 1974, South Africa's position deteriorated rapidly. The liberation of Mozambique and Zimbabwe inspired protests against Apartheid in South Africa. Black workers staged strikes, and open rebellion erupted in the black township of Soweto. Six hundred black people died as rioting spread to other cities of South Africa.

Black conscious leader Steve Biko's suspicious death in police custody gave rise to more protests and sanctions. The Apartheid government, enacted a Tri-Cameral Parliament constitution in 1984, to stem the tide of unrest. They introduced Coloured- and Asian representation to the political system. A transformation that failed; the majority black community did not accept the change.

The ANC's armed wing *Umkhonto we Sizwe* and the PAC turned to military revolt and active resistance. Previously they avoided violence.

The Apartheid government labelled the liberation struggle as *terrorism*. Interesting, the British colonists, labelled the Boers in the Anglo-Boer War as *terrorists*; now the tables have turned. Once the Boer-Afrikaners came under threat, the oppressed black people became the *terrorists*. It is incredible how the terrorist label rubs. The moment a nation is threatened the risk become a *terrorist*. It is all in the eye of the beholder.

Conspicuously the support of the West to South Africa in opposing Communism, sublimated into thin air; they changed their stance to favour democratisation. Post-World-War-Two introduced a turn-around; a support of the previously oppressed peoples materialised. The revolt against fascism and racism replaced capitalism and colonialism.

Angola and the Slave Trade: 15th to 19th Century

In 1483, the Portuguese arrived in Angola for the first time. In 1575 the Portuguese founded the town Luanda. Angola became a primary Portuguese trading station for slaves in the 17th and 18th centuries. The Portuguese slave trade flourished between 1580 and 1680. In the 15th century, the Portuguese endeavoured to mine for gold, but the slave trade was a more lucrative commodity on the international market.

In 1587 the Portuguese fortified the town of Luanda with 400 Portuguese settlers. The slave trade became the primary business of the colonial economy. A million men, women and children were captured as slaves and shipped from Angola to Brazil. Even banning the slave trade in 1836 by Britain, did not stop the Portuguese; they continued slavery up and until 1875. The Portuguese eventually encountered problems due to the slave trade ban. The question was how to make productive use of the subjugated African labour. The Portuguese transformed slavery to full colonisation and land-grab involving local labour exploitation. The comprehensive settlement converted to occupation synonymous to colonising South Africa.

The race for land-grab in Africa was fierce. The Portuguese found it challenging to compete with the Dutch in Asia, and the Americans, British and French rivals in the rest of the third world. The Angolan Colonial Government made land grants to settlers in regions inland from Luanda. The awards resulted in the settlers encroaching on the land of the native Angolan peoples. The colonists developed coffee, cotton and sugar plantations, similar to Mozambique. The land encroachment gave rise to outbreaks of warfare with local rulers and peoples. Angola was an unsettled region during the 19th-century European scramble for Africa.

In 1891, at the Berlin Conference, European powers recognised Portugal's Angolan claim, setting boundaries by negotiation. Naturally, native Angola was not consulted by Europe. At that time, Portugal was in control of only a small part of Angola. Theoretically, the Portuguese Colony was enclosed by native Angolan Tribes. But the Portuguese settlers expanded in opening up the interior.

Back in Europe, Portugal had been through two transitions. Portugal moved from monarchy to a Republic in 1910, followed by a military coup in 1926. The effect of the European and Portuguese changes resulted in the initial tightening of Portuguese control in Angola. Endemic warfare raged between the Portuguese and African rulers in a conquest for land. One by one the local kingdoms were attacked and subdued. The 1920s brought about fully established Portuguese colonial control. Almost the entire Angola became a Portuguese Colony.

Slavery abandoned, but the plantations operated with African forced labour. No relief from oppression and subjugation for the natives of Angola. When the Angolan colonial government banned the Portuguese Communist Party, the enslaved Angolans responded by establishing three rival guerrilla groups. The first liberation movement was the *MPLA (Movement for the Popular Liberation of Angola)*, founded in 1956 and supported by the USSR. In the following year, the *FNLA (Front for the National Liberation of Angola)* emerged with aid from the USA to oppose the MPLA and Russia. A third liberation movement *UNITA (United National Independencia for Total Angola)* formed with little foreign assistance. It had considerable tribal allegiance in Southern Angola.

The communistic inspired MPLA was not Portugal's biggest problem, the 1961 rebellion of workers in the North plunged the country into chaos. The Lisbon Government responded vigorously, sending scores of troops to the conflict area. The supplementary migration of Portuguese peasants to Angola was an effort by Lisbon to populate Angola with Portuguese nationalists. Furthermore, to appease the Angolan community, the colonists introduced reforms to education and health.

The sequence of events in Southern Africa followed similar patterns. First, it was South Africa, then Mozambique and Zimbabwe, now Angola. The colonial masters in Europe supported by the West launched military efforts to quash the resistance as standard modus operandi. The prime objective was to retain colonial minority rule and oppression. The numbers of settlers were also increased by the colonisers to swing the demographic balance favouring the imperialist powers.

One by one the African kingdoms were disbanded and destroyed. Almost the whole of Angola came under the control of Portugal. Slavery abolished, but the plantations worked on a system of forced labour. The characteristics that gave rise to Apartheid are ever present during African colonisation. The main feature was control of the oppressed native population. Throughout the 1960ˢ and into the 1970ˢ the liberation movements rebelled against the colonial powers.

When one considers the western colonisation, the question arises; was communist interference a tempering effect on Imperial expansion. This curved ball question poses an uncomfortable position in the western-inclined mind.

The 1974 *Coup d'etat* in Portugal, brings an end to the country's long-established right-wing dictatorship. The change of regime in Lisbon had immediate consequences in Africa. The new government in Lisbon was not prepared to continue expansionism in Africa.

Lisbon granted the occupied colonies independence. First Portuguese Guinea in September 1974, followed by Portuguese East Africa in June 1975. Lisbon gave new names to the territories, Angola and Mozambique. Both liberations experienced violent decolonisation.

In 1975, I was touring Namibia bordering Angola and South Africa north and south. Similar to Mozambique, the freedom did not go without bloodshed.

A fleeing exodus of Portuguese from Angola into Namibia ensued. Convoys of fleeing Portuguese colonists crossed the northern Namibian border; they ultimately entered South Africa. Once again the South African army erected large refugee camps. The South African Civil Defence did not mobilise for the same reason as the Mozambican exodus. Not to come to the aid of the refugees when colonial powers are defeated. The South African public kept at bay.

Before the official Portuguese withdrawal in 1975, civil war in Angola broke out. The Portuguese colonists were keen to leave as quickly as possible; they abandoned Mozambique and Angola without formally handing over control to any incoming government. The warring factions in the Civil War of Angola brought the western world to intervene. First to oppose Communism and finally for peace. The UN in 1994, at the UN intervention in Lusaka, mediated a somewhat shaky peace deal. However, progress was far from convincing.

All traces of agreement ended in December 1998. A full-scale civil war ensued while the rest of the world hardly noticed. Compared to Kosovo, Angola was less of a priority. Angola had an appalling start to independence. Potentially Angola can be a prosperous country with ample natural resources. But, the nation suffered from colonialism and self-inflicted civil strife. The unrest intensified by interference from the West and the Communist East.

Countries spared the Suffering of Decolonisation

Next, I will research the three states, not subject to full decolonisation and liberation. Their saving grace was that opportunity and time did not suit. Alternatively, the availability of abundant resources was not that enticing to the capitalists from the West.

Namibia: German South West Africa

In 1884, Germany seized the Agra-Pequena, *formerly a* Portuguese small cove settlement in Lüderitz. The occupation was the first German scramble for Africa. Initially South West Africa was occupied by Portugal, but, eventually, it became a German colony. The Germans over the next hundred years ravaged the Namibian native tribes. An oppression followed by South Africa as a British administrative authority. The early days of the German presence were calm. By 1896 only two thousand German traders and farmers lived in German-occupied Namibia. Relations with the Herero Tribe, were, for the most part peaceful.

In 1897, a natural disaster gave the German settlers an unexpected advantage. South West Africa became ravished by a previously unknown cattle plague. In 1889 the *Rinderpest*, formerly ravaging distant Somaliland, crossed the Zambezi. It devastated the livestock of the Herero Tribe as a cattle-raising people. In desperation, the Herero forcibly sold their pasture and half of their surviving cattle to the Germans. The Germans bought the land and livestock at well below the market value. Once the Herero was at its weakest the colonial settlers, step in and exploited the situation. The balance of power as a characteristic of colonialism and capitalism made an appearance, favouring the colonists. The God of Mamon will forever be a changing factor in world politics.

Prompted by their loss, the Herero attempted a desperate uprising against the Germans. They believed that the Germans were the cause of the Herero's misfortune. In January 1904, Herero warriors killed every German capable of carrying guns. The Herero spared the women, children, German missionaries and Europeans in general. German deaths amounted to not much more than one hundred. However, the uprising was incredibly vicious.

The killings prompted reprisal from Berlin. The Emperor William II in revenge tasked General Lothar von Trotha to attack the Herero Tribe. The Emperor instructed Lothar to select the nastiest possible army of men to carry out the attack. The order was to put down the uprising *by fair means or foul*.

Trotha engaged with the Herero and forced them into the Kalahari Desert. He surrounded them with his German army, leaving only one exit from the encirclement, leading further into the desert. The objective was to prevent the tribesmen from returning to their place of residence. Von Trotha placed guard posts preventing the Herero return. With no water, in extreme temperatures the Herero was defenceless. Some eight thousand men together with their women, children and remaining cattle perished.

In October 1904, Von Trotha followed this action with a *Vernichtungsbefehl* - extermination order. The command was that any Herero found within the German colonial borders must be killed. This order amounted to ethnic cleansing. It was an example of the century's most shameful genocide under colonial occupancy.

News of von Trotha's action profoundly shocked Germany and the rest of Europe. Berlin countermanded the extermination order. In 1905 von Trotha was removed from his command and recalled to Germany. Astonishingly, the Emperor decorated him on his return, for devotion to the fatherland. He carried out his orders, *by fair means or foul.*

Once again Europe came to the rescue of colonialism. They quashed the rebellion with overwhelming force. Von Trotha's Vernichtungsbefehl as an extermination order is synonymous to Lord Kitchener's Scorched Earth Policy. The Anglo-Boer-War was another example of colonial genocide; the BBC described the camps as murder camps. And again the question of war criminals and war heroes come into play; in whose eyes? Indeed the Herero's and Nama people won't agree with the decoration of von Trotha.

In retaliation, the Nama Tribe rose in support of their traditional enemies, the Herero Tribe. The combined forces lodged successful guerrilla raids on the German troops.

But eventually, most of the Nama tribe were confined to labour camps on the occupier's railways development, aimed at increasing colonialism. For many of the Nama's and Herero's, this proved to be a death sentence.

A census in 1911 revealed the reduction of 45% for the Nama Tribe; from twenty- to nine-thousand. The Herero, reduced by 80%; from eighty- to fifteen thousand. These statistics reflect genocidal practices; way more than half of these nations exterminated. It seems like the German colonial powers almost succeeded in the ultimate success of colonisation, similar to Canada, Australia and New Zealand. They nearly annihilated the native population to a level where the demographic balance swung in favour of the colonists.

The Nama's and Herero's were probably relieved when South Africa colonised Namibia in 1915, ridding them of the Germans. Colonialism shifted from the German oppressors to the South African colonisers. What followed might be less atrocious but equally evil and oppressive.

South Africa and South West Africa 1915-1988

The First World War changed the future of Namibia. Britain commissioned South Africa to invade South West Africa. The invasion reflects an interesting coincidence. The Dutch lost in the Napoleonic Wars. The British used the vulnerable position of the Dutch to occupy the Cape. Now South Africa as a British dominion, claims Namibia because Germany lost World War 1. The League of Nations commissioned South African administration over South West Africa.

Namibia's prosperity increased after World War II. A buoyant market for diamonds and beef gave its economy a boost. But, the wealth accrued, went exclusively to the white Europeans and South African occupiers. The Herero and Nama Tribes as the indigenous tribes did not benefit.

South Africa's Apartheid laws after 1948, added to the distress of the black people in Namibia. In 1958, the *Ovamboland People's Organisation (OPO)* established to resist the occupation by South Africa. The Ovambo tribe straddled the border between South-West Africa and Angola. In 1960, the OPO claimed a broader remit, changing its name to the *South West Africa People's Organisation (SWAPO).*

SWAPO launched a guerrilla campaign against the South African administration and soon became the leading political force in South West Africa. In 1960, Harold Macmillan's *winds of change* speech introduced the end to Imperial expansion. It dramatically sped up the process of African independence, spurred on by the revolt against fascism induced by the defeat of Nazism.

In 1961 South Africa became a Republic. The South African protection and support in opposing Communism from Britain and the West diminished and came to an end. The changes also marked the beginning of South Africa's long spell out in the cold. Sanctions and trade embargoes became commonplace as a resistance against Apartheid. The West turned its back on South Africa.

When Tribal leaders in South West Africa petitioned the UN against South African rule, the time was ripe for liberation. South Africa disputed the authority of the UN in this matter. South Africa argued at length before the International Court of Justice in The Hague. Eventually, in 1967, the UN actively supported the liberation of Namibia.

In the 1980s, the South African war against SWAPO escalated and carried far north into Angola. The war drained the reserves of the South African government. South Africa, already inundated with significant and increasing internal unrest became more under threat. Some 2500 South African soldiers died in the conflict, the cost of the war became extreme.

I was part of the military conscription programme, forcing men after leaving school to undergo military training in the South African Defence Force. Many of the South African young people served against liberation movements. They waged war against oppressed fighters, to quash the uprising of liberation struggles. I was spared military call-up and never served on active military duty. However, I can remember my neighbour, a young police officer killed in the so-called *border war*.

In 1988, the South African border war effort collapsed. The policy of stalling Namibia's independence abandoned.

The UN supervised the provision of a new constitution and elections. In the 1989 elections, SWAPO won 57% of the vote. The party's leader, Sam Nujoma, became president of Namibia.

In March 1990, Namibia formally gained independence. Nujoma pursued a policy of reconciliation. White settlers remained in their government jobs. The agreement also included a peaceful coexistence with South Africa.

Decolonisation or civil war did not characterise the liberation of South Africa and Namibia. There was no bloody exodus of colonists from the two countries, but signs of reconciliation marred by the manifestation of decolonisation and de-whiting.

Zimbabwe, Angola and Mozambique taught colonies some lessons how not to decolonise. Namibia seems to be one of the success stories of liberation; bar the manifestation of de-whiting and decolonisation.

The colonisation release was peaceful and resulted in a democratic dispensation. But, the price paid in the form of genocide was excessive and painful. Post democratisation did not materialise in peace and tranquillity. Namibia is not free from farm murders and black-on-white discrimination. In 2015 *Africa Today* reported on the escalation of race-related murders.

South Africa is the fifth country liberated. However, earlier I covered the liberation thoroughly. The next objective will be to consider the countries that were British protectorates and not fully fledged European colonies.

Countries under British Protection and not Colonised

The countries researched so far suffered formal colonisation and had liberation struggles to free the oppressed African nations. The following three Southern African states had explicit intervention from Britain. But, no liberation strife and continued oppression materialised.

Bechuanaland – Botswana: British Protectorate

Bechuanaland, in 1885, became a British protectorate, with the intention to merge it with the Cape Colony in the south or with Rhodesia to the north; Bechuanaland would eventually become part of the British Empire. The plan was frustrated by the resolute action of tribal chief Khama III, king of the Ngwato.

Along with two other local chieftains, they travelled to London to negotiate. They persuaded the colonial secretary Joseph Chamberlain, towards the continued protection by the British Crown. In return, Britain gained territory for the construction of a railway line to the North.

Inevitably, the countries bordering South Africa were economically dependent on their industrialised neighbour with the British-owned mines and industries. Bechuanaland provided migrant labour for both the Transvaal and the Cape Colony. The British owned Anglo-American mines profited greatly from the cheap migrant labour from Bechuanaland.

The decolonisation of South Africa came about after the signing of the Vereeniging Peace Treaty, ending colonial rule.

In 1910 the Union of South Africa came into being with constant pressure to incorporate Bechuanaland. But, the British government held to Chamberlain's pledge, confirming that no transfer of sovereignty will happen without the agreement of Bechuanaland and the British government.

However, Westminster's implicit involvement in the politics of Africa became evident in 1935. Seretse Khama, the grandson of Khama III, and heir to the leadership of the Ngwato people studied at Oxford University and married a white British woman, Ruth Williams.

The South African government proclaimed laws against mixed marriages. Racist laws compelled Britain to prevent Seretse Khama and his wife, as a mixed-race couple, from returning to Bechuanaland. The Apartheid government's racial policies obliged Britain to introduce the embargo against Seretse and his white wife's return to Botswana. Six years expired before Seretse was allowed to go back to Botswana as a private citizen.

In 1965, Bechuanaland became independent. Seretse took his rightful place as the head of his nation. He was elected Bechuanaland's first Prime Minister.

The liberation of African colonies led to the dismantling of the British Empire, as a result of the Balfour Declaration. The inauguration of the British Common Wealth followed.

Seretse Khama changed the name from Bechuanaland to Botswana and founded the Botswana Democratic Party in 1965.

After fair elections, the Democratic Party formed a national assembly. The Botswana National Front, also dating from 1965, constituted a legitimate parliamentary opposition. Botswana enjoyed prosperity due to its export of diamonds. Blessed with the wise leadership of two long-serving presidents. Botswana experienced a peaceful existence.

During the 1970s, Botswana allied with Zambia, Tanzania, Mozambique and Angola to exert pressure on Rhodesia and South Africa for democratisation. The unrest in Rhodesia and South Africa resulted in a flood of refugees to Botswana; many of them political activists. During the 1980s South Africa executed frequent raids on Botswana.

Lesotho

South African borders land lock Lesotho and the Orange Free State; previously the Boer Republic of the Orange Free State.

Inhabited by the Sotho people since the 16th century, they mingled peacefully with the earlier Khoisan. Their history features in rock-art at various sites in the Lesotho Mountains. Boers started to occupy territory within Lesotho posing a threat to the Lesotho nation. King Moshoeshoe I, paramount chief of Lesotho, asked the British Crown to intervene; preferring British protection to annexation by the Boers.

Lesotho became a British Protectorate in 1868. Britain had a vested interest in Lesotho due to the labour offer from Lesotho to the South African mining industry owned by British colonists and founded by Cecil John Rhodes.

Lesotho also resisted incorporation into the proposed Union of South Africa in 1910. Its primary natural resources consisted of diamonds, sand and clay. The wealth gain was not convincing enough for full colonial settlement; capitalism was probably not that interested. Also, the democratisation of nations in Southern Africa, at this late stage, did not favour colonialism. There was never a need for liberation of an oppressed country.

Swaziland

The Nguni Swazi Kingdom was under the leadership of King Sobhuza I. He absorbed the non-Nguni people and enlarged the Swazi territory by conquering their land. King Mswati II merged the Swazi Kingdom as an independent country and avoided colonisation.

The rivalry between the British and the Boer Republics kept the probable colonisers at bay. Swaziland was administered by the Transvaal Boer Republic from 1894 until 1902 but did not incorporate Swaziland into South Africa.

The British defeated the Boers in 1902 when Swaziland came under British control. British control lasted until Swaziland's independence in 1968. King Sobhuza II governed Swaziland from 1921 to 1982. He is considered to be the second-longest reigning monarch in world history. Swaziland was along with Lesotho and Botswana fortunate as a result of timing; colonisation did not happen.

Modern Time Black Perspective on the Rule of Law

According to *the Guardian* of 12 August 2017; Grace Mugabe whipped a twenty-year-old South African model with an electrical cord. Gabriela Engels filed court papers challenging the South African legislative authorities who granted Zimbabwe's first lady Grace Mugabe diplomatic immunity. Police placed a *border red alert* preventing Mugabe from leaving the country. But, South Africa's international relations minister over-ruled the alert by granting diplomatic immunity to the wife of Robert Mugabe. The diplomatic immunity granted after the incident and the red border alert became front page news. The Mugabe's sneaked out of the country from the military airport *Waterkloof* in a hired plane.

Afriforum decided to back Engels in a legal case. Gerrie Nel, the prosecutor who secured a murder conviction against Olympic and Paralympic star Oscar Pistorius, will be handling the case. Afriforum's chief executive, Kallie Kriel, said: *"We want to set aside the granting of diplomatic immunity to Grace Mugabe."* According to AfriForum's CEO, Kallie Kriel: *"AfriForum is a civil rights initiative to mobilise civil society and specifically minority communities, in order to take part in democratic debate. Kriel further stated that AfriForum would like to achieve balance in South Africa."*

This incident illustrates the arrogance of black politicians to the Rule of Law; who is subject to the law is flexible and relevant to the person not the miscarriage of justice. Astonishingly, it is white law practitioners challenging the injustices of black politicians.

Conclusive Comments on Liberating Southern Africa

The occupation of Southern African countries commenced in the late 15th century with capitalism as the driving force. Initially, the slave trade and later full colonisation plagued Africa. Liberation struggles were initially peaceful but turned to violent protest and warfare. The capitalist-inclined colonists only surrendered control in the face of international condemnation after the Second World

War. The West withdrew support from Apartheid South Africa and capitalism; they could no longer benefit from oppression.

In Zimbabwe, Angola and Mozambique the countries were decolonised with violent expulsion of colonists accompanied by deaths and bloodshed. Robert Mugabe in 2000, changed land ownership in Zimbabwe, resulting in thousands of white farmers forced off their farms and out of the country. White farmers owned 70% of the most arable land in the country inherited from a colonial past. Many white farmers lost their lives and property in black-on-white hate crimes. Farm murders became an international concern as a result of the Zimbabwean farm murders scenario. The Mugabe government either supported the farm murders or turned a blind eye to the atrocity.

Grace Mugabe's misconduct that went unpunished illustrates how black politicians can manipulate justice and put the Rule of Law in disregard.

In July 2015, forty years later, Mugabe's people hinted that white farmers are welcome to return to Zimbabwe. Mugabe's government realised, killing white farmers was in effect killing the farming industry in Zimbabwe. The conflict that plagued decolonisation demolished the agricultural sector with no ability to recover. The destroyed agrarian sector left liberated countries wanting. Matters got worse before they got better in the post-liberation era.

There is evidence throughout Africa that the West, specifically America, entered the power struggle to oppose communism. The intervention had a determining effect on colonisation and liberation. Today Communism has a significant stake in Southern Africa.

Hopefully, improvement and normalisation should gradually set in with full and efficient democratic rule. But, time is telling a different story. After twenty-two years of democracy, South Africa is facing threats of decolonisation and de-whitening. Wrecked by maladministration, corruption and black-on-white hate crimes. South Africa experiences dire times. The ANC government governs

South Africa as a failed state; it also turns a blind eye to black-on-white hate crimes. To date, few liberated countries transformed into economically viable and democratic accountable nations.

Capitalism and Communism will always be lurking on the horizon to pounce and exploit vulnerable countries in some shape or form. Southern Africa paid the price of destruction, bloodshed and genocide in the struggle for liberation. It happened when European colonists repeatedly enforced their superiority with military force. The moment the native peoples of Southern Africa resisted colonisation and oppression, a superior colonial power subdued them and killed thousands.

The countries that suffered the least are the countries that experienced the lowest level of expansion like Swaziland, Lesotho, and Botswana. They are also the countries with long-standing and stable governments. Namibia had severe liberation struggles but in the end reconciled.

The problem for Southern Africa was the imbalance in military power. A well advanced Europe in the technology of war, conquered nations of lesser ability. Cheap slave labour, diamonds and gold enticed the capitalists, under the banner of imperialism to overcome and exploit Southern African countries. Imperialism was for the enrichment of Europe.

In the next chapter, I will focus on hate crimes and the change of discrimination; from white-on-black to black-on-white oppression. Also, I will investigate the interference of Britain in the affairs of South Africa that led to so much disruption and complications.

CHAPTER 8

DEMOCRATISATION AND REVERSE DISCRIMINATION

Misconceptions and Culturally Cursed

Mindsets within South Africa are and were always diverse, even to this day and age. The diversity was inevitable due to racism and discrimination. The South African nation never saw eye-to-eye across skin colour lines and even language differences. Conflict and distrust were prevalent and reached a crescendo in the 1960's to 1990's.

I am part of the white Afrikaner Nation that ultimately legalised Apartheid. I endeavoured to explain myself in previous chapters, but there are many facets of my life still to be clarified in chapters to come. My mindset was cultured by the history of the Afrikaner. The Afrikaner elders made sure that we young ones knew how our ancestors battled and suffered under British colonial rule and the Anglo-Boer-War. The interaction with black tribes was fresh in the older folks' minds. They made sure that we understand how the Boers had to fight for survival. The battle of *Blood River,* where the blood of the Zulu warriors and the Boers coloured the river red, is still to this day an Afrikaner memory of Boer suffering. For the Zulu people, it will be a memory of Boer occupation of their land.

While growing up, tales of Boer suffering were impressed on the young generations of the 20th century. We were conditioned to be appreciative of what our forebears had to suffer; to make life comfortable and safe for us, the generations to come. The cultural curse of Apartheid and being an Afrikaner-Boer were impressed on our makeup and mindset, from the moment we were cognitively aware.

A coin always sports two sides, metaphorically that is the case to almost every story. Apartheid as a standard coin has two dark sides. I will shine the spotlight on both sides, the *white-on-black* as well as the *black-on-white* Apartheid. Knowing that there are some grim descriptions in this chapter, I would like to ease the mood with a humorous start before I embark on the dark path of genocide and murder in the history of South Africa, plaguing the nation, even today. Black-on-white hate crimes in the post-Apartheid era are rife and getting worse in South Africa. The atrocities that happened under white Apartheid, progressively recur today under the *dictatorial-democratic* and Communist-inspired ANC government; it contributes to the distorted mindset of all South Africans.

Sometimes two people will consider the same thing but understand two different concepts. Differences not addressed and reconciled become deep-seated and extended over periods of time, even repressed over centuries. Disparities can turn into civil strife and even war.

The *Hot Totty* incident was straightforward and easy; effortlessly resolved. Apartheid and its legacy is a different kettle of fish. Maybe I can explain delusionary perceptions with a metaphor; an episode between a young Scottish lady doctor and myself. It was an incident that resonates so true to my early life's confusion within Apartheid. Delusionary Afrikaners and Peoples of colour inherited mindsets that culturally cursed and nurtured them into some delusions and mal-perceptions.

Hot Totty: The Misunderstanding

The incident that serves as a parable is real. The *Hot Totty* represented a trivial incident that happened to me quite recently. I use the parable to illustrate the ambiguity in people's understandings; sometimes resulting in differing perceptions and feelings. The *Hot Totty* experience is light-hearted and humoristic. Apartheid perceptual differences were severe to the extent of death and genocide as an outcome of pre- and post-Apartheid. White-on-black Apartheid was discriminatory in the Afrikaner Apartheid era. Black-on-white decolonisation in the post-Apartheid era seems worse.

The start of My Hot Totty Parable:

I arrived in the UK and lectured on Tuesdays and Wednesdays at the Derby University. This particular Wednesday, I took the one-hour drive to Derby feeling a bit under the weather. At first, I did not give it much thought. The introductory two-hour lecture went well, but I felt poorly halfway through the second two-hour session. At the break I contacted my supervisor, informing him of my discomfort. We agreed that I cut the final hour short. I did that and apologised to my students.

I called my wife, telling her that I felt dreadful and asked her to get me some medication. I explained my symptoms of cold-fever and a body that was shivering like a rattlesnake's tail. We concluded that I must have some flu-bug. My wife wished me a safe journey home, and promised to concoct me a proper African *Hot Totty*; so I can *sweat it all out.*

I arrived back home; my whole body was trembling. Boy, did I sweat; like a pig. Chilling trickles of cold sweat ran down my spine. My teeth chattered, and my body shook like a vibrator. I went straight to bed with the *Hot Totty* remedy. Later my wife gave me a second dosage. It tasted awful, but I welcomed it grumpily, trusting the treatment to rid me of the bug. I survived the night lying in a pool of sweat. The fever dissipated overnight. I got some well-needed sleep.

The next morning, I made an appointment at the local Medical Centre. A young Scottish lady doctor administered the consultation. She was new to the practice, rather attractive, with dark brown eyes and a white almond skin against the wavy spread of black hair. She had a strong Scottish accent. Her demeanour was professional; she displayed all the paraphernalia, stethoscope, white coat, etc.

I sat down and explained my ordeal of the previous day. When I got to the *Hot Totty*, I sensed a puzzled and amused discomfort in her body language. She was not comfortable with this *Totty* term, and *hot* confused it even more. I suddenly remembered, in my infant days, mothers affectionately referred to little boys penises as *totties*.

So I felt compelled to explain: A Hot Totty is an old African folk remedy. You mix a decent measure of whisky or brandy with a teaspoon of crushed ginger, add a tablespoon of sugar, lemon juice and two Aspirins. Pour it all into a mug of boiling water, and drink up. Straight to a warm bed; sweat out the bug that is messing with your body. I explained candidly; hopefully discarding any misunderstanding. Not likely.

A frown as big as a coat hanger crossed her brow, she started to giggle. I felt a creeping discomfort in my stomach. Her response sent a shiver of confusion down my spine. Her response was a *Totty* of confusion.

She responded in her thick Scottish accent: *"Ye went to bed with a Hot Tiddy? Wir I cum frim, aye Hot Tiddy is aye sexy yung thing; generally, aye young sexy and willing gal."* It took me an uncomfortable and grossly-embarrassed moment to comprehend this misunderstanding.

No, no, no, I blurted in defence, that's not it. I was shocked and momentarily silenced. In my condition? No, I would never have been able to cope with that kind of cure. And what's more, my wife would never have agreed to that remedy. Especially a double dose, on one night within the space of two hours, and in our home, in our bed, under her supervision. No! That is not my Hot Totty.

We both doubled over with laughter at my embarrassment; that was pure, authentic humour. The incident will stay with me for a long, long time. The lovely young doctor took some samples and very professionally diagnosed the bug. I had a bladder infection.

"Ye git yir butt to the chimist, pick up the antibiotic and complit the intyre curs. Yir discimfirt will go, I'd sey within a fiw days, stey awei

frim the Hot Tiddies" she mocked me with a smile twirling her lips. The dark Scottish flavour to her voice left a grin on my face. I left her rooms, walking down to reception with that smile still lifting my spirit. I could hear the young doctor still chuckling away; that was a good laugh.

End of the Hot Totty Story.

In the short-term within our day-to-day lives, two people will consider something but understand it differently. We listen, and we compare the concept to our understanding and formulate a self-centered viewpoint. The differences become a fundamental delusion, in need to be put right and move on. The doctor and I, both appreciated the misunderstanding. We laughed, corrected the confusion and moved on.

In real-life, delusions sometimes develop over centuries, and we become obsessed with our understanding to such an extent that people would rather die or kill before they resolve differences and move on. Serious conflict, wedged over centuries in the minds of opposing nations, led to wars. And that happens as a result of unresolved political differences. Millions of people will die as a result of dictators and politicians not able to resolve disputes. The people targeted in hate crimes do not even understand they are part of a severe political difference. They just pay with their lives, innocent and vulnerable.

The Apartheid delusion stuck within me, as a result of cultural brainwashing as an Afrikaner. I grew up in an Afrikaner family, still reeling from the shock of what happened to the Boer-Afrikaner nation at the hands of the British colonisers.

The Anglo-Boer-War incidence included the dreaded concentration camps and partial genocide of my Afrikaner nation. The psychological wounds for my generation were significant. Even though we were supposed to be a born-free generation of the Anglo-Boer-War, the trauma still affected us. Our grand and great-grandparents were part of the Anglo-Boer-War. Our parents would tell the gruesome stories to us children, with an intense sense of distaste and even hatred. I wrote extensively about the Cronje family sufferings in earlier chapters.

Some of the black people of South Africa did not forget the oppression suffered by their ancestors. Opposing perceptions exist today and give rise to continued discrimination and even death. Reconciliation of differences did not happen with democratisation. It just seems like the Afrikaner, and today's white population of South Africa are cursed and traumatised by the conflict of civil disorder and genocide. Decolonisation as recently propagated and induced by the mass democratic black movements like the *Rhodes Must Fall (RMF) and Black First Land First (BFLF)*, is once again emerging. I discuss decolonisation extensively in later chapters. Decolonisation can have many facets. The approach presently pursued by the black mass democratising movements relate to the removal of colonial symbolism, like the statue of Cecil John Rhodes. Farm murders and black-on-white hate crimes refer to decolonising the country, removing white people; the colour of the colonists and the West.

Based on Mandela's legacy and the South African Communist Party's constitutional declaration that; *"South Africa belongs to the people that live in South Africa"*, it is fair to conclude that decolonisation is inappropriate and misplaced. South Africa decolonised in 1910, but the renewed drive started, even as the 1995 democratisation is fresh in the mind of South Africa.

The question that springs to mind and needs answering. Is this Ethnonationalism? Is it majoritarianism and political demagogues blind-siding the ordinary people's minds, leading to Apartheid once again? Discrimination and segregation based on ethnicity and skin colour are a serious matter that derails democracy and the integration within a nation.

Democratisation and Genocide

The unification of 1910, to a great extent, successfully minimalised the animosity between the English- and Afrikaans-speaking whites in South Africa. However, the delusional tension between whites and blacks increasingly became distraught and reached a crescendo during democratisation. There is pressure on both sides of the colour spectrum. Some whites left the country in the so-called brain drain. Qualified whites moved abroad, seeking a new life, away from civil unrest and violence. There were also radical black groups that favoured decolonisation; manifesting in hate crimes and murders, ethnic cleansing of whites.

On white farms, there are a concerted effort by black groups to drive whites from their farms. This form of ethnic cleansing was and is prevalent in Zimbabwe, Angola, Mozambique, Namibia and South Africa. Hate crimes and actions synonymous to genocide continues even to this day. I restrict my reference to two hate crimes, yet there is a myriad of examples.

I chose to limit the gruesome reference to one incident in the first year of democracy, 1995. The second happened as recent as March 2017. I do this to illustrate the characteristics of Apartheid, ethnonationalism, majoritarianism; atrocities based on skin colour differences. During Apartheid we had white-on-black discrimination. The following black-on-white hate crimes are only two of many examples. One happened four months after democratisation in 1995, and the second occurred in March 2017.

Orffer Family Murder: Black-on-White Hate Crime

I recall this grim murder to highlight the underlying tension and volatility between black and white people. The psychotic perception of fear, distrust and discontent among South Africans, resulting in hate crimes, crossing the skin colour divide.

The murder of the Orffer family was gruesome and shocked South Africa. I lived in the town of Stellenbosch, Western Cape, within walking distance from the Orffer family residence. I drove past it several times a day.

Ted Botha in March 1995, gave a detailed report on the household murders, he researched the case and had interviews with one of the killers, MKhosana.

Botha starts his story by describing Stellenbosch as a liberal, prosperous and lovely university town. A pleasant place to live, similar to anywhere in the new South Africa. Nelson Mandela was the revered black President that stood for reconciliation and not retribution; he spent twenty-seven years in jail. He made a promise of peace and tranquillity.

Botha describes Andile MKhosana as a black drifter who butchered the white family. The Orffers were his first employer, giving him his first real job. MKhosana murdered Pieter Orffer, his wife Lida, their two children as well as their maid. One of the most gruesome and inexplicable crimes ever committed in South Africa. The murders are incomprehensible to Botha, but I have an understanding of the underlying motive; it was a black-on-white hate crime.

Botha recalls that they found the two murder suspects within twenty-four hours of the crime. One was dead, and the other shot in the head. Botha points out that this time, they suspected the police of murder. The 1994 democratic elections that ended Apartheid concluded just four months ago, and already the most severe test of tolerance faltered the reconciliation process. Botha asks the question, *"Was racial harmony possible or did the legacy of hatred simply run too deep?"*

I lived in Stellenbosch from 1985 to 2000. I never felt threatened and as Botha reports: *"Even the street names conjure up visions of goodness and health."* The Orffer family lived at 2 Saffron Lane, The Orchard. Violent crime was not something that happened in this peaceful town; it happened *out there*, somewhere else. Probably in the black shanty townships.

Botha reported that the father Pieter worked in the liquor industry but lost his job. Lida, the mother, was a high school teacher. Both in their early thirties with a daughter, Eulalia aged four, and a son Jean aged six. Pieter started his joinery business and was looking for an assistant. He enquired from friends, who made mention of a possible candidate, an ex-convict. Pieter didn't mind; he decided to give the guy a second chance.

Botha continues his report saying that Andile Sydney MKhosana, the murderer was thirty-two, the same age as Pieter when he died. MKhosana, a father of three, spent eight months in jail for violent assault. He was released on parole and given his freedom under the post-election and post-Apartheid amnesty.

According to Botha, MKhosana acknowledged after the Saffron Lane killings, that Pieter gave him a second chance. MKhosana even said to Botha that, *"I owe him everything, we worked well together. I used to eat breakfast with them. I drove the children to school. They gave me enough clothes to wear. They used to let me drive the pickup on my own. Pieter called me Sea boy; he trusted me."*

Botha recalls that on Saturday the 30th July, Lida's brother, Will Theunissen, called the police, he was the first to visit the horrific scene. The murder spree took place over a period of five hours on a busy Friday afternoon; no one had noticed the drawn curtains.

Botha explains the crime scene by saying that *"The bodies of Pieter, Eulalia and Jean, as well as the coloured maid, Sus Jacobs, were lined up next to each other on the living room floor, covered in blankets and cushions."* All had died from numerous axe blows to the head. *"The mother Lida was lying on her bed, her face covered with a pillow, her pants around her ankles, she had been raped and then axed."* The incident was so gruesome and shocking that police officers were in tears, they had never seen anything as gruesome.

Botha recalls that in late October 1995, he visited MKhosana in Polls Moor, the prison where they imprisoned Nelson Mandela. MKhosana's left eyelid was sewn down. MKhosana filled in the pieces of what happened on the morning of 29th July to Botha. I quote Botha's version of events verbally in the words of MKhosana: *"Pieter Orffer left home early to run various errands. He was on his way to see possible buyers of his pickup (LDV), and he had to organise things for his son, who was going to a school for the deaf from the following week. While they were out, Amos Nxara, a 23-year-old unemployed former taxi driver, arrived at the Orffer's house. The two men had got to know each other in prison and, like MKhosana, Nxara was released under the amnesty arrangement. Nxara was looking for work; MKhosana said there was none at the Orffers.*

They sat in the garage and began talking. Nxara spoke about how he was struggling to make ends meet. 'Then he said we should do this thing', MKhosana tells me (Botha) suddenly. 'Do you mean, kill the Orffers?' I (Botha) asked. 'Yes.' He replied. The maid, Sus Jacobs, left the house at midday to fetch Eulalia from nursery school. When they returned, Nxara killed them both.

Pieter and his son arrived back three to four hours later. MKhosana recalls what happened after they walked through the front door: 'Pieter said to me, I treated you like a brother, why are you doing this?' So I told him: 'I am going to kill you.'

Nxara, whom MKhosana always refers to as the accused, restrained the Orffers' son, Jean. When he saw his father roll over dead, the boy sat down submissively. MKhosana brought the axe down on him too. Then he dragged the four bodies to the living room and covered them, so they were not visible from the front door. He arranged several rugs to hide the bloodstains.

When Lida Orffer returned from netball practice after 5 pm, she immediately saw that something terrible had happened. She ran to her bedroom, locking the door behind her. The windows were barred, and she couldn't find the key to the porch.

The killers kicked in the bedroom door. Of all the victims, says MKhosana, she put up the most vigorous struggle. If he shows any remorse now, it is for this last killing. The accused [Nxara] started to rape her, and I asked him: 'Why are you doing this? You have a girlfriend already.' He said that he'd never tasted a white woman before. She pleaded with me not to kill her. She told me she would not tell and we could get away. I wanted to let her live. But while I was looking out the curtains of the living room, I heard him hitting her, three times, I think."

Botha continues his report saying that the police found MKhosana the next Sunday, attending a church service, they arrested Nxara later. Within twenty-four hours, Nxara would be dead, and MKhosana would be lying in a hospital bed with one eye shot out.

I remember, Stellenbosch was stunned, people fitted burglar proofing and employed security firms; racial tension rose. Botha recalled that white housewives were speculating: *"You looked at your maid and your gardener and suddenly wondered: Can I trust them? They could just turn on me."*

Botha does not put the murders down to political motivation. Afrikaners felt particularly shocked and vulnerable. My family shared the distrust of the times. I do not share Botha's reason for the crime. In my mind, it was an authentic racial revenge crime; it was a black-on-white hate crime.

Lida Orffer's grandfather the famous Afrikaans poet, Uys Krige, a literate and liberal Afrikaner, supported the reform process that led to the democratisation and the election of the ANC-government.

Botha reported on a somewhat racist letter published in an Afrikaans newspaper, *Die Burger (The Citizen)*. The letter written by Lina Spies, a professor of Afrikaans at the University, she expressed what others dared not say. Spies wrote that the Orffers had gone out of their way to give MKhosana, a black man and a convicted criminal, a second chance. *"Their courage cost them their lives,"* and *"The reward for trust was rape and an axe."*

According to Botha, the black township Kayamandi residents reeled with similar feelings as their white neighbours. They felt that: *"What they (MKhosana and Nxara) did to the Orffers, could just as easily have happened to us."* Doreen Hani, a town councillor and cousin of Chris Hani wrote: *"We have daughters and children, too".* Chris Hani was the Communist Party Chief, assassinated in 1993; the killing was a definite white-on-black race-related murder. A Polish far-right anti-communist immigrant named Janusz Waluś killed Hani.

I do not agree with Doreen Hani's statement. She could have instead said; *'I share your grief, it happened to my family, I (Doreen Hani) begrudge black-on-white and white-on-black, violent killings in the name of decolonisation and Apartheid.'* That would have been the truth.

Chris Hani's murder was an incidence of white-on-black racial hatred, congruent to the black-on-white Orffer murders. Doreen Hani wrote a public letter expressing her sympathy with the Orffer family and called on all women in town to meet and talk, if not for themselves, then for the sake of their children. I applaud Hani's outreach. It is just a pity she did not call it for what it was. The whites declined Doreen Hani's proposition.

Botha referred to the reaction of white people when the police brought MKhosana to the crime scene. Botha recalls that: *"The response of most whites was unexpected. Instead of hatred and anger, they showed pity. MKhosana wasn't a stranger to them, not a faceless black man who'd crept through a window at night. He was someone they'd known and employed. In trying to rationalise what had happened, they asked themselves whether a man who'd led an ordinary life could have committed such an atrocious act. Was MKhosana himself a victim of Apartheid? Who was actually to blame: the man who'd held the weapon, or the system that had made him into what he became? Guilt dissipated their anger."* Personally, I believe Botha is much closer to the truth in his later speculations.

When Botha asked MKhosana why he killed a family he cared for, he answered; *"The God's truth is, I don't know what happened to me. The devil was in me. Pieter gave me everything. I still see his face in my head. I have to live with that; he doesn't. It's a scandal, a real scandal."* What MKhosana didn't say, was that Nxara fired the wrath within him, the rage that transformed him into a racial killer. That will be my observation, his motivations to kill.

Thinking on the Orffer murders I can only surmise that MKhosana and his prison friend perceived the Orffers to be the *haves* and the two of them are the *have-nots*. When MKhosana told Nxara that there was no job for him, it might have tipped the scale. The deep-seated wrath against white oppression might have got the better of Nxara and triggered the killer instinct. They revolted against their sense of nothingness, distraught at being the *have-nots* at the mercy of the *haves*; the white man and oppressor of centuries. Nxara at twenty-three was naïve and revengeful and dragged MKhosana, already disgruntled and with underlying wrath, along with him in the murder spree. They vented their deep-seated resentment and anger of a century and more, against the white Orffers. The maid was an unfortunate collateral-damage-murder.

According to Botha white people didn't want to consider the motive they feared most, racial hatred. The notion of refraining from the obvious is common among white South Africans. Aware of the Apartheid-wrong, and realising that it had to go; they placed a high premium on Mandela's preferred future for South Africa. Reconciliation and peace for the Rainbow Nation.

Botha refers to Roland Grazer, head of criminology at Durban-Westville University, who contemplated; *"A deep-seated bitterness could have caused MKhosana to kill a white man, even someone he cared for."*

Botha reflects on the 1994 stabbings of Grazer's parents while they lay in their beds in Cape Town; the motive was race-related. Botha continue quoting Grazer: *"For a long time whites have seen blacks as inferior. By the same token, blacks have resented them for it. There's a lot of hatred and misunderstanding. Someone who doesn't have a high value of life for himself doesn't have a high value of life for others."*

The case according to Botha did not end with the arrest of MKhosana and Nxara. He recalls that: *"On the same day that Nxara was arrested, MKhosana was transferred from Polls Moor to the Cape Town suburb of Bellville, where the police murder and robbery unit has its offices.*

Very early the next morning, the two prisoners were taken from their respective cells and driven away by the unit chief, Des Segal, detectives Snakes Huyshamer and Andries Bosman. Less than an hour later, both prisoners had been shot in the head.

The police told reporters that the detectives were taking the two accused to point out houses which might contain weapons in Lwandle Township, ten kilometres from Stellenbosch. MKhosana, they said, had a penknife, which he'd somehow smuggled into prison. As they approached Lwandle, he reached over the seat, grabbed hold of Detective Bosman and cut his chest. Nxara, meanwhile, grabbed Bosman's gun and pointed it at Segal. A shoot-out followed, in which both of the accused men were shot."

According to Botha, MKhosana relates a different course of events. He recalls that at 3 am on 10 August, he and Nxara were handcuffed together and transported to somewhere near Muizenberg, which lies in the opposite direction of Lwandle, the minivan stopped.

According to MKhosana, he could see no lights and no other traffic. MKhosana says one of the detectives got out, pointed a gun at him and Nxara, and told them to get out. MKhosana refused because he knew, they wanted to kill them. MKhosana believes, he was shot twice in the head and kicked; he woke up in the hospital.

Botha concludes that under South African law MKhosana version of events is allegations made by a prisoner awaiting trial, not allowed as evidence. However, Botha says that there are convincing circumstantial conditions, implying that his words are more than the rantings of a killer, trying to save his skin.

In my opinion I agree with Botha; in the same way that the two murders had deep-seated hatred towards whites, the same might be true of white police officers. They have to deal with gruesome murders, like that of the Orffers, on a regular basis.

Botha recalls a conversation shortly after the killings and before the murderers were arrested; *"A reporter Terry Nel said she had heard a policeman conjecture 'that the accused would never make it to trial. If they catch the suspects, I wouldn't be surprised if they don't live'."*

One can speculate that the Police are not beyond suspicion. But most white people concurred as Botha put it; *"The consensus was that MKhosana and Nxara had got what they deserved. They had perpetrated an unspeakable crime. There was no doubt about their guilt."*

Conclusively Botha recalls MKhosana telling him: *"I could get death. I could get life, or maybe the police will take me on a ride and reshoot me."* No one has bothered to explain to MKhosana that there is a suspension on death penalties.

Even writing this part of my book I wrench at the cruelty, the hate and the deep-seated resentment; there is hatred on both sides of the skin colour. This fear, distrust and resentment are even today prevalent in South Africa; I write extensively on the topic in later chapters.

The Orffer murders happened four months after democratisation in 1994. The next black-on-white hate crime occurred in 2017. It is the year I write on the subject of hate crimes and twenty-two years since democratisation.

Ethnic Cleansing: Murder of Sue and Robert Lynn

As recent as March 2017, a British woman Sue Howarth and her husband Robert Lynn, woke when three black men broke into their remote farmhouse in Dullstroom, in the rural north-east of South Africa. They were tied up, stabbed, and tortured with a blowtorch; bundled into their truck, and driven to a roadside where they were shot. Mrs Howarth, 64, a retired pharmaceutical company executive, was shot twice in the head. Mr Lynn, 66, had a wound in the neck.

Miraculously Mr Lynn survived, he flagged down a passer-by. Mrs Howarth, had multiple skull fractures, gunshot wounds and *horrific* burns to her breasts. According to a newspaper reporter of the local paper; *"Sue was discovered amongst some trees, lying in a ditch, her rescuers managed to find her by following her groans of pain and then noticing drag marks from the road into the field. Her head covered with a towel, her eyes were swollen shut. She was partially clothed with just scraps of her shirt remaining. Her breasts and upper body were bloody. The plastic bag, shoved down her throat, took some effort to remove because her jaw was clamped down tightly. How she managed to breathe with the bag in her throat remains a mystery. One of her rescuers later recalled how Sue was unresponsive except for the constant groaning. While the man ran back to the road to see if an ambulance has not arrived yet, she managed to curl one of her arms around her breasts in a last attempt to protect herself."* Sue's British nationality, resulted in her murder attracting lots of overseas media attention.

The next web blog I reference about hate crimes is an Australian blog. The publisher asked one of the South African expats in Australia whether he feared that South Africa would become another Zimbabwe. Another Africa country killing and displacing white farmers. The respondent, a Mr Kruger was uncertain:*"My family back in South Africa have chosen not to (get out), and they love living there,"* he said. *"They have a very comfortable, pragmatic view, but they are also concerned. South Africans have got this undying ability to believe in the bigger picture, and I'm talking about many blacks as well as whites. There are lots of beautiful people of all colours, who find all of this stuff to be wrong. The question I would ask, given the rhetoric; 'is there a future for farming in South Africa? It's not just about, is there a future for white farmers. It's three times more dangerous to be a farmer than it is to be a policeman. It's sad — it's not what we want."*

Remarkable, farming concerns him, not so much white farmers. I later write about *Fanie and Jabulani,* reflecting on farms going to waste when expropriated. White ownership passed onto black tenure resulting in isolated and unproductive farms.

According to statistics relating to farm murders: *"The South African farm attacks are an ongoing trend of violent attacks on farmers in South Africa. Between 1994 and March 2012, there had been 361,015 murders in all of South Africa. Many white farmers perceive the attacks to be racially motivated."*

White Genocide in South Africa: A Plea for Prayer

R Radmin of *The New American organisation* relates the following transcript on their web blog: *"On the 22nd of April 2017, Christians of all race groups are coming together to pray for our country. God has given Angus Buchan some one million people who will be attending. For South Africa, this is a significant number considering that we are 40 million inhabitants in the country. The prayer meeting will take place on a farm outside of Bloemfontein. Our nation is in a terrible state with corruption, rape, hijacking and the most heinous murdering and torture ever imagined (especially on farms). With the greatest of respect to all Americans due your sufferings and problems, you guys have no idea of the utter violence and disrespect of life that goes on in South Africa. The government has no control, and the quietness from them sends a positive and supportive message to all evil-doers. The standard murder rate (in the world), as I understand it, is seven people killed for every one hundred thousand citizens. In South Africa, it is one-hundred-and-thirty (almost twenty-fold) the 'standard rate'. Farmers are murdered and tortured in ways you cannot imagine. A clear statement made that white people in this country are going to be murdered."*

South Africa is Facing White Genocide, a Total Communist Takeover. While most of the world refuses to acknowledge what is happening in largely communist-controlled South Africa, the non-profit group Genocide Watch declared last month that preparations for genocidal atrocities against white South African farmers were underway and that the early phases of genocide had possibly already begun. In the long run, Genocide Watch chief Dr Gregory Stanton explained; powerful communist forces also hope to abolish private property ownership and crush all potential resistance."

Today, I am physically writing; it is September 2017. That is how recent and dire the situation of hatred, retribution and fear is in South Africa. Over time various forms of genocide materialise. Today it is Communist-supported racial hatred and decolonisation under the ANC rule. In the Anglo-Boer-War the British killed 15% of the Afrikaner-Boer nation; it might have been a war but in effect another genocidal experience to the Afrikaner nation.

In the decolonisation effort of wrath ridden black revolutionaries, they endeavour to drive white South Africans off their land and property. In the process, they impart the fear of death into the people; this is an absolute form of genocide. Is Ethnonationalism emerging; segregating the nation instead of integrating society?

The prognosis for a peaceful South Africa is dire when one considers the position of white farmers in South Africa. Similar to Zimbabwe, the situation is symptomatic of decolonisation and genocide; a movement presently advocated by some black mass organisations. I write more extensively on new-age political manifestations, related to African decolonisation, in later chapters.

Like the *Rhodes Must Fall movement (RMF)*, the *ANC Youth League* along with the *Mass Democratic Movement (MDM)*; the question arises what these movements understood under democracy when the ANC came to power? Does it mean getting rid of the people they perceive to be the colonists; the white people from the West? The people brought to Africa by Europe? The people led and inspired by Cecil John Rhodes and his fellow pioneers during imperialism?

In considering Cecil John Rhode's legacy, the *Spectator* asks the question: *"Slavery was a cruel and odious institution. Does that mean that organisations that benefited from its profit, must be made to atone by agreeing to engage – now – in acts of public degradation and contrition? And how far up (or down) the scale of gross moral turpitude are devotees of Rhodes Must Fall prepared to go? They do seem to me to have been curiously selective in their choice of targets."*

The vengeance of these revolutionary groups has no barriers. They will not stop before the legacy of colonialism is removed from Africa and even the world along with the whites of Africa. Where and when are they prepared to draw a line in the sand? Acknowledging enough is enough, and an eye for an eye will leave the world blind!

Even Rhodes, as quoted by the same blog, admitted: *"I could never accept the position that we should disqualify a human being on account of his colour."*

I relate to hate-crime to create an understanding of the mindset on both sides of the skin colour spectrum. Worldwide the divide between the ethnic and skin and colour-divisions, result in segregation that intensifies and grows. The distrust on both sides is still widespread when integration comes into play.

My *Hot Totty* comparison was funny, a misunderstanding quickly fathomed and corrected. We laughed and moved on. Perceptions of people that violently differ and oppose in a juxtaposition can turn into wrath and hatred. If allowed to embitter, it can become an extreme resentment; it will culminate in murders, genocide, decolonisation and even war.

I am no psychologist, but what is happening in Africa post-colonisation and post-Apartheid, clearly show an unhealthy manifestation of wrath, revenge and destruction, inclusive of decolonisation, Ethnonationalism and murder.

The crimes are recent; It makes me wonder who the racists are? The white or black peoples of South Africa? Racism is spread over centuries and culminating in the 21st century. Both sides, black and white are guilty. But, the developing conditions in South Africa, convince me that the black extremists have taken over, they became the new-age racists of South Africa.

Pardon me but, I could not refrain from repeating Rhodes's attitude typical of imperialistic times, extrapolated over five centuries; it establishes some sense of understanding of European delusion during Imperialism. Rhodes delivered his famous Oxford speech, his words might sound archaic, but correct to imperialistic times: *"I contend that we the British, are the first and preferred race in the world and that the more of the world we inhabit, the better it is for the human race. Just fancy those parts that are at present inhabited by the most despicable specimen of a human being. What an alteration there would be in them if they were brought under Anglo-Saxon influence. If there be a God, I think that is what he would like me to do; paint as much of the map of Africa as British Red as possible."* Imperialism and slavery practised Apartheid same as the Apartheid government did in the 20th century. The Imperialists and Colonists introduced these atrocities to Africa; it was as standard as breakfast and sex, even in the 15th century.

The Boer-Afrikaner nation foolishly and obstinately continued, even constitutionalised this lousy policy that became Apartheid. Even though colonialism was dead, the Afrikaner forcefully tried to reach the future through the past, or maybe they carved tomorrow from the tombstone of colonialism.

All rulers of South Africa practised Apartheid for centuries; slavery and subjugation performed as part of colonisation. The British conquest followed the colonial and slavery atrocities. Some *Apartheid* legislation even served as statutes of West Minster. And finally, the Afrikaner Apartheid government constitutionalised Apartheid.

It is just so ironic that Britain repeatedly enters the South African scene to add to the problems of the country.

British Interference and Anti-Apartheid Activism

A Boer-Afrikaner perspective on Britain's involvement in South Africa conjures terrible memories. Britain commenced association with Africa as slave traders. British colonisation not only colonised land, perceived by the Boers as Afrikaner land; they also engaged in the Anglo-Boer-War scarring the Afrikaner nation. Fifteen percent of the Afrikaner nation wiped off the face of the earth. Tens of thousands of black Africans, along with vulnerable Boer women and children were killed in the British *murderous concentrations camps.* Britain robbed the Afrikaner nation of their Transvaal and Orange Free-State Boer sovereign Republics. Britain also exploited and raided Africa of gold, platinum, diamonds and mineral wealth. Sneakily, Britain dispossessed the Afrikaner Boer's sovereignty and property as war loot during Imperialism and the Anglo-Boer-War.

Ultimately in 1917, fifteen years after the Anglo-Boer-War, as an act of; shall we call it *remorse or repentance,* the British washed their hands off imperialism and its atrocities. Britain announced the Balfour Declaration. Ex-British colonies were *set free* to be self-sufficient with *no interference* in each other's affairs. Britain became an *equal partner* in a British Common Wealth along with the ex-British colonies. Allegiance to Britain remained paramount. So, if the Common Wealth assured *non-interference* in the internal affairs of South Africa, why did Britain return in the late 1960's with British Anti-Apartheid Activism interference? Is that not dishonouring the Balfour declaration of *non-interference and self-determination?*

A British boycott movement coined as the Anti-Apartheid Movement (AAM), developed, opposing South Africa's system of Apartheid; it supported South Africa's oppressed non-whites. The *ACTSA: Action for Southern Africa, emerged in 1994 as a follow-up to AAM.* South Africa democratised in 1994 after multi-racial elections. What is ACTSA's stance on reverse discrimination, black-on-white Apartheid and murders?

It is interesting to take into account that communism was a matter of concern for Britain's secret service investigations, during the Anti-Apartheid years. ACTSA's members were investigated and suspected of being communist agents at the early days of the organisation's existence. According to the Guardian of March 2015, British secret service section MI5 investigated Labour Party members suspected of being communist agents. British Police spied on Labour Party activists even after their election as British MPs. The special police branch had Peter Hain on record, dating back to the Anti-Apartheid Movement. The same applies to Labour MP Politicians Jack Straw, Harriet Harman, Jeremy Corbyn, Diane Abbott, Ken Livingstone, Dennis Skinner and Joan Ruddock, along with Tony Benn and Bernie Grant. They were all named by Peter Francis, undercover police spy and former *Special Demonstration Squad*, turned whistle-blower.

In later chapters, I write extensively on the influence of communism during the liberation of Southern African nations, previously colonised by the West. A liberation era marred by severe rivalry between Russian communism and Western capitalism. I also highlight the South African Communist Party and its determining influence on the present-day ANC government in South Africa. In fact, communism is seriously changing South Africa under ANC governance. Did Communist involvement coincide with Peter Hain's interference as an AAM/ACTSA organisation? Did Peter Hain help the Communists to achieve its final objective; removing all western remnants from South Africa?

Given the continued interference of Britain and its agents in South Africa's affairs, I find it incomprehensible that Europe, especially Britain and America can so quickly wash their hands off present-day atrocities. These wrongdoings are happening in South Africa today under communist inspired ANC governance. The West with Britain at the forefront played capitalism versus communism warfare games in Africa for close on a half-a-century; especially in the final decades before democratising South Africa.

The West financed Apartheid-South-Africa to oppose liberation movements, the likes of Frelimo and SWAPO funded by Russia.

Western interference financed the RENAMO anti-liberation movement, initiated by Ian Smith's Rhodesia UDI government and supported by South Africa. They used the Afrikaner Apartheid government to do their dirty work.

During the liberation of the Southern African colonies, Southern African nations paid an incredibly high price with Western interference opposing Communism. I highlight these atrocities and write extensively about communist involvement in later chapters.

And after all the western support to the Apartheid government, the West hung the Apartheid government out to dry during the democratisation era. Suddenly the world turned to be the ultimate philanthropist. The West had a change of heart, shocked by the Hitler's genocide, fascism and racism; they came to the aid of oppressed people. Hypocrisy undoubtedly accompanied the change of heart and attitude.

British liberation interference in Southern Africa went hand-in-hand with genocide and white murders under Zimbabwean and ANC governance. The murders are the outcome of anti-British/Rhodes' colonialism. In the post-democratisation era, the wrath against colonial wrong-doings plagued South Africa. Like so many British expansionist and interfering undertakings, ancient and recent, Britain's meddling in the affairs of third world countries is suspect. Yesteryear was Africa, over the past years it resurfaced as Iraq and Lebanon.

As I reminisce on historical developments from slavery through colonisation, the *Balfour white-wash*, anti-Apartheid interference and democratisation; I sense a grievance taking hold of me. I experience an *Afrikaner rant* against British and the West intrusion and meddling. Bear with me, as an Afrikaner minded writer I have a right to engage in this rant. Like me, the Afrikaner nation was and still is not impressed by the likes of Hain and Corbyn with their hypocritic interference in South African affairs. But, even more, hypocritical their silence on today's atrocities undertaken by the people of colour they helped to liberate.

Don't get me wrong, *Apartheid is wrong and forever will be a mistake*. But after all the British slavery and imperialism followed by hypocritic arrogance; having British Anti-Apartheid Hain involved, just added insult to injury for the Afrikaner nation.

I researched the Wales-online *website* with Hain's contemporary tirade on Apartheid, along with his take on ANC failures in South Africa. Reading his comments and attitude my sense of fury re-ignited. Peter Hain, as a British Labour Parliamentarian with his anti-Apartheid cronies, were very enthusiastic and forthcoming to engage when white-on-black Apartheid was opposed. Where are Britain and the West Anti-Apartheid central character now, when black-on-white discrimination is worse than under the Afrikaner apartheid government? The ANC atrocities overshadow the wrongs of Afrikaner Apartheid.

Why Hain, are you not aggrieved and forthcoming in 2017? Did Afrikaner Apartheid kill 70 000-plus black people in the Apartheid era? Were there murders brutal like the Orffer and Lyn families under Apartheid; white-on-black genocide?

I turned twenty-five when Peter Hain started his campaign against the Apartheid regime in South Africa. He was not a pleasant person in the eyes of the white people supporting Apartheid and extenuating British colonialism and abuse. At that stage, I was still supporting Apartheid. I was aware of the demonstrations and violence, but it happened in areas far from where I lived. The TV screen was my only visual cognisance of black revolt. The Boer-Afrikaner struggle and wrath against the British oppression still over-shadowed my mindset. I was always firmly set on the Afrikaner's right to govern themselves free from abuse and subjugation by the British.

Peter Hain on the Wales website recalls that Nelson Mandela told his supporters: *"If the ANC does to you, what the Apartheid government did to you, then you must do to the ANC what you (the liberation fighters) did to the Apartheid government."* In short, Mandela advised; *drop the ANC, if they treat you like Apartheid treated you.* Will the blacks of 2017, remember the advice and respond? I wonder, maybe I doubt that they will. The majority is still stuck on skin colour-revenge or, staying away from the ballot box!

In the post-Apartheid era Hain, expresses his concern about the *cancerous* corruption and inequality created by the corrupt ANC-government. He describes it: *"As the revolution of rising expectations and frustration, as ungovernable as in the darkest years of Apartheid".* Hain says he *"Cannot ignore the growing constituency of people who sacrificed so much for the freedom struggle. They are now dismayed at the squandering of Mandela's legacy."* Hain states that; *"Cronyism has replaced merit, not only in the public services but also in the state-owned enterprise (SOE's)."*

Interesting that comrade Hain recognises the communist *State Owned Empires (SOE's)*; introduced to South Africa by communist China, in support of the ANC. The SOE's replaced the Apartheid created infrastructure; described *by Hain* as the: *"Clean as the cleanest in the world."* Foundations established by white Apartheid South Africa. Hain continues by saying: *"South Africa has fallen into disrepair and is shamefully imperilled."*

Up to this point, I am in agreeance with Peter Hain; he appreciates, and confirm that what Apartheid created for South Africa, was the; *"clean as the cleanest in the world,"* destroyed by the Communist and corrupt ANC Regime.

But, Hain you lost the plot! You are obsessed with being a self-righteous communist *COMRADE.* You lost sight of the evil face that Communism brought to the present day, South Africa!

Hain did not change his opinion on the *white Apartheid privileged,* referring to them as the *jaundiced (cynical) whites.* Hain, is this still the Afrikaner responsible for establishing the *"cleanest in the world,"* facilities to South Africa?

Hain states that: *"I know some of these people only too well: they continually troll me on Twitter. I choose to ignore them, just as I ignored those whites who attacked me during the long, bitter battle against white supremacy and its police state."* Hain continues by saying that such individuals and their children are *"Part of a whingeing ex-pat community in the UK. Their privileged South African education has opened doors for them in Britain, but they have conveniently forgotten the debts they owe to the land of their birth."*

Well, Hain, tell that to the Orffer's, Howard and Sue Lynn's and the thousands of farmers being murdered today in South Africa. Did they pay the debt with their lives? Assassinated in black-on-white hate crimes, was that their debt to pay?

Do you want the *whingeing ex-pat community in the UK* to remain in the communist-governed ANC South Africa, and wait to be killed as part of the decolonisation extravagance? The likes of the Mass Democratic Movements and the RMF movement broadcast precisely that; the de-whiting of South Africa? Shall I spell it out to you, Hain? The *Rhodes Must Fall* resistance revolt against British colonial oppression *is a cancerous outcrop of British imperialism and colonialism.*

Hain at least acknowledges ANC blunders, when he states; *"In 2013, Parliament passed Zuma's Protection of State Information Bill, informally known as the Secrecy Bill. It invokes draconian powers to prevent journalists from exposing corruption, nepotism and state abuse."* Well, that is surprising, communism and dictatorial oppression are taking shape in Africa. I just wonder if Comrade Hain recognises communism; similar to a country like Cuba?

You might try to ignore this Hain, but it is a reality and part of your legacy; live with it.

However, I must applaud Hain's positivity. He sounded a signal of hope: *"A vibrant civil society, forged initially during the anti-Apartheid struggle, continues both to challenge any attempt by the ruling party to undermine democratic structures and processes, and to demand a renewed leadership in harmony with the Mandela vision."*

High hopes Hain, it is not going to happen. If the sound-minded remnants of capitalism and logical citizens of South Africa, meaning all colours and ethnicities, do not make it happen, it will not materialise. Hain, please keep your dirty Communist hands off Africa.

Conclusive Comments on Reverse Discrimination

Hain, Europe and Britain, you brought the problems to Africa, when you colonised Africa in your imperialist expansionism. America and the West you were intensely involved in the capitalist exploitation of Africa. You used Africa to play your devious West versus East and Capitalism versus Communism game on African soil. Now it's time for you to step up to the plate. Or, are you shit scared of Communism and Russia, frozen into oblivion?

Herbert Morrison, British Labour Politician in 1951, considered political freedom for black African countries, as ludicrous as: *"Giving a child a latch-key, a bank account and a shotgun."* Considering South African President Jacob Zuma's track record, Morrison sounds like a prophet. The January 2017, Times Magazine front cover portrays Zuma as; *"A Fraud who can't read or count, has five wives, twenty-plus children, and he shagged his best friend's daughter."* This so-named *Fraud* is the ANC President, presently governing South Africa as a failed state. He bought eleven cars in three years for his five wives at the cost of £374,000, and for himself, a shining new presidential jet, at £1.75 million; and he is still the President.

Jacob Zuma is the same President of South Africa who chanted: *"We are going to shoot them with machine guns. They are going to run. The Cabinet will shoot them, with the machine gun, kill the Boer. We are going to hit them. They are going to run."* Herbert Morrison, you were a clairvoyant prophet!

Even Comrade Peter Hain has to retrace his communist steps of the 1970's, and regretfully reflect on the failures he along with the West introduced to South Africa. And Hain, atrociously, after twenty-two-years of black rule the people of colour is still the impoverished ethnicities; even more miserable than under white Apartheid. One of my black professors once said; *"The western vehicles do not run smoothly on African soil"*.

Dr James Watson is a Nobel Prize winner for his contributions in unscrambling the intricacies of DNA and human genetics. Watson suggested that the West's approach towards African countries wrongly assume that black people are on par with their white counterparts relating to intelligence. Considering the manifestation of British interference in Africa, Watson's perspective manifests truthful. The Western world not only exploited Africa, but they are also forever getting it wrong when interfering with Africa and its people of colour. I wrote extensively on Watson's findings earlier.

I opposed Apartheid in my late forties when I delivered my Master's Degree Script and conclusions. In my Thesis, I criticised the government's civil defence and Apartheid. After two decades of local administration service, the Apartheid Bureaucracy blacklisted me. They forced me out of my career; I was left jobless in 1995.

Sitting here today and reflecting on the reverse (black-on-white) Apartheid, as experienced by white South Africans; I just wonder, was it all worth it. Why did we democratise? To create this monster of a communist inclined ANC government that embarks on the same atrocities as the Apartheid government and much worse.

But, life goes on, there is no sense in delving into the wrongs of the past. The future lies ahead, and a positive outlook is essential for survival. If only the colonists, expansionists and the Hain's of the past will be big enough to step up to the plate and come clean. At least acknowledge *your debt and guilt* in the process. Stop placing the blame exclusively on the Afrikaner and Apartheid. Britain started colonialism in 1806, and after they destroyed Africa, they tried to put it behind them with the Balfour Declaration. And, once again they messed it up with the help of Hain and his cronies.

It is with a mindset shaped by all the atrocities of the past that I pondered for more than four years and ultimately punched my thoughts onto my laptop. I published my biography: Apartheid; The Blame – Past and Present.

In the next chapter, I focus on Post-Apartheid South Africa; what changed after democracy. How happy or devastated is the outcome of democratisation to the nation?

CHAPTER 9
SOUTH AFRICA TODAY, POST-APARTHEID

Tribalism: A Tourist Attraction for South Africa

Tribalism as we knew it in the times before the white man came to Africa, is for all practical purposes only a historical remnant and national heritage in South Africa. Tourists love to visit the Bantu tribal villages, watch the Zulu dances and antiquities of the Bushmen. Africans have adopted the civilised western culture as their own, and much relinquished their tribal culture. The South African nation-state is a mix-match of western induced culture within a multi-cultural and ethnically-divided population. Presently a nation gripped in a psychosis of fear, distrust and cynicism. As an introduction to what South Africa is today, this is a gloomy statement which should be substantiated. I will, first of all, study what the experts, and the people at grass-roots level, have to say about post-Apartheid South Africa.

A Future Perspective: A Time Travelers Guide

A report by Dr Frans Cronje leaves a distressing prognosis of South Africa's future. Cronje is the *Chief Executive Officer* of the *South African Institute of Race Relations (IRR),* he is also the author of the publication *A Time Traveller's Guide to our Next Ten Years after 2014.* Cronje denotes typical scenarios that contribute to the problems of South Africa.

Slow growth and unhappiness

Cronje predicts that the rest of the developing Third-World will lead the global growth, while South Africa will be dealing with a dilemma of *social ills*. South Africa he predicts, will experience limited economic growth. The decline will be due to an increase in corruption in government and unemployment. Cronje foresees that the developing East and South Asia will have an annual growth of more than six percent, while South Africa will remain at two percent. This weak growth he states will leave the citizens dissatisfied and disgruntled with poor economic prospects. Cronje concedes that the populace's dissatisfaction gives rise to more and more demonstrations and increasing disturbances that will require more resources to safeguard the country.

During May 2016, a fire destroyed the Johannesburg University's 1000 seater *Sanlam Auditorium* along with computer labs at the Kings-way *Campus*. One more protest and a hundred million Rand down the drain.

Activism by Abstinence

According to Cronje, a passive and absent majority at the polling booth is the next dilemma for South Africa. Forty percent of eligible voters choose to stay away on Election Day. The stay-aways are more in number than the electorate voting for the ANC. This statement implies that the ANC government is a problem to the country. Cronje continues by saying that the South African economy has stagnated since the 2008 global financial crisis. South Africa harbours a significant difference in economic equality; probably the highest in the world.

Cronje's findings and projections are bad news, but maybe there is a light at the end of this ANC doom-tunnel. The results of the 2016 Municipal elections show a shift in political support. The BBC report of 6 August 2016, announced a swing to the Democratic Alliance away from the ANC. It seems like, after twenty-two years of democratisation, people are now voting on political issues and not on skin colour. It might just be that the wheel is turning. Strong opposition to the corrupt ANC Government might be surfacing. Ultimately, the hope is that political will materialise from the logical reasoning and not from the colour of their skin.

What is happening in South Africa reminds me of Alibi's words quoted in earlier chapters; *"Why can African elections not produce politicians that can govern their country professionally; providing well-organised services for the people, systems that will run industries and service homes. I blame the failures on poor leadership. Why must Blacks always suffer poor leadership; is that not a manifestation of unintelligence?"*

Why-oh-why is Africa burdened with bad politicians and governments? Africa is such a promising continent regarding resources and natural beauty. Alibi's words can be applied verbatim to South Africa in the post-Apartheid era. The immediate question that surfaces; what corruption is attributable to the Afrikaner Apartheid government.

Corruption Pre- and Post-Apartheid - Herman Giliomee

Herman Giliomee delivered a paper at Stellenbosch University titled *White-led Opposition Parties and White Minorities under South Africa's liberal Dominant Party System*. In this article, Giliomee quotes Pierre Van den Berghe: *"If your constituency has the good fortune to contain a demographic majority, racism can easily pose as a democracy. The ideological sleight of hand can be an inscriptive and racially-defined majority. It (overall majority) is a far cry from a (democratic and accountable) majority made up of shifting coalitions of individuals by a commonality of beliefs and interests."*

Elif Şafak, as discussed later, reverberates van den Berghe's sentiments when she states; *"Democracy is fragile don't let it slip into majoritarianism, it can quickly move into a one-man majority, with unbridled authority."* Later on, I write more extensively on Eli Şafak's findings.

Does this imply that the ANC's outright demographic majority, might contain racism disguised as a democracy? Racism, in this case, a *phantom justice*, seems to be a concerning statement. It almost rings true when constitutional discrimination legislates affirmative action and black job-reservation and preferences; even after a quarter of a century of democratic rule?

The Apartheid government excluded the majority blacks from the political scene. Thereby the white government maintained a false majority in government. Strangely majoritarianism even materialised in the Apartheid minority government.

Brink: Institute of Internal Auditors of South Africa

Dr Eugene Brink is a senior researcher at the *Solidarity Research Institute*, also an affiliate of the *Institute of Internal Auditors: South Africa*. Brink states that the South African monetary loss due to corruption paints a pretty dire picture. He sees the declared waste by the ANC government as only a *drop in the ocean*. According to Brink, it is not possible to put a figure on the size of corruption in South Africa. Brink says that fraudulent incidents are going unnoticed and unpunished; the amounts published are only warning signs. According to Brink, corruption is endemic to Africa and reverberates within the post-Apartheid ANC Government. He calculates that dishonesty lost some R700 million (£35 million) in the first two decades of democracy. This loss poses severe concerns and Brink considers it to be the most severe catastrophe in South Africa.

After twenty years of ANC rule, there should have been a correction in some of the past mistakes and progress to a better future, a brighter prospect. Let's have a look at South Africa today. It should be a democratised country, free and flourishing with Mandela's dream of a *Rainbow Nation*. In earlier chapters I considered the dreaded life of non-whites under Apartheid; what changed? Do the non-whites of South Africa have a dream coat to wrap around their shoulders? One that will pack a smile on their faces, or at least a contented prospect?

Twenty-Two Years of ANC Rule: Post-Apartheid

Race-segregation still runs central to South African politics. Imperialism followed by Apartheid gave rise to a segregated society. The *Rainbow Nation*, romanticised by Mandela and prophesized by Desmond Tutu, is today supposed to be a twenty-two-year-old multi-racial *democracy*. In real-life, the so-called Rainbow Nation is a disintegrated and segregated state. Amalgamation did not happen. Indications are that the nation lives in fear and discontent. They mistrust the government and have little faith in the future of South Africa.

Apartheid-era symbols are deep-seated with the dream of freedom and democracy. The imposed symbolism, adopting an inclusive anthem, did little to induce integration and unity. The Anthem combines the African liberation song *Nkosi Sekelel Afrika - God bless Africa*, with the Afrikaner-Boer anthem *Die Stem van Suid-Afrika / Voice of South Africa*. As a medium, the song uses three of the nine officially languages; Xhosa, Afrikaans and English. Only Xhosa is not an imported colonial language. There is a clear indication of the Anglo-Saxon way of life ingrained in the South African society.

People, in general, adjust to the new South Africa. The majority just get on with life while the vociferous minority demonstrate and destroy existing infrastructure. There are those that prefer to go back to what they had under Apartheid. Then there are those aggrieved by Apartheid past. They would instead pursue retribution, genocide and decolonisation.

The South African nation, its politics, culture, and the economy have not dispersed the wrongs of the past. Even after twenty-two years, democratised South Africa is still in turmoil. Segregation is always endemic. Towns and cities with separate neighbourhoods for white, black, coloured, and Asian race groups, dominate the socio-political environment

But to be realistic, the divided state of affairs cannot change within twenty-two years. Relationships and intermingling across racial lines have improved. Mixed marriages appear increasingly within South African society; crossing racial divided barriers is commonplace in South Africa. But, the different race groups still voluntarily seem to prefer apportioned residential areas. It might be that they cannot afford to integrate. Wealth inequalities might be the stumbling block. Separate townships are not a unique situation to South Africa. It is a phenomenon worldwide and is presently intensified giving rise to Ethnonationalism.

National statistic still collated and published by race groups, again reflecting the demographic spread of the nation; race is always core to demographics. Is there even the dream to build an integrated and harmonious *Rainbow Nation*? Maybe the craving for integration is over-emphasised. All over the world, census statistics reflect your race as a standard. The moment you try to identify your heritage, you look back at your racial origin. Skin colour still seems to be a tool to determine one's ethnicity and to introduce universal discrimination. The problem arises when ethnicity becomes an instrument in the hands of oppressors and discriminators.

The following analysis of the demographic layout of the South African nation gives a clear overview of the ethnic divide.

The 2011 Census Data:

79.2% Black Africans (41 million)
8.9% Coloured (4.62 million)
8.9% White (4.59 million),
2.5% 'Asian' (1.29 million) and
0.2% 'Other' (280.4 thousand).
Total Population: 52 Million

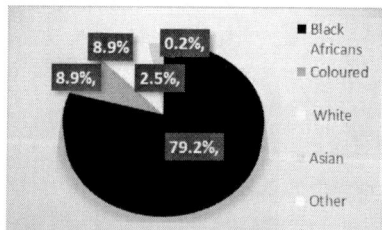

Statistics published by the Department of National Statistics South Africa

The Provincial Population Spread

Distribution within the nine Provinces also paints a pretty segregated picture. The first seven regions noted in the table show a skewed demographical spread with the majority of the population being black. Demography leans 80% plus towards black people with some concerning variations; the statistics underpin segregation rather than integration.

Province	Black	Coloured	White	Asian	Other
Eastern Cape	86. 30%	8. 30%	4. 70%	0. 40%	0. 30%
Free State	87. 60%	3. 10%	8. 70%	0. 40%	0. 20%
Gauteng	77. 40%	3. 50%	15. 60%	2. 90%	0. 70%
KwaZulu-Natal	86. 80%	1. 40%	4. 20%	7. 40%	0. 30%
Limpopo	96. 70	0. 30%	2. 60%	7. 40%	0. 20%
Mpumalanga	90. 70%	0. 90%	7. 50%	0. 30%	0. 20%
North West	89. 80%	2. 00%	7. 30%	0. 70%	0. 30%
Northern Cape	50. 40%	40. 30%	7. 10%	0. 60%	1. 60%
Western Cape	32. 80%	48. 80%	15. 70%	0. 70%	1. 60%

Statistics published by the Department of National Statistics South Africa

Decline of White People: 1910 to 2001

The following statistics only refer to the black versus white proportions of society. I focus on a dwindling white population due to the Anglo-Boer-War deaths, decolonisation, farm murders ethnic cleansing and the *white brain drain.*

Since democratisation, the so-called *brain drain* relocated 15% of the white population to western and industrialised countries. Well qualified white individuals in the prime of their lives and financially able left the country for the hope of a better life within more secure environments. The decrease in the white population

241

correlates with the decline in the maintenance of infrastructure under ANC rule. Also, the inability to integrate society emerged as a causal factor for some leaving the country. The failure of the ANC government to impart trust, along with the cynicism to believe in a prosperous and accommodating South Africa, led to many whites leaving the country.

Considering the statistics contained in the following table, over 90 years, the proportion of blacks increased by 24% (from 67.5 to 91%) while whites decreased by 13% (from 21.6 to 9%). The movement reflects a 37% swing in favour of the black population.

	1911 Total %		1960 Total %		50 Yr % growth	2001/4	2001	100 Yr % growth
White	1,1 Mill.	21. 6%	3,1 Mill.	19. 3%	168%	4,3 Mill.	9%	367%
Black	3,5 Mill.	67. 5%	11 Mill.	68. 3%	213%	34,2 Mill.	91%	980%

Statistics published by the Department of National Statistics South Africa

In 1991 Census statistics indicated that there were five million whites in South Africa. During a single decade of the *Brian-drain*-migration, more than 750 000 white people or 15%, left the country. The migration reduced the white population to four million in 2001. Under normal conditions, there should have been an exponential growth and not a decline in the white community.

During the first half of the 20th century, the white population increased by two million (from 1.1 to 3.1 million); this represents a growth in the white community by a 2.81 factor or 281%. If extrapolated to the second half of the 20th century the population should be close on 9 million and not 4.1 million (3.1mil. x 2.81 = 8.68) by 2001. Population growth, as a rule, increases exponentially. Therefore the white population should have totalled more than 10 million whites.

Take the exponential 10 million and add the 1 million plus that left in the brain drain, the white total should be 11 million. Add the 15% lost in the Anglo-Boer-War, and the white population could have been in the region of 12 million whites, at the start of the 21st century.

The losses explained and suffered, fleeced the white population to 9% of the total population. White people could have been 35% of the South African population. The calculation relates to twelve million as a share of thirty-four million of the total population in 2001.

I do not hold the calculations and deliberations as perfectly accountable. People of colour also died in the Anglo-Boer-War and the also migrate. But, the proportions are much lower. The calculation is just an effort to determine a trend. And, the tendency is the definite decline instead of growth in the white population.

Typifying the migration as Brain drain means that, the people that leave are well-qualified and in the prime of their lives. They are the cream of South Africa's workforce, essential for the growth and development of South Africa. The bad news is that the *brain drain* has not petered out, it is still going, and it is the white rich and qualified that migrate.

The majority of the one's left behind are the less well-off and those not well-qualified they are forced to sit-it-out and hope for better days. In fact, poor migrants from developing countries, the so-called *South African Developing Countries (SADC)*, to the north migrate southwards and become a burden to the state. Africa is not a favoured destination for well-qualified and experienced economic migrants from industrialised nations. The South African scene does not entice migrants. The society lives in fear and distrust due to violence and bad governance.

Losing much needed and necessary expertise is a significant problem for South African growth and prosperity. Losing intellectuals have already hampered development and infrastructure maintenance, and it will continue if not curtailed. Since democratisation in 1994, South Africa experienced severe problems with infrastructure degradation. A lack of sound government administration and economic growth presents serious challenges. The deterioration of infrastructure after liberation and democratisation is not unique to South Africa. It is endemic to Africa and liberated countries. Even Zimbabwe, since 2010, long for their white farming community to return to the state; the white farmers Zimbabwe murdered and drove away in decolonisation and genocide.

The white decline has already reduced whites to a single percentage figure; it might go down to a fraction of a percentage. The white population, representing the white Afrikaner Nation, might become insignificant, even extinct. Contrary to the white decline, the black community in proportion grew substantially. It might just be that the protagonists of decolonisation and de-whiting have precisely this in mind.

Africa over centuries suffered a less creative environment aggravated by colonisation and occupation. Is it sensible to add insult to injury by driving intellectual whites from Africa? They are the people that add value to a creative environment? Common sense should prevail, and the intelligent whites should be appreciated and retained.

Languages of South Africa

Two of the most common languages are European tongues, introduced to South Africa during the Imperial era, English and Afrikaans. English seems to be the champion style, the universal language of education, business, and politics. Afrikaans seems to be a common language in the more rural areas. As long as the business and work environments dominate, it will control the linguistic tendencies of society.

The bias towards specifically English is a global phenomenon in pre-colonial countries. The indigenous languages gradually play second fiddle and diminish progressively; Coloureds in the Western Cape do not speak the language of the Khoikhoi anymore.

Adding the number of people, speaking Afrikaans and English together the total is 22.7% or 11.7 million; more than the indigenous and largest African isiZulu ethnic language.

Bantu languages in developed areas are losing importance; they are not conducive to cross-ethnic communication. Afrikaans and English emerged as the Lingua Franca of South Africa. A relatively small number of people will only speak a tribal language. However, almost 80% of the nation's citizens talk as a first language one of the tribal languages; the most significant proportion speaks isiZulu. The following diagram and table illustrate the communicative dispensation within the six more prominent languages of South Africa.

Language	%	Mill.
Isi Zulu	22.40%	11.6
Isi Xhosa	15.80%	8.2
Afrikaans	13.20%	6.8
English	9.50%	4.9
Sepedi	8.90%	4.6
Setswana	7.90%	4.1

Statistics published by the Department of National Statistics South Africa

The statistical information thus far is of interest but what is of importance is wealth and economic progress. Did South Africa improve or did it go downhill?

Wealth Segregation - Access to Wealth and Amenities

Reducing the disparity in wealth should be a positive indicator for growth after democratisation. It would prove South Africa's success in redressing the wrongs of the past. However, the table below illustrates the persistent and glaring disparity between race group wealth. The situation has not changed since Apartheid; in fact, it deteriorated. The Whites are still the wealthiest, followed by the Asians; both European ethnic groups migrated to South Africa. The Coloureds and Blacks are still impoverished; they are the original natives of the land. Access to amenities persistently epitomises the disparity between the various race groups. Blacks are still worse off, 28 to 41% are deemed unemployed. Distribution of household income re-iterates the unbalanced distribution of wealth.

The table below shows no column for whites, they are the control statistic. For instance, whites not schooled will veer towards 0%, while the 10.5% blacks will not be schooled. Also, the whites live in formal dwellings while almost 80% blacks live in squalor. Asian household earns 60% of what the white family receives, Coloured families, make 22% of what the white family gets and the black family receive 13% of what the white family makes.

A significant concern is that the earnings of Coloured and Black households have stagnated and deteriorated after democratisation. Even though the statistics reflect optimal wealth for whites, the position of white people has worsened since democratisation. The only conclusion based on the figures contained in the table is that wealth imbalance between white and black has deteriorated.

Indicator	Percentages %		
	Black	**Coloured**	**Indian**
No Schooling	10. 5	4. 2	2. 9
Higher& Secondary Education	15. 2	32. 6	61. 6
Household Income *(White R 419 K)*	R 61 K	R 112 K	R 251 K
Informal Dwelling	16. 4	8. 1	1. 3
Formal Dwellings	22. 7	90. 2	97. 5
Less than three rooms / dwelling	48. 1	32. 1	14. 1

No Access to Piped Water	10. 9	1. 5	0. 6
Flush Toilet Central Sewage	43. 1	85	94. 7
Electricity used for lighting	81. 4	94	98. 5
Electricity used for cooking	69. 8	89. 9	92. 1
Refuse Removal	54. 5	87. 5	95. 4
Refrigeration	62	82. 5	96. 7
Cell (Mobile) Phone	88. 3	83. 7	92. 9
No Internet Access	70. 6	64. 3	41. 7
Unemployed	28 to 40	24 to 29	10 to 16

Statistics published by the Department of National Statistics South Africa

Criminality and Violence

Violent crime is still high in South Africa, and there is an increase in poverty and inequality. South Africa is failing as a country to secure confidence and respect for the rule of law. The 2013 / 14 Crime statistics contains the following data:

Children murdered	827
Children assaulted	21 575
Women murdered	2 266
Women attempted murder and assault	141 130
Men murdered	13 123
Rape cases per year	500 000
Vehicles hijacked	10 933

The information tabled reflects a very insecure society. The dire situation re-iterates the assumption that the ANC government has governed South Africa to a failed state. Until the government address these deficiencies, South Africa will remain a failed state.

ANC Government Inability: The Failed Legal System

The South African courts of law and prosecution systems don't seem to cope with the workload, at best only half of criminal cases make it to court. Concluded and solved court cases do not correlate with the crimes committed.

Earlier, I referred to the Khoikhoi killed by Pierre Cronje. Banished from the Cape, he did not serve his sentence. Due to administrative incompetence, the penalty not concluded he just carried on farming. The legal system failed the Khoikhoi. Is the ANC legal system as ineffective as the 17th century colonial years?

Continued violence and traumatic experiences result in deteriorating physical and psychological health. The country's ability to raise a new generation of safe and healthy children is questionable. These far-reaching problems do not end with the trauma inflicted on society. Attitudes depreciate as a result of a failing criminal justice system.

During the years of Apartheid, South Africans had little reason to respect the law. There were no confidence and belief in the rule of law. The laws were not only unjust, but they secured white domination. The security forces ensured that all South Africans lived in fear of the police state, regardless of their race. The Apartheid state harboured corruption while widespread abuse prevailed in the application of the law. The culprits were predominantly politicians and bureaucrats not challenged in a court of justice. There was no consistency in inter-racial violence and crime. Black male murderers received harsher sentences than their white counterparts. Inequality in rape-case-treatment between black and white women was standard; fairness and equality did not prevail. Injustices resulted in a lack of respect for the law.

In 2009, Judge Kate O'Regan questioned the fidelity of the Rule of Law. She reasoned that wrongs of the past put the allegiance to the Rule of Law in question. The unfair practices during and after the Truth and Reconciliation Commission had weakened any sense of abiding by the Law. By not punishing gross human rights violations under Apartheid, South Africa commenced restitution on the wrong footing. Amnesty granted in exchange for telling the truth, resulted in criminal charges dropped as pardons. Pardons as a consequence of truth and reconciliation, corroded trust in the Rule of Law.

As a result, South Africa entered its current dispensation with immunity to criminal actions. Protection entrenched in the system and amnesty awarded to those who held positions of power. The superior influence flaunted the objective of amends. Northern Ireland struggles to this day, burdened by the same restitution problems.

Accessibility and Equality under the Law

South African laws have changed for the better since democratisation. The Constitution protects the rights of all South Africans, guaranteeing treatment equal before the law. The equality seems to be a worthy achievement in Post-Apartheid South Africa. Or is this equality a farce?

A real inequality example is Oscar Pistorius and Jacob Zuma, where wealth is once again the deal breaker. They are both wealthy to pay for good lawyers and can use psychologists to help them deal with trauma and stress. Over and above the said preferences Zuma is regarded as a one-party government abusing power. For 650 000 bourgeois victims of crime, access to the police is uncertain.

Democratisation is not necessarily a model process of solutions. It is an involved and time-consuming progression towards a full resolution. It does not always cure all the ills of the past. The post-Apartheid ANC government considers *discrimination to be fair* in redressing the wrongs of Apartheid-past. Discrimination of this kind is precisely the danger of majoritarianism as explained by Şafak and supported by Johnston, discussed elsewhere. *Democracy* turns into racism when majoritarianism emerges as a result of a landslide electoral victory. I describe the new age phenomena of majoritarianism, demagoguery and populism in depth in later chapters.

The process of affirmative action is deemed appropriate in the constitutional approach for Post-Apartheid South Africa. It is understandable that the disadvantaged non-whites under Apartheid deserve restitution, but is reverse racism and discrimination the answer? I do not think so. The affirmative action just ingrains the wrongs of the past and reflects the adverse outcome of democratisation.

Credibility of the ANC Law in the Post-Apartheid Era

The following list of unlawful behaviour undermines the reliability of the law. It illustrates the attitude of South Africans towards the Laws of the country. Vehicle drivers are not wearing seat belts and driving under the influence. Teachers still beat children at school, police officers are breaking traffic rules, and drivers ignore traffic rules. Disregarding the law result in the steady erosion and disrespect of the Law. Unlawfulness leads to a lack of confidence in the legal institutions of the country. It deteriorates trust in the system, especially when politicians and officials break the law; the very code they are responsible for enforcing. Officials holding office must maintain an unwavering regard and respect for the Law. They must always act with absolute certitude. Any cynical abuse of the criminal justice system will put the Law in serious disrepute. Abuse of power and shirking responsibilities undermine the legal system.

Corruption in the Post-Apartheid ANC Era:

President Jacob Zuma tops the list of corrupt South African politicians with his home in Nkandla costing the South African taxpayer 246 million Rand, the equal of £ 12.3 million. Zuma claimed that the money spent was for the essential security of the head of state. Democratic Alliance spokesperson Mmusi Miamane alleges that Zuma is personally liable for at least R52.9 million; the expenditure allegedly expended for the non-security upgrades to his private residence.

Jacob Zuma after seven years in office may yet stand trial for corruption. Zuma had five wives and bought 11 new cars in three years for his wives, at the cost of about 8.6m rand (£374,000); money supplied, helpfully, from the police budget. This extravagance happened during a budget of severe austerity. The President bought himself a shining new presidential jet, at the cost of £1.75m.

The Telegraph of April 2016, reported that President Jacob Zuma faces criminal trials in South Africa's High Court, charged with 783 counts of alleged corruption, fraud and racketeering. February 2017, *Time Magazine* published an image of Zuma with the following caption: *"Jacob Zuma: A Fraud who can't read or count, has five wives, twenty-plus children and he shagged his best friend's daughter."* Between 1999 and 2005, Zuma received an annual bribe of £40,000 from a French defence subsidiary company. Zuma accepted bribe payments of £280,000 from Schabir Shaik, Zuma's financial adviser. Zuma irregularly adorned contracts and favours on Shaik in return for bribes. The court convicted Shaik in 2005 of bribing and sentenced him to 15 years in prison. Shaik served three, released on the grounds of ill health. The corruption charges against Zuma is plentiful and rife. The question is; when the wheel will turn? He is the most corrupt statesman in modern times.

Local government

In a statement made by Bongi Mlangeni from the Corruption Watch, he urged a rethink on the systems of accountability at all levels. Mlangeni claims that mismanagement of public funds and abuse of resources by officials are rampant. Local administration is the most corrupt institution in the country.

Management of State Tenders

More than eleven billion Rand expenditure was found to be irregular in the Orange Free State Administration during 2013 14. The administration did not comply with policy guidelines.

Sixty percent of auditees reflected fiscal uncompetitive and unfair procurement procedures.

Electricity Prepaid Meters

City of Tshwane electricity billing administration proved to be corrupt and expensive. PEU is a black-owned and black-managed investment holding company, established in 1996. The Tshwane local authority paid the PEU company R830 million to install 800,000 metres. PEU had to install more than 435,000 during the first two years, a target it was highly unlikely to achieve; the company had to manage the project for eight years. PEU only installed 12 930 meters, less than 2% of the contract at the time of cancellation.

The South African Police Service

Bribes to Police officers thwarted cases under investigation and undermines democracy. Ordinary citizens left with little recourse to justice; they do not even have the means to bribe police officers. Ordinary people cannot even expect the cops to do the work for which they receive a salary.

The Metropolitan Police

The *Tshwane Metro Police Department* fired sixty-seven members of the *Anti-Corruption Unit*. According to *Business Tech South Africa*, the department dissolved the Unit in 2012. Out of 2,600 Metro Police Officers investigated, only 184 prosecuted, less than 1%. The prosecution was for corruption between 2009 and 2011. The dissolution of the anti-corruption unit left a serious question.

Scorpion is another anti-corruption unit that was dissolved by President Jacob Zuma to curtail criticism of the government on nepotism and corruption. I write about the *Scorpion* dissolution and the Zuma/Gupta state capture in later chapters.

My Personal Experience of Police Corruption

During my 2016 visit to South Africa, and Mozambique I experienced bribery among the Police first hand. While driving in Mozambique, we were careful not to exceed the speed limit. Four of us was on the look-out for speed signs without fail. We alerted the driver of speed restrictions because we were pre-warned of the corruption. Stopped by a young female traffic police lady, she said we exceeded the 60 km speed limit by 20 km/hour.

We had a SATNAV in the car warning the driver of speed restrictions. I pointed that out to the Police Officer and explained that there were no speed limit signs. I offered to go with her so she can show me the sign. We were not in a built-up area. There was only a small settlement way-off the roadside. She became uncomfortable and asked me for my driver's licence. Once she had my driver's licence, she said, after I paid the fine I can have my licence back. I asked her what the penalty will be. She stated 1000 meticais (£15). I asked her if I will receive a written receipt. She replied, if I pay 1000 meticais at the nearest town they will issue a receipt. When I return and showed the receipt, she will give me my licence back. I said I only have 500 meticais on me. She agreed, if I pay her 500 meticais, I can regain my licence and carry on driving. I did not feel the debacle was worth the inconvenience, and I needed my driver's licence back. I paid the 500 meticais (£7.50). Relieved she said that would be okay, but no receipt issued. That money went straight into her back pocket. She earned bribe money posing as an official police lady of the state.

We crossed the border into South Africa. Stopped again after travelling less than 25 kilometres with the same story as in Mozambique. This time, I addressed the traffic officer in the Lingua Franca of the African Mines, Fanagalo. I provided the same explanation, no signs, and the SATNAV. No he said, the SATNAV does not work in this area. In the end, I soft-soaped the officer and explained that I have lived in this country for decades. I played

253

the standard fellow-citizen card, appealing to him for reasonable treatment as a fellow African. It worked, but as we drove off, he immediately stopped the vehicle behind us. I doubt this guy was as lucky as I, it was a black man. They don't seem to have empathy towards their black fellow citizens either.

Passenger Rail Agency of South Africa (PRASA)

November 2015, PRASA purchased unsuitable locomotives by tender and lost the country £ 133 million. The inappropriate locomotive tender resulted in the most significant financial debacle in South Africa. The public prosecutor found that ex-Chief Executive Officer, Lucky Montana was responsible for the maladministration. He was found guilty of large-scale abuse of power and wasteful expenditure during his tenure.

False qualifications

According to the *Institute of Internal Auditors of South Africa*, September 2015, the ANC spokesperson Carl Niehaus lied about his skills. According to the *Business Tech RSA*, many government bigwigs falsified their qualifications. No scandal of this kind was more significant than that of Pallo Jordan. He was the former Arts and Culture Minister and struggle stalwart. Jordan lied about obtaining a PhD qualification. He holds no tertiary qualifications whatsoever.

Home Affairs

According to *Business Tech RSA* of 22 September 2015, *Marabastad Refugee Office* is a hotbed of corruption and bribery. The *Department of Home Affairs* recorded 781 cases since the hotline started in 2004.

The Cabinet and Parliament

According to the *Mail Guardian* of October 2006, fourteen ANC members of Parliament, as lawmakers, pleaded guilty to theft and fraud charges, they were all penalised. In a case known as *Travelgate*, these members of Parliament abused parliamentary travel vouchers; more than ten officials named in the report.

News 24 asked the following question on 4 December 2017: "In a country of 51 million people, how can 3.3 million pay 99% of all income tax? It's a policy that can only lead to a financial crash." Needless to say the majority of the 3.3 million are white tax payers. And then the wasteful ANC is predominantly black.

Corruption during Apartheid

Corruption is rife within the post-Apartheid ANC Government, but what was the situation during Apartheid? *Business Day Live* stated that time might both heal wounds and erase the memory. As an example, *Business Day* refers to an argument made by former *Democratic Alliance* leader Tony Leon. Leon claimed that the Apartheid political elite was *morally more responsible and internally accountable.* There might be some truth in the *more*, but the jury is still out on the accuracy of that claim. Leon's statement signifies that far too many South Africans tolerate this delusion. Apartheid South Africa was guilty of severe corruption blunders. Comparatively, the new ANC government seems to be more corrupt and lazier in applying the Rules of Law, especially economic crime soared, while public accountability withered.

The Rule of Law spells out principles enforced by the government on its officials and agents, as well as individuals and private entities. Everyone is accountable under law for any acts of corruption, maladministration and abuse of power. The *Apartheid Government* had some severe failings; Open Secrets that might have slipped into oblivion.

The Lifeboat Scandal

The *Daily Maverick* of 17 March 2017, refers to an unresolved example of Apartheid-era corruption as the *Lifeboat Scandal* of the

1980's. Apartheid Finance Minister, Barned du Plessis signed off on the so-called lifeboat scandal, relating to loans by the *Reserve Bank* to some of the country's largest banks. Lifeboats represent loans converted into gifts. The said loans benefited the Finance Minister Du Plessis's brother who served on the board of one of the banks.

Oil Sales and Swiss Bank Accounts

The *Progressive Federal Party's* leader van Zyl Slabbert reported information relating to oil sales to South Africa. The evidence implied alleged corruption in the oil trade. President PW Botha and the advocate-general were handed the proof and lodged an investigation. The investigation did not produce any results. The matter might have been too hot to handle for the political elite.

The Smit Murders and Secret Accounts

In 1978, the assassination, of Robert and Cora Smit, left a shadow over the integrity of the *Apartheid Government*. Robert was a former *International Monetary Fund* representative for South Africa. He was also a *National Party* parliamentary candidate. Rumours had it that there was foul play. Smit stumbled onto secret information relating to overseas bank accounts of the Apartheid elite. Apartheid Minister of Finance, Diederichs, had links to a secret bank account in Europe. No investigation into the murders and financial corruption followed. The oversight damages the integrity of the Apartheid government.

South African Defence Force (SADF) Secret Funds

Three-point-seven-eight billion Rand was spent to buy weapons for secret defence projects. The transactions represent covert corruption with no scrutiny by the *Auditor-General*. Secrecy in international arms trade was endemic. The abuse by individuals, corporations, and financial institutions were rife. These incidents were never exposed and communicated for public scrutiny.

Tax Breaks for White Companies in Black Homelands

Apartheid Bantustans (homelands) allowed special tax breaks for white companies. These tax breaks represent a further instance of corruption. The tax breaks involved the evasion of exchange control laws. Improper dealings between South African business and the homelands were suspect. One of these deals included the gaming business person Sol Kerzner who paid R20m in bribes and facilitation fees. The bribe to Transkei Chief George Matanzima was for gaming licences. Kerzner's defence was that the allegations were extortion. All charges were dropped by the Transkei Attorney-General Christo Nel in 1997.

International Criminal Network

The 'published report titled *Resolution of the Second National Anti-Corruption Summit* held in Pretoria/Tshwane in March 2005, dealt with the Vito Palazzolo case which represented some shady deals of the Apartheid Government. These deals rooted to the top and linked the government with organised crime in Italy. Vito became a state representative for the Ciskei government. Rumours had it that they used him to clean *hot* money for arms and nuclear co-operation. A National Party parliamentarian provided Vito with an illegal residence permit. The government in 1993, approved residence permits for Palazzolo. At that stage, Palazzolo was a wanted fugitive running from the Italian police.

South African Defence Force and Ivory

A report on elephants slaughtered during the civil wars in Angola and Mozambique, to fund *Defence Force* spending, reveals some concerning information. Ivory is still a source of civil conflict funding in Africa. The slaughtering served as a source of revenue for the Apartheid Government border-war-effort. The funds raised were for the benefit of leaders of resistance movements against liberation, the likes of RENAMO, supported by the West. I wrote extensively on RENAMO in previous chapters. The *Kumbleben*

Commission after democratisation in 1994, found proof of corrupt SADF involvement. The SADF worked through a front company. No action was taken to hold the transgressors to account.

Apartheid Death Squads

The *Civil Co-operation Bureau* had an annual budget of R116m. Individuals received massive amounts of cash *in faith* to execute their duties. About forty-five million Rand was found to be improperly authorised. No legal consequences followed the corruption.

Exchange Controls Amnesty

Treasury Exchange Control exposed forty-three thousand flight cases at a total of sixty-eight-point-six billion Rand. The trials investigated, included individuals and corporations making one-off payments. The payments violated exchange controls and income tax regulations. No evidence exists of prosecutions or legal action taken. Economists suggested that this was a considerable underreporting of illegal flight capital.

Comments on Government Corruption

Corruption was and is endemic on both sides of the divide; the ANC as well as the Apartheid government. The ANC government had without a doubt an element of personal enrichment from the President right down to low-level bureaucrats. There is no doubt that the corruption is crude and ruthless with little regard for the nation. Accountability and servitude to the country vary from suspect to grossly absent.

Incidents of corruption, disregard and abuse of powers, by the Apartheid government happened more frequently in the latter two decades of Apartheid. Apparently, crime often coincides with desperation to cling onto power and to save the *white bacon* in the face of democratisation. Syphoning money before the ANC took over, resonates vigorously and echoes similarly to pre-bankruptcy syphoning of funds.

On both sides; corruption is unacceptable. Apartheid was democratically illegitimate, but the ANC government is supposed to be the legitimate and democratically elected government.

White South Africans: Life in the Post-Apartheid Era?

I already touched on some perspectives on the future of the South African economy. It is worth getting an insight on how people at grass-roots level see life in the post-Apartheid era. The depressing investigation on corruption pre- and post-Apartheid leaves a gloomy perspective on South Africa. I do not intend to do a comprehensive survey, but there are some interesting publications on the subject; comments and reports are plenty and varied. Some are critical and damning of the ANC government. Some less perilous but still no real uplifting news, the ANC government is not perceived to be a model regime.

South African ANC politics promised peace. The question remains, will it be Canaan or Kosovo? Probably, it will be the hanging *knot* of Kosovo or should it be the ANC hanging *snare*.

Into the Cannibal's Pot – A Perspective by Ilana Mercer

Ilana Mercer published *Into the Cannibal's Pot* as perceptions on Post-Apartheid conditions in South Africa. Mercer acknowledges the need to enfranchise black people as the previously disadvantaged. She also condemns the *terrible injustices* of the Apartheid Regime, recognising the unacceptable seven thousand plus murders a year during Apartheid. Mercer equates the Apartheid death statistic with the Western-celebrated ANC government's annual figure averaging twenty-four thousand-plus deaths a year; *threefold the killings of the Apartheid era*. This crime record represents only the first eight years of ANC rule. According to her, these statistics rank Post-Apartheid South Africa worse than the drug-cartel-infested Mexico, projecting a sad reflection on the ANC Government.

According to Mercer, white Boer farmers murdered since the end of Apartheid amounts to more than four thousand. The *Times of London* corroborated this statistic. *Genocide Watch* gives South Africa a rating of six on a scale of one to eight for genocide. Mercer claims that the black-on-white crime rate is approximately 95% of the total crime rate. President Jacob Zuma himself contributed to the carnage. Zuma in 2013 led a crowd in a song promoting the killing of the Boers. According to Mercer, Zuma as the President of South Africa chanted: *"We are going to shoot them with machine guns. They are going to run. The Cabinet will shoot them, with the machine gun, kill the Boer. We are going to hit them. They are going to run."* Mercer claims that after this chant, the murder rate of white farmers quadrupled. Mercer petitions that Zuma's song aggravated the killings.

The Incidence of Rape in South Africa

When considering rape in South Africa, Mercer quotes Emily Craven, Policy and Program Manager to *Action Aid South Africa*; Action Aid was the first charity to document corrective rape. Mercer refers to South Africa's rape crime statistics as being appalling. Under the ANC Government, approximately half a million rape crimes occur on an annual basis, of which only 10% is reported. This atrocious dilemma amounts to 133 rape cases per 100,000 people per year. According to Mercer, this statistic is the highest in the world. Some of these rapes are of the so-called *corrective* variety, carried out by legions of black men believing it will *cure* lesbians. By way of contrast, South Africa became the first country in the world to outlaw discrimination based on sexual orientation in its 1996 Constitution. Is the nation out of touch with the Constitution? The people appear to have a different idea when it comes to rape.

Mercer continues by saying that there is a sense of entitlement to women's bodies among the black male population. She refers to Craven from *Action Aid* who underlines this as the cause of the widespread rape pandemic. According to Craven, there is a common notion that women need men for economic support and sexual pleasure. She argues that this attitude is threatening and entrenches patriarchal values; values that result in 24 out of 25 men acquitted when brought to trial for rape. This derogative situation contradicts the constitutional position on discriminative actions relating to abuse. Mercer states that these misconceptions resonate a twisted culture among black people.

According to the research group *Community Information, Empowerment and Transparency (CIET)*, as quoted by Mercer, twenty percent of rapists explained that the victim *asked for it*. A quarter of Soweto school boys claimed their behaviour was for *fun*.

Mercer proceeds by naming another concerning concept, that of *jackrolling*. Jackrolling relates to the perception among black men, *how to be real women and what does a real man taste like*. Many *corrective rape* survivors gave evidence to this effect. Furthermore, many criminals are not content with rape crime. Thirty-two women were raped and then murdered in the last fifteen years. As a result of under-reporting, rape crime incidents remain rampant and much more widespread than official statistics imply. The charity *Luleki Sizwe* contends that more than ten women are raped or gang-raped on a weekly basis.

Apartheid in Reverse; Reverse Discrimination

Mercer highlights another wrong-doing when she deals with the incidence of *reverse Apartheid*. She refers to it as the prime cause of a deteriorating economy in South Africa. The ANC established the *Black Economic Empowerment (BEE)* programme.

Mercer explains that the BEE systems focus on affirmative action; or would it be reverse discrimination. The system requires all enterprises public and private, to *make their workforces demographically representative.* Under this programme Mario Rantho, an ANC parliamentarian sets out his party's vision for government. He proclaims that it is imperative to get rid of *merit* as the overriding principle. According to Mario qualifications and experience should not feature in the appointment of public servants. What is this? Quality does not count; skin colour is the determining factor when recruiting staff? The most deserving and suitable candidate will not get the job? Instead, the skin colour will determine who is successful? This practice is pure racism, discrimination based on skin colour. That was the equivalent of job reservation for whites under the Apartheid government. Now the ANC implements the same atrocity. This attitude is reverse discrimination *par excellence*. Will this be the *acceptable and affirmative action* discrimination of the ANC Constitution? This misguided policy can only give rise to an inefficient public sector; an attitude that South Africa can ill-afford. South Africa can just degrade and become poorer; a prediction that Mercer subsequently claims. South Africa has been paying the price for this type of discrimination ever since democratisation. Along with the so-called *Brain-drain*, reverse discrimination is without a doubt one of the leading causes for South Africa being a failed state.

The quality of South African sport suffers for the same reason. Players selected on skin colour instead of merit. That is why some of the best South African sportsmen and women in Europe are South African white players. They play for clubs and nations in Europe.

Mercer states that the income of black households shrunk by nineteen percent under ANC rule; it happened within the first six years of the ANC taking office. Since the ANC's ascension to power citizens living in *absolute poverty* had doubled.

Mercer's findings reverberate the statistical revelations at the beginning of this chapter. South Africa's population, especially Black's and Coloureds, are paying the price for democratisation under the ANC Government.

White Farmland Confiscated and Farm Murders

Mercer sees the white farmer debacle, as a bone of contention in the post-Apartheid era. Farms seized during affirmative action from whites as part of a land-sharing agreement harm the economy. After the expropriation of land, the farms remain barren and unproductive. It happened in Zimbabwe; it is now happening in South Africa. Zimbabwe after half-a-century of black rule is making noises inviting white farmers back to Zimbabwe. I wonder why? The farms were in full production in the hands of white farmers. But, once confiscated it turned into a wasteland under black farmers not proficient in farming. This phenomenon I dealt with earlier in the fictitious Fanie and Jabulani tale, based on some real incidences. *Black First Land First (BFLF)* is on the forefront destroying agriculture with black-on-white discrimination and hate crimes in South Africa.

Deterioration of Health and Infrastructure

Mercer refers to the life expectancy of South Africans. The living age declined from age sixty-four at the end of Apartheid to age fifty-six in the post-Apartheid era. The *Economist* corroborates this backwards move. The report states that public healthcare, roadways, ports and road infrastructure is deteriorating. This insidious effect bears testimony of discrimination against whites in the workplace; standards and quality of service are diminishing.

Mercer continues by stating that more recently, economic growth has plummeted. The National debt increased by forty-four percent, the value of the South African Rand is deteriorating at an alarming rate. There was a twenty percent decline in the value of the Rand, only in 2013. The level of unemployment is as high as twenty-five to forty-one percent. The city of Durban does not resort any longer among the world's fifty largest container ports.

In 2016, I was astonished at how lucrative it is to have a holiday in South Africa with British currency. A bottle of wine cost £2 in South Africa, the lowest £5 plus in the UK. A hamburger cost fifty pence in South Africa, £ 2.50 plus in the UK for the same quality burger.

Mercer describes South Africa with the ANC Government like a *one-party state*, even though other parties partake in elections. This description reverberates van der Berghe's statement quoted earlier as echoed by Elif Şafak. This loaded-dice political dispensation hands a blank cheque to the ANC government. The ANC, not held in check for their actions in the absence of a strong opposition, give rise to racial discrimination and corruption. ANC insiders are handed government jobs, irrespective of qualifications and ability. Mercer mentions that regardless of the corrupt track record, the black electorate put President Zuma back in power in 2014, for another five years of corruption.

Mercer refers to Leon Louw as a think-tank theorist and supporter of liberation and democratisation in 1994. He helped to defeat Apartheid in the struggle era. Louw characterises the crime and corruption in South Africa as *"A clear manifestation of the breakdown of the state. The government is just appallingly bad at everything it does, education, healthcare, infrastructure, security, everything that is a government function is in shambles."* Even the anti-Apartheid activist Lord Peter Hain of Britain supports the claims on deterioration in South Africa as I elucidated earlier.

Mercer is not enthusiastic about the future of South Africa. She states that it is not likely to get any better. Mercer attributes her negativity to the Communist-aligned ANC's firm hold on political power. She bases her despondency on the ANC receiving 62 percent of the vote during the 2014 election. The Democratic Alliance had only a paltry 22 percent of the ballot. Interesting to note, if the white voters were 35% of the population total, as previously resignedly extrapolated, the situation could have been different. Is this the final objective of the *Rhodes Must Fall (RMF)* and decolonisation protagonists? De-whiting South Africa?

Mercer is not surprised by the nation's broken justice system, beyond imagination. She quotes Ruth Hopkins as described by the *Daily Mavericks*; *"South Africans are battling a dysfunctional court system, where lengthy delays put presumed innocent suspects behind bars for years. Overworked state-funded lawyers do not bother to question glaring inconsistencies. Soddy evidence and lying police officers are not investigated."*

Mercer further re-iterates the unfairness of flourishing politically-driven favouritism and nepotism. The Head of the Police's crime intelligence section, Richard Mdluli, charged with an extensive list of criminal charges, was pardoned. All charges dropped and reinstated as head of the intelligence section. His release came after promising to help Zuma win the election in 2014. Crimes Mdluli committed included murder and attempted murder. Mdluli lives an extravagant lifestyle even after suspension in 2012; all paid for by the South African taxpayer. Renewed calls to prosecute Mdluli remains in politically influenced limbo. Mdluli's case is one instance where Zuma interfered. Politicians manipulate the *National Prosecuting Authority (NPA)*.

Mercer's viewpoints and theories might not meet with the agreement of everybody. But it portrays a picture of disillusionment and discontent at the grassroots level. A sad sensitivity not limited to Mercer and like-minded disgruntled South Africans. Discontentment seems to be a widespread perception in South Africa. The resentment adds to the detrimental psychosis gradually sedimenting and intensifying throughout South Africa.

South African Singer - Steve Hofmeyr

The famous South African singer, Steve Hofmeyr vociferously agrees with Mercer, he almost verbally repeats Mercer's shocking statistics. Among the claims, the following were examined by Africa Check: *"Whites murdered at a rate faster than any previous period in South Africa's history. A white farmer killed every five days.*

The ruling ANC, led by President Jacob Zuma, is central to corruption; inclusive of the highest rates of rape experiences in the world."

Africa-Check agrees that these type of comments and perceptions is quite common in South Africa. It also confirms that South Africa has one of the highest crime rates in the world, characterised by a high incidence of violent crime. But, *Africa Check* warns against the creation of a situation of fear based on unconfirmed allegations.

On Facebook 27 October 2017 Steve Hofmeyr quoted the following statistics:

What is worst Decide for yourself		
War	**When**	**Killed**
Anglo-Zulu War	1879-1899	6700
Anglo Boer Wars	1899-1902	100 000
Apartheid	1948-1990	21 000
ANC Rule	1994-2015	328 244

Africa Check is a non-profit organisation set up in 2012 to promote accuracy in public debate and the media in Africa. The goal of their work is to raise the quality of information available to society across the continent.

In principle, I agree with *Africa-Check*. Comments should be made with caution not to cause a psychosis of fear. However, one cannot ignore reality. South Africans at the grassroots level are caught up in fear of violence and lawlessness, stagnating into a psychotic culture of terror and distrust. The detriment of this kind of observations can amount to scaremongering, but the truth should be acknowledged.

I can only but rest my case, psychotic fear and distrust are standard, a sad situation that threatens harmonious integration and nation-building. Even though the truth might just be partially correct, the psychosis will escalate if not addressed and curtailed.

Reasons to be happy: The new-born generations

South Africa moved forward from democratisation after 1995, and we live in the present anticipating the future or will it be the failure. Memories are strewn out like a patchwork blanket with varying textures and colours. Does Post-Apartheid warm to the South African nation; a transformation to behold? A comfortable and memorable Dream coat. Will it be South Africa's version of a *Dream Coat*, merging the good with the bad and promising a bright future, something to cherish?

South Africa has an Apartheid-born-free generation aged 20 years plus, after democratisation in South Africa. I have dreams and precious memories to treasure; treasures from my childhood days under Apartheid. Do the born-free generation of South Africans share my *something to be proud of*; my childhood-dream-coat? It just seems like the *Apartheid Dream coat* is more comfortable than the *post-Apartheid dream coat*.

My Patchwork Blanket of Memories

The present and the future is a product of the past, standing here and now, bring back memories. I look back decades into the Apartheid era. What would be my reasons to be cheerful? Might it be memories I can drape around my shoulders; wrapping a smile on my face? For my dream coat, I go way back to my life in South Africa, especially my childhood memories on Grandfather's farm *Vrolikheid*, meaning happiness. As a kid, I spent holidays on the farm and accumulated so many pleasant memories. Encounters that I patch into my dream coat.

I remember a farmhouse, no electricity, no in-house running water. Kids bath-time was once a week on Saturday mornings. The big zinc tub filled with steaming hot water, placed in the bedroom or on the veranda in the summertime. It was great fun. Children scrubbed pink all over until they were shiny clean. The rest of the week, feet washed in a foot tub. Faces and hands up to the elbows cleaned at the enamel basin on the wash table. Afterwards, Mum checked and rebuffed; *"...scrub behind your ears."*

Kids would compete to wash Grandfather's feet. I remember taking off his shoes; no socks and the shoes were handmade. Shoes made from animal skin, he made shoes for the family all his life. I remember his tools; the cast iron cobbler, gouge, paring knife, edger, sharpening stones and most important, those hands. Grandfather had worker's hands and puffy feet. They looked tired and calloused. He worked and walked all day. Most of his days Grandfather would irrigate the vineyards by hand with a shovel, opening the furrows. The water gravitated, from the high-up reservoir. He had to check for mole holes. The holes would drain off the water away from the roots of the vines.

Drink water we collected in buckets from the fountain. A ten-minute walk away from the farmhouse, late afternoon when it was cooler. We would place the pails on the water-table in two rows of three, covered with linen cloths. If you want water, you don't dunk your cup in the bucket of water. There will be trouble. Use the fat transfer-beaker. And, don't dare drink from the transfer-beaker. You'll get a clip around the ear.

The farmhouse floors were compacted with broken ant-heap suds, crumbled and stamped solid. Then we would cover the almost level dirt floor with a mix of cow dung and water. We had to collect the cow shit, still hot and wet, with our bare hands. Then we mixed it with water to a creamy paste. Much fun for our kids, messy and mucky. Once combined we carried the smooth dung mix indoors, all furniture removed. We smeared the floor by hand with the cow-dung-mix, what fun. We made cutesy patterns with the shitty blend, circles, squiggles and zigzags. No ridges, all had to be smooth and flat.

When the new floor cover dried, it was dust free and hardwearing with an apple green colour. *"Don't drag your feet"* Gramps would often say. The floors were not level, and dragging feet wore the cover. We treated the floors every six weeks. The cover kept the flies at bay. I never understood why flies will go for wet dung but are driven away by dry shit on the floor.

There were no refrigerators or freezers on the farm. My grandfather slaughtered cattle for the kitchen and the workers on the farm. We would get up at two in the morning. Oil lamps scattered on the worktables. Everyone had a job butchering the meat, making sausages, biltong and whatever.

We also made soap from the solid pork fat in substantial three-legged black iron pots over open fires. Fridges were cool-boxes hanging from trees they were handmade. Evaporation cooled the contents down. The cool-boxes had moist water-logged-cinders housed in the double-walled gauzed box-sides. That was Grandfather's improvised farm refrigeration.

To preserve meat, we would cook and store it in used-, cleaned-and sterilised paraffin tins. Still preparing we sealed it with a layer of boiling fat. Finally, we would cover the tin with a linen cloth. Some cuts of meat will be dry-cured in the open-hearth fireplace.

All foodstuffs we stored in the larder. The pantry contained all sorts, dried fruit, cured meat and fish, jam preserves and the like. The pantry was dark and a no-go area for kids. We did sneak in from time to time, to pinch a bit of dried fruit, nuts or biltong, *dried meat jerky*, naughty, naughty.

Milk time, mornings and eves, you would sit lowly on tripod-stool milking cows. Afterwards, we had to operate the cream separator. Every turn of the handle a bell would make a *cling* sound; the revolutions per minute had to be perfect. Otherwise, the creamery will not work. The ring helped set the rhythm. We had to churn the cream into butter. Season it with salt to taste. Then we rubbed the water out of the butter with a wooden spatula. The butter we shaped into one pound bricks and wrapped it in waxed paper.

Granddad would coffee-time steal a slug of cream for his coffee.

He called it *coffee capital*, pinching some of the creamy riches. That will be the worth he got from bartering with the Koopmans-De Wet Grocery Store in town; his *capital*, cream turned to goods when swapped. Memory serves me right, Susan Nel was helped by Margarethe Koopmans after her ordeal in the British Concentration Camps. I told Susan's story earlier. Might just be that in later years her family had a hand in the Tulbagh grocery store; who knows? The name might even be different nowadays, but then it was *Koopmans*.

I drifted a bit. Saturdays were market days, and we packed eggs, butter, cream and veggies, into baskets. All of the goods produced on the farm. Loaded onto the horse-drawn cart, we would travel at a leisurely gallop to the Tulbagh town. Granddad in his white dust coat would barter his fresh farm produce with the only Grocer, *Koopmans*. He would exchange it for stuff that the farm does not produce, coffee sugar clothes and candy.

No money needed to change hands. Bartering was Grandad's way of capitalisation. He accrued a positive monetary balance on the Grocer's books. Sometimes he would need cash. He would draw some money from the Grocer's book balance. Grandfather required small change for church collections on Sunday. The whole family will go to church, and everyone, young and old needed something to drop into the collection tray.

Those are my memories. My *patchwork blanket, my Dream Coat*. I suppose that would be my reasons to be cheerful. I meander among my youth special moments, exceptional experiences and recalls. I often do shoulder glances and wrap it around me; they are thoughts that make my life special. Not the economy, just things that contribute to my quality of life.

Everyone should have a memory dream coat. The government should make it possible, creating an environment that will avail patchwork blankets for all its peoples. It is unacceptable that the *Apartheid Dream coat* is comfortable while the Democratic *Post-Apartheid Nightmare-Rags* harbour fear, distrust and disenfranchisement.

Conclusive Comments

I set myself a challenge but find it difficult to meet the essentials of a dream coat for all. The born free generation of South Africa does not produce dream-coats to drape around their shoulders. The majority South African twenty-year-olds do not harbour fond experiences and memories of the land of their birth. They do not have reason to experience South Africa positively. The ones that can afford it and have the educational advantage, leave South Africa to find a better life elsewhere. Even the previously disadvantaged black youths are at the forefront of demonstrations, protesting against the ANC governments rule. There are glimpses and pockets, like my memories relating to my grandfather's farm. But those memories date back to an era before the ANC came to power. For the majority of South Africans, the picture is bleak. South Africa is the end product of three and a half centuries of oppression and exploitation. First, the land and wealth grabbing colonists, then the Apartheid debacle. When finally democratised, South Africans experienced corruption in the public sector. And, topping all of that, an economy unable to produce or generate the wealth needed to upgrade South Africa out of its third-world and deteriorating status.

Democratised, the so-called Post-Apartheid South Africa is a failed state. Two decades of majority ANC government brought about a situation where the people of colour is still the disadvantaged ethnicities of South Africa. They are even worse off than under the Apartheid government.

The ANC government, born out of a liberation struggle, cannot blame colonisation and Apartheid anymore. After two decades the situation has not improved; not even incrementally. In fact, it got much worse, that is what lies at the door of the corrupt communistic inclined ANC government. The struggle-freed ANC government fail miserably with no sense of accountability. When corruption remains unchecked within a dictatorial regime, resolving maladministration issues will not be forthcoming. The much-needed trust to instil confidence will be lacking, and the reconciliation outcome will be suspect.

Pardoned conciliation incidents stay active and are not forgotten. After the Truth and Reconciliation Committee, it would have been better to uncover the real face of injustice and enforce accountability. Today millions need to swallow the bitter pill of truth but no genuine conciliation. In secretive societies, people, are prone to unimaginable crimes of blood and money, a reality under Apartheid.

Why should the poor man carry the burden of corruption and a failing ANC government? The corrupt ANC government with an outright majority of support, outstrip any sense of real democracy. Bribery for personal gain, maintain a despicable record of maladministration that destroys the country. An underperforming economy along with never-ending protests and distrust gives rise to further discontent and destruction.

The corporate character of Apartheid crimes and fraud is not surprising. It was a means to retain control by the minority Apartheid government. Personal enrichment was inevitably present in corruption cases. But, the crime ultimately served the Apartheid government. Contrary to Apartheid, the ANC corruption is purely for personal gain and self-enrichment.

One can quickly fall into the trap of statistics and comparisons, it is so simple, especially with a biased presupposition. Negativity will only serve to contribute to the underlying social fear and distrust. But more importantly, misinformation and delusions create and entrench racial divisions. It perpetuates unfound fear and hatred among races. A situation where the people of South Africa feels unsafe and vulnerable.

Low employment and an unbecoming growth rate cannot generate growth. The overbearing self-interest among corrupt officials, fail South Africa. The country needs a social environment where everybody feels safe, cared for and acknowledged.

Ethnonationalism refers to people reverting to their *ethnic-safety bubble,* entrenching separatism and segregation. *Ethnic-safety bubbles* harbours distrust and even fear. Until Ethnonationalism breaks down, integration of the entire nation will be a pipe dream. Countries in Europe in modern times suffer from Ethnonationalism, which along with colonial revenge, give rise to terrorism.

Apparently, Post-Apartheid South Africa, after twenty-two years of democracy is struggling. Described as a failing state by the *Economist.* The question is what will be the solution.

In part three I will investigate payback for imperialism and colonialism, I examine some of the modern-day political phenomena. I endeavour to understand the changes and manifestations within the political arena. Changes and expressions that influence the lives of people; not only in South Africa but throughout the western world.

Part Four:

PAYBACK FOR IMPERIALISM AND COLONIALISM

Colonial powers butchered Africans in their hundreds of thousands when they rebelled against exploitation and oppression. Crushing rebellions by colonists inflicted unbelievable human suffering. France and England, as colonial powers are today targeted for revenge and payback. Self-righteous imperial efforts counteracting the anti-colonial revolt will probably generate more retribution. Ex-colonial revulsion to historical imperialism continues to evoke actions of vengeance.

In June 2013, *Foreign Policy in Focus* reported that in the early 1960s, the British secretary of state for the colonies launched a cover-up manoeuvre, by authorising the obliteration of colonial documents to prevent Her Majesty's government from being embarrassed.

Apologists of British colonialism emphasise the *benefits* of colonialism. They endeavour to balance the *achievements* with the *sins* of colonialism. British abolishment of slavery, annihilating rogue governments, and the establishment of free markets are claimed as credits for imperialism. Imperial countries claim advanced communications, technologies, good governance and the rule of law as colonial achievements.

The publication *Empire: How Britain Made the Modern World*, is an example of how the British commend themselves for the merits of innovation to British colonies. However, intentional *wrongdoings* brought about some *incidental benefits;* all for exploitation and enrichment of the Empire.

The feeble apologies enraged ex-colonies for half a century. Today Africa's colonies are impoverished with failing economies, dependent on western aid.

Trying to understand political, economic and social consequences as a follow-on to imperialistic exploitation, requires a detailed and encompassing investigation. Exploitation of the less-developed countries involved the systematic exploitation and transfer of resources from the developing countries to the wealthy and developed imperialists.

Century-old rural and tribal economies were forcibly transformed to produce wealth for capitalism. An ancient tribal existence that worked adequately, replaced with a market economy and administration with enforced foreign decrees. Opportunistic landlords, unscrupulous people in business and speculators turn tribal structures into disrupted and contaminated communities, starving millions in the process. The biased outcome served imperialism, not the colonised populations.

Lack of local native investment and growth, over centuries, left developing countries in a self-perpetuating state of dependence on the industrialised western world.

Wealthy capitalists and opportunists from the West invest in maintaining the under-developed status quo. They will bribe monarchies, dictatorships, fascists and rogue government-elitists, to retain power and to subdue the masses. The wealth created leaves the developing country, exported for the wealth of the industrialised West.

The industrialised regimes will support everything backward, medieval and totalitarian. The exploitive capitalists will prevent or destroy social revolutions aimed at local progress, when and where they occur.

The outcome of imperialism and the mutilations inflicted on ex-colonies, result in violence and terrorism; retribution that threatens western societies in modern times.

Part of the solution might be truth and reconciliation. Foreign policies of western countries will be much better based on historical fact and acknowledgement. And not repeated efforts, denying the reality and hiding behind, *colonialism made Africa better*. In part three I will endeavour to uncover some of the past and present exploitive colonial practices that give rise to modern day terrorism and retribution.

Part Four consists of the following:

10. *Politics Post Imperialism* *277*
11. *Political Manifestations in South Africa* *310*

CHAPTER 10
POLITICS POST IMPERIALISM

New-age Politics: Our Changing World

Modern day political expressions are changing our world-society. Scientists research problems and publish papers on various political manifestations. The events I investigate were introduced by the expansionist exploitive and imperialist era. Events I believe influenced the past but once again returned to haunt modern-day society. It is essential to consider these expressions to understand what happened and still happens as a result of imperialism and exploitation.

Architects that Devastated South Africa

Most of the *designers* involved in nation-building, Boers, Afrikaners, African Tribes, British and European countries, all must take responsibility for turning South Africa into the failed state of 2017. Over several centuries neither Britain, Apartheid nor the ANC democratic government solved South Africa's problems. In fact, the problem got worse and compounded.

During the slave trade and imperialism, *corrupt African Tribal Leaders* sold their people and the country's resources to the western imperialists and capitalists. The tribal kings and chiefs of Africa traded the sovereignty of their nations for personal enrichment and gain. But, buying and selling slaves is only part of the truth. The Portuguese was the first to raid West Africa and captured Africans as slaves. Effectively they abducted people and trafficked them to America. It does not matter how the West accrued slaves. It introduced the epoch of slave labour. It brought about the atrocity of oppression and exploitation. Slavery is the ultimate of the derogative class system. It established the master-slave relationship.

Following the slave trade, Ethnonationalism in the form of Apartheid exploited and oppressed the nations of Southern Africa. Imperialism left South Africa as a segregated society. South Africans live in fear and distrust of each other. The overall feeling is that of disenfranchisement with a sense of deprivation. Identifiable ethnicities feel denied of what they believe should have been theirs. What is this perceived dispossession? Is it the lack of peace and tranquillity promised by Nelson Mandela in his dream of a *Rainbow Nation*? Or, is it what they believe the West stole from them during Imperialism?

To ask for the resolution of all South Africa's problems in two decades of ANC rule will be delusional. But, after twenty-two years, there should be some improvement. There should not be further degradation. The democracy established by Mandela turned into a dictatorial Junta State. The so-called freedom included black-on-white discrimination and murder. The present political dispensation is in effect Apartheid in reverse. It surfaced as a new configuration of Apartheid; just a new-age formation of Ethnonationalism.

The revelations uncovered in the previous chapter are startling. Inequality and Ethnonationalism are still rife. The people of colour is in a state of civil unrest harbouring racial hatred. The different ethnicities live apart and hate each other. It is *Aparthate* all over again. The campaign to *de-white* Africa of western symbols is the outcome of Imperialism. The Western world introduced Ethnonationalism to Africa. Astonishingly the West, seems to be out of touch and delusional about contemporary Ethnonationalism.

Decolonisation protagonists are prepared to go to the extremes of genocide. Black-on-white discrimination and murder to *de-white* South Africa happen almost daily. They don't even spare the remnants of imperialism in Europe their wrath. They insist on the obliteration of statues and buildings recalling the critical figures of colonialism and slavery. In history, we attempt and acknowledge the wrongs and the worth of the past. It allows us to make amends and develop a better future. You cannot erase history.

Why the Contemporary African Revolt against the West?

Is the wealth of the West, built on the exploitation of Africa? In August 2005 the *Guardian* published an article by Dr Richard Drayton. It is titled *The Wealth of the West; Built on Africa's Exploitation*. Drayton is a senior lecturer at Cambridge University, United Kingdom. According to Drayton, Britain spearheaded the slave trade during imperialism. In his paper, he refers to the *BBC Channel Four's* programme on the documentary *Empire Pay-Back* by Robert Beckford. Beckford appeals to Britain to take stock of imperial exploitation. In the program, Beckford asked why Britain did not apologise for African slavery. Britain apologised for the Irish potato famine. Beckford even hinted that there should have been a *"Substantial public monument of national contrition equivalent to Berlin's Holocaust Museum."*

Drayton quotes Beckman when he asks: *"Why, most crucially, was there no recognition of how wealth (was) extracted from Africa (that) made the vigour and prosperity of modern Britain possible? Was there not a case for Britain to pay reparations to the descendants of African slaves?"* Drayton concludes that politicians should heed appropriate and related issues. The invasions such as Libya and Iraq are new-age international bones of contention.

Drayton quote Beckford's documentary saying that Britain's debt to Africans run into the trillions. He even questions the trillions benchmark. Drayton considers the obligation to Africa as infinite and immeasurable. He makes the statement that if it were not for Britain's Africa and Caribbean exploitations the modern Western World, we enjoy today, would not exist.

Drayton points out that the *well-meaning* Western World would not admit that there should have been a *quid pro quo* settlement. He urges the profit-making Western companies to grant an excellent *pay-back* to Africa. Altruistically the *pay-back* should have been in the form of improving and uplifting the disadvantaged nations. They were the nations exploited during imperialism and colonialism. This modern-day lack of empathy seems similar to the colonists of the 17th century

The West often slant the IMF interventions in the form of international aid and debt forgiveness, as Western altruism. Taken into account the history of exploitation, the Western IMF claim of debt relief amounts to hypocrisy.

Drayton asserts that South African mines under the ownership of British and American capitalists secured Britain's contemporary prosperity and its monetary stability. He further vows that the gold in the *International Monetary Fund's (IMF)* vaults, allocated to pay for Africa's debt relief, had in effect been stolen from Africa. He inferred that the IMF African debt relief allocation is in fact, not a *gift*; *"It was what the merchant bankers would call a debt-for-equity swap; the equity here being national sovereignty."*

The term equity can refer to *even-handedness and parity*, or it can relate to the *worth of value and right of possession*. Does Drayton equate African *sovereignty* to *self-rule and the loss of it?* Or, to the wealth, *resources* exploited during the colonial era? Whatever the equity balancing components may be, the essence and significance of his statement are clear. The IMF debt relief is not a *gift, offering or endowment*. It is effectively a western debt for exploitation not yet honoured over centuries. Drayton apparently finds the altruistic attitude of the West with debt relief hypocritical.

The IMF proclaimed in February 2008 that debt relief of some $42 billion, delivered to nineteen African countries, brought substantial benefits to Africa. The IMF pompously claimed that: *"Debt relief under two international initiatives has helped reduce significantly the debt burden of heavily indebted poor countries in Africa and freed up additional resources for poverty reduction and social expenditure."*

Considering Drayton's claim that the West's debt to Africa on exploitation is trillions of pounds, and in effect incalculable. $ 42 billion is not even a drop in the ocean. Ironically, Drayton points out that; *"The sweetest bit of the deal was that the money owed, and already more than repaid with interest, had mostly gone to buy industrial imports from the West and Japan, and oil from nations who bank their profits in London and New York. Only in a bookkeeping sense had the debt relief ever left the rich Western world. No-one considered that Africa's debt was trivial compared to what the West owes Africa."* Drayton implies that the West's IMF debt relief payment to Africa in effect bought more wealth for the West while Africa is once again paying the price.

Drayton when quoting Beckman concludes that the gains from the slave trade, sugar, coffee, cotton and tobacco do not reflect the full truth. It represents only negligible aspects of the wealth story. What is of real importance is how the gains transformed Western Europe's economies. He states that: *"English banking, insurance, shipbuilding, wool and cotton manufacture, copper and iron smelting, and the cities of Bristol, Liverpool and Glasgow, multiplied in response to the direct and indirect stimulus of the slave plantations."*

Drayton continues by saying that: *"African slavery and colonialism are not ancient or foreign history; the advanced and wealthy world they created, is around us in Britain. Africa underpins and paid for the modern experience of the white British and Western privilege."*

In conclusion, Drayton refers to the then British Prime Minister, Gordon Brown who told journalists in *Mozambique: Britain should stop apologising for colonialism."* Drayton rebuts Brown's comment by stating: *"The truth is, Britain has never even faced up to the dark side of its imperial history, let alone begun to apologise."*

Western Complicity on Capitalist Mining Exploitation

Drayton dealt with exploitation in the colonial era. Kabemba touches on the imperial period but focuses more intently on

281

contemporary exploitation. In March 2014, Claude Kabemba from the *Open Society Initiative for Southern Africa (OSISA)*, published a paper titled *Undermining Africa's Wealth*. Kabemba criticises Britain's role in Africa during the imperial era scrambling for Africa's resources. He confirms that Africa's resources were plundered to enrich Britain and Europe with a negligible contribution by the colonisers to the development of Africa. In effect according to Kabemba, Africans have little to show for centuries of exploitation? He states that poverty in Africa is as unhealthy as ever with severe, if not worsened inequalities. He claims the disparity gives rise to recurring conflicts between exploitative western companies and African communities.

Kabemba continues by declaring that there is a definite correlation between the mining company's wealth and the poverty of people living in the mining communities. The wealthier the mining company become, the more impoverished the Africans are left behind. This paradox has its roots in the colonial period extenuating the way that Britain and Europe exploited the African resources; purely for the enrichment of the West. There is little to no concern for the welfare of Africa or even the advancement of African societies.

Kabemba points out that due to globalisation and the mobility of capital, only a few British mining companies are operational in Britain today. However, the UK maintains a high profile in global mining. Kabemba considers companies headquartered in the UK, formed under the UK Companies Act and listed on the London Stock Exchange as British companies. This benefit Kabemba ascribes to the gains Britain reaped from imperialism that ultimately accumulated in Britain's financial strength and renowned stock exchange.

Along with its technological expertise exported to poor and developing countries, Britain maintains a high profile in the global mining industry. Kabemba continues by saying that British mining companies in Africa provide the capital investment, planned to ensure maximum benefit to the Western enterprise. The skewed profit distribution in favour of mining companies is claimed to endorse the risks within unstable environments. Kabemba says that British companies do not hesitate to invest in countries at war. These countries suffer from human right abuses, systemic corruption and extreme poverty. They ingeniously employ private security companies to protect their interests. Benefits awarded to the African governments in taxes, royalties and bonuses are scant compared to the riches gained by the exploitive western companies.

A small African elite political group, with dubious unaccountability and corruption, often reap the benefits in scandalous falsification and bribes. African nations as a whole do not advance in development or gain. Capital greed inspires British companies, despite their moral rhetoric, to just relent and accept Africa's irrationality of corrupt authoritarian personal rule and benefit. They pay bribes to close suspect deals that undermine democracy while conspiring with unscrupulous elite African groups. There are those that dispute that elite African tribal chiefs and kings sold their people and sovereignty in the imperial era. Present-day bribe transactions reiterate the unscrupulous gullibility of Africa's elite politicians.

I previously referred to the recent Algerian oil scandal involving Netherland's Royal Dutch Shell company and Italy's Eni company. The scandal included $1 billion bribes paid by Royal Dutch Shell and Italian Eni to Algerian politicians. Later in this chapter, I consider the *state capture cum Coup d'etat* collusion between the wealthy Gupta family and President Jacob Zuma of South Africa, in the *Zuptoid* scandal. Just my thoughts in passing on the gullibility and corruption of Africa and its elite politicians; back to Kabemba.

Kabemba subsequently refers to the Angolan example where the British government conveniently ignore human rights abuses and rogue regimes, in return for significant oil interest of British

Petroleum. Kabemba finds it unacceptable that Britain keeps quiet on Angola's bad human rights record and the severe embezzlement of funds by the ruling elite.

Kabemba asserts that Africa is the world's poorest continent, where people have insufficient access to clean water, decent health care, education and electricity. Effectively Africans struggle to survive in the face of high levels of unemployment, poverty and inequality.

Kabemba continues by relating to the Perenco Anglo-French oil and Gas Company with headquarters in London and Paris. Perenco has activities in Cameroon, Gabon, the Democratic Republic of Congo, Tunisia and Egypt. The company's oil extraction has not only decimated sea life but destroyed vegetation. Exploration carried out in the proximity of poor Congolese suburbs, with no outcry from the British authorities.

Kabemba once again asks the question: *"Why does the British government allow its companies to invest in countries with questionable records on human rights and corruption, such as Angola and the DRC? And, why does Britain permit them to operate with impunity?"*

Kabemba comes to the supposition that: *"The love affair between many African governments and international companies obscures harsh realities, excluding Africa from benefiting from the exploitation of its own resources. In many of these supposedly high growth countries, citizens now believe that they are paying too high a price for economic growth, which does not filter down to them; the nation as a whole and owners of the resources."*

Kabemba recounts severe clashes around mining activities in Africa. These conflicts involved British companies, including the Marikana massacre in South Africa where they mine platinum. Another atrocity includes the execution of Ogoni activists in Nigeria. The collusion between British businesses and the corrupt African political elites were the cause of the uprising. Fact is, British companies are happy to extract resources without trying to improve the lives of workers and mining communities. According to Kabemba, British businesses that perpetuate misconduct refuse to change their ways, despite the cries of communities and civil society. He refers to the recent study in Zambia, titled *"Copper Colonialism: Vedanta-K CM and the copper loot of Zambia"* where it became apparent that: *"This British company does not respect human rights or the labour laws of the host country or international standards to which Britain is a signatory."*

The continued contraventions result in a revolt by the Africans exploited, ending in consternation and riots that give rise to bloodshed and lives lost. Kabemba also mentions the Zimbabwe debacle where the De Beers mining company removed diamonds under cover of supposedly geological surveys. De Beers did not declare the diamond extractions to the Zimbabwean government. De Beers claimed they could not find any diamonds but subsequently since 1996, a significant diamond rush transpired.

Kabemba concludes that western extractive companies continue to take advantage of weak governance structures in most African states. He sees the West as the *big man elite clique*; making secret deals with corrupt and authoritarian African elite groups. The disproportionate contracts closed, allow the western companies to run extremely lucrative, but usually environmentally destructive and socially damaging operations.

The exploitation highlighted by Drayton and Kabemba represents some of the actions by the players I coined *architects of destruction* that harmed South Africa for centuries and even to this day. The *destructive architects* are not only the *big man elite clique* from the West but also the *corrupt authoritarian political African elite* selling out their country's resources to the West for bribes under the table. The impoverished African nations are paying the price as collateral damage for the exploitation by the West. Secret collusion between the capitalistic western companies and corrupt African politicians, as condoned by western governments, ultimately warrant *pay-back-*

time. The price the world of the west needs to pay as a result of imperialism.

In the final instance, *pay-back* manifests in contemporary *fall-outs* in the shape of modern *terrorism, de-whiting and decolonisation*. The aggrieved ex-colonial nations want to rid their countries of symbols and remnants of western exploitation. The West and any form of western symbolism become the target of revenge and retribution.

Based on Drayton and Kabemba findings, it just seems that there might be *new faces and formats* of modern imperialism and colonisation, invented by western capitalism. Colonial destruction and the memory thereof manifests in modern-day terrorism. Black-on-white discrimination, killings and even genocide are just one of the manifestations.

Why continued Modern Day Exploitation: Is Africans Still less Intelligent?

Earlier I investigated the question of black intelligence. Based on the extensive evidence it was confirmed that there is a disparity between European and African intelligence. The variation came about due to the less-intelligent and less creative environmental exposure of Africans over centuries. Is it the responsibility of the West to wipe out the difference and establish parity in intelligence between Africa and the West?

The Western Industrialised World brought the responsibility on themselves by exploiting Africa over centuries and building its super development on the sweat and labour of enslaved nations and colonised countries. However, the continued exploitation of Africa by the West, in the form of new-age colonialism, is symptomatic of a still backward intelligence on the part of African people. If that is not the truth why do Africa even in 2017, succumb to exploitation by the West? Why do corrupt African elite politicians once again sell-out their nations and countries to unscrupulous capitalists, taking bribes in return for personal enrichment?

The West has a responsibility that is undeniable. But, Africa has a counter-acting liability; it will have to be a reciprocatory act of restitution. Africa primarily has a responsibility to wipe out the disparity, by first of all eradicating corruption. The answer lies first and foremost in education. Where African people experienced good education and a creative environment, there is no difference. Intelligence is not laid down in genetics. There are differences among individuals due to genetics, but that is standard in all colours, ethnicities and races. You will always have the talented and less bright people.

The third and first world can meet and find a solution. Both will benefit by the levelling of development and intelligence. It is a two-way street and a dual responsibility. In the final chapter, I endeavour to do a value judgement on the South African situation and make some suggestions towards a possible settlement to the problem under the title *South Africa, a future perspective.*

Modern Day Revolt and Retribution

The exploitation highlighted by Drayton and Kabemba should have been corrected by a democratised South Africa in 1994; it wasn't. Majoritarianism materialised in South Africa with the adverse outcome of authoritarian- and dictatorial one-party ANC rule.

In Europe, the post-colonial era brought new forms of retribution as a *pay-back* for colonial wrongs. Contemporary terrorist attacks frequent Europe. The incidents emerged from deep-seated vengeance as a backlash from colonialism. There is also the perturbing phenomenon coined as Ethnonationalism, a form of ethnic segregation. Ethnonationalism or separatism and discrimination is the outcome of intolerance based on ethnicity, the cultural- and skin colour differences. Ethnonationalism develops in modern European societies. Ethnicities are unable to integrate as one nation. They revert to opposing ethnic groups distrusting and hating one another. Separatism and Apartheid within society, produce the festering ground for home-grown terrorism as well as migrating terrorism.

In the USA the opposing factions like the *black-lives-matter, white-lives-matter, Ku-Klux-Klan, and Nazism* are in a dangerous stand-off and aggressive conflict. All four camps perceive the police as the *enemy* while especially the African-American community does not trust the cops. Four terrorist attacks launched in England in as many months in 2017 are of great concern. The world harbours grave and conflicting societal unrest.

Decolonisation, as a new-age form of black-on-white Apartheid, surfaced within the black mass democratic movements, like the *Black First Land First (BFLF) and Rhodes Must Fall Movement (RMF)*. RMF and BLFL aim to drive the whites out of South Africa and strip the country of Western remnants and symbols. Decolonisation is a grave concern for South Africa, primarily due to its predisposition to Communism. Progressively farm attacks and murders by black extremist groups drive whites off their land and make the white ethnic group unwelcome in their country of birth. This practice represents a form of genocide. Decolonisation of this kind emerges, notwithstanding the 1910 unification, decolonising South Africa and finally severing all ties with the British colonial masters in 1948. In 1961, South Africa turned into a Republic finally severing all imperial relations and relinquished its *British Common Wealth* membership.

The white-on-black Apartheid Government was corrupt, but the ANC Government seem to do a better job at failing the nation with black-on-white discrimination. After the rest of the world had its will and outcome of liberation, democratised South Africa is a nation in shock, fear and disenfranchisement. The people do not believe in the ability of the government to rule for the good of the country. They mistrust the law and order agencies to protect them. The economy does not grow to provide in the needs of the nation, and the *Rule of Law* is not upheld and respected.

Tarnished democratic values, throughout the political, bureaucratic and social environment, result in discrimination and non-compliance with fundamental human rights. Hopes and dreams for a liberated and integrated free South Africa sublimate into thin air. Democratised South Africa, left to its own devices by the international world, is going downhill. The South African nation rightfully is asking the question: Quo Vadis South Africa, where are we heading?

South Africans should be enjoying the land where the sun never sets, where mineral resources and natural wealth is available aplenty. South Africa has the skills and ability to answer in all the needs of the country. Due to majoritarianism, ethnonationalism, demagoguery, discrimination, corruption and mismanagement, South Africa has turned into a failed state.

Libby Lane is the first woman bishop in the UK. She delivered an address at the 2017 Bath University graduation ceremony where she made the powerful statement that: *"Driven by fear our lives spin out of control, what we need is hope, hope that nurtures our lives and enables society to believe in the future."* One just wonders whether there is any hope of bringing the conflicting factions within society together? I suppose *the jury will remain out on that issue* for a long time to come. Just maybe, conflict is endemic to the DNA of society.

In this day and age, there are a variety of political developments surfacing and affecting South Africa. In fact, these political trends change South Africa as well as the world socio-political environment. To establish an understanding of the dreaded vicissitudes, I will research the more prominent manifestations and developments based on published papers and books.

Imperialism: The cause of Today's Terrorism?

Is there a correlation between Imperialism and modern-day terrorism? Yes, Drayton and Kabemba implied this, and some modern events confirm such an association. Decolonisation terrified and vigorously traumatised countries like Mozambique, Angola and Zimbabwe in the 1970's. It will forever be an atrocity; an African pandemic caused by European imperialism and colonisation. In African ex-colonised countries, the wrath against the British Empire manifests as decolonisation and hate crimes. Vigour aimed at clearing Southern Africa from the perceived white colonists. The *de-colonisers* see whites as the autocrats and exploiters, the remnants of colonisation from the West. Africa plagued by exploitation, first by the colonial West and presently by the communist east.

In the imperialistic European countries of yesteryear like Britain and France, the *pay-back* for colonialism materialises as terrorism originating from revenge and retaliation because of imperial expansion. Home-grown and migratory fanatic extremists, inflict death and destruction, in Europe; the countries of yesteryear's perceived oppressors. Effectively they are hate crimes committed as terrorist attacks in revenge following colonial oppression and exploitation.

ISIS as a threat to the West is a matter of great concern worldwide. It is a movement in revolt against western values that need consideration. On 28 June 2017, *BBC Two's News night* interviewed Souad Mehkennet on her new publication, *I was told to come alone.* I researched her book and unearthed some staggering truths. The following is a transcript of my findings on Sound's publication.

I was Told to Come Alone: by Souad Mehkennet

Souad Mehkennet wrote about her meeting with the ISIS leader Abu Yusaf in 2014. Souad is a reporter for the New York Times, Washington Post and some major German news outlets. Souad regularly reports on Islamic militancy across Europe and the Middle East. The meeting took place in Antakya Turkey, three weeks before ISIS became an international household name. The release of the video, containing the beheading American journalist James Foley, made headlines all over the world and brought ISIS to the world political stage. Souad could only bring a pen and notebook to the interview. She noticed that Abu had three mobiles with him; she suspected that he was armed.

Souad became aware at an early stage that ISIS will become a significant player in world politics. She made extensive efforts to secure the interview. Being of Moroccan-Turkish decent, born and raised in Germany, Souad had unique access to underground Islamic militant leaders. She took severe risks in procuring the opportunity to meet Abu Yusaf. Souad was well aware of journalists kidnapped and murdered. One must commend her for her courage. Understanding the ISIS culture, she secured her safety by pro-actively making it clear; she is married and is not *in the market* for marrying a Jihad fighter. She made sure that there is no risk of being kidnapped.

Souad's revelations in her book contain revealing aspects of ISIS. She alarmingly later learnt that Abu Yusaf oversaw ISIS hostage program inclusive of the likes of Jihadi John. John is the British-born assassin of James Foley. Western forces killed Jihadi John in a drone attack in 2014. The meeting took place at 10:15 pm, even though Souad asked for a daytime meeting.

Her go-between picked her up, and after a long drive they met up with Abu Yusaf, he seemed to be in his twenties, dressed in a way to unobtrusively blend in with any European environment.

Abu was well-educated and conversant in several languages. As they drove, Abu explained the ISIS vision: *"If the US hits us with flowers we will hit them with flowers. If they hit us with fire, we will hit them with fire, inside their homeland and the same within any Western Country."* Abu continued by saying: *"You just think we have nutcases coming to join us."* He exclaimed that ISIS have *brothers* with university degrees from Britain, Pakistan, Somali, Yemeni and even Kuwait.

Souad asked Abu why he joined ISIS to which he answered that he got fed up with the hypocrisy of Western governments.

They propagate human rights and religious freedoms but relegate Muslim communities to second-rate citizens. Abu stated that the West would never accept the Muslim community as their equal. Abu referred to the invasion of Iraq and the human right abuses: *"... and then they point fingers at us for how barbaric we are."*

Souad challenged Abu on kidnapping and killing innocent people to which he replied: *"Every country has the chance to get their people free, if they don't think, that's their problem. We did not attack the West they attacked us, the Americans colonised Iraq; now we fight the Jihad to free the Muslim world."*

During the interview, Souad thought back on how her father told her about her grandfather fighting the French colonists. As a freedom fighter, when the French colonised their Moroccan ancestral land, he opposed the colonisation. She remembered that her father told her that killing people was not the ways of Jihad. Her grandfather's rebellion was nothing like the horrors perpetrated by ISIS. Souad challenged Abu once more telling him that Syria and Iraq are not ISIS land to which he replied: *"This is Muslim land, the country of Muslims."* Souad countered by declaring that she grew up in Europe and progressed in life based on European values, to which Abu countered: *"Why do you believe the European system to be fair and just?"* Souad responded by asking what will be the alternative, to which Abu responded by saying: *"The alternative is the caliphate."*

Souad reported that the conversation got heated when Abu challenged her by asking: *"Why are you doing this to yourself, do you believe that the West respect us? Treat us Muslims equally? The only way is our, the caliphate way."*

Even though Souad could identify with much Abu said, she could not agree that ISIS and the Caliphate are the answer to the problem. She told Abu: *"You may be right that we face discrimination and the world is unfair, but this is not the Jihad, what you're fighting.*

Jihad would be if you stayed in Europe and made your career. It would have been a lot harder. You have taken the easy way out."

The interview ended and Abu took Souad back to her hotel. Upon reflection, Souad remembered that Yusaf had spoken with confidence and fury saying: *"Whoever attacks us will be attacked in the heart of their countries, no matter if it's the USA, France, Britain, or any Arab country."*

Souad's contemplation concluded with the thought: *'We're losing one after the other. This guy could have been somebody different. He could have had a different life.'*

Souad was thinking of all the Muslims youngsters being radicalised and joining ISIS. The attitude of ISIS, as Souad's report expose, is a grave concern to the West. Abu Yusaf response confirmed that Ethnonationalism is one of the prime reasons for ISIS's aggression towards the West.

Are Suicide Bombers and Terrorists Cowards?

Immediately after a terrorist incident enters the newsrooms of the world, it is condemned by politicians as a *cowardly act*. I suppose it takes guts to sacrifice your life to make a point or to die for a cause. One must be cautious in attributing any positivity to the stealth and spineless character of terrorist acts. The attack is always planned as unsuspected and with the benefit of surprise and secrecy. The terrorist knows that if he is open and honest, he will have to face counter-action and a target that can defend itself.

The stealth character implies that the terrorist knows that *to go toe-to-toe* with the *enemy* will mean he will be on the losing end. The stealth approach is what makes terrorism a faint-hearted act. To believe that the stealth approach in conflict and battle is something new is delusional. *Kamikaze bombers* and *guerrilla warfare* incorporate stealth attacks. But, the opponents are military and armoured units. They are *hard targets*, not innocent civilians.

Pop concerts are *open events,* which is what makes terrorism *pathetic.* A brave and genuine warrior or soldier give himself and his opponent a 50/50 chance to live or die in battle. The mutual understanding and consent make stealth and surprise, acceptable in a soldier to soldier conflict. Hard targets that can defend themselves and warriors that are willing to enter into battle; they are prepared to face each other man-to-man.

To attack civilians during a pop concert, innocent of any atrocities, and not guilty of past colonial and wrong slavery doings, is like killing a baby in a crib because his ancestors are exploiters. That is what makes terrorism a cowardly act. In my mind, the young man and women succumbing to terrorism grooming should brave-up if he or she wants to claim the accolade of heroism. Only cowards kill defenceless people. There can be no doubt that terrorism is a cowardly act. Society can morally never condone the cowardly actions of the aggrieved terrorist.

To the angry terrorist and groomed sympathiser I say; grow some balls if you want to go to war, be brave enough to face your enemy. Do not hide behind sneakiness, cowardly secrecy and attack targets in surprise; they are defenceless and innocent. To honour the ISIS terrorist is morally pathetic. Brave up, do not lower yourself to cowardice in condoning terrorist activities

When I refer to *braving up,* I do not only reference acts like suicide bombings. I also see to hate-crimes where deranged murderers kill unsuspected people in their sleep. Also, I relate to defenceless farmers, *soft targets*, murdered in surprise assaults, as is the case in genocidal acts in South Africa.

Maybe, if the above understanding is incorporated in anti-terrorism propaganda, the cowardly terrorist and disgruntled groomed young and misguided Muslim, will reconsider his/her delusion of heroism. I agree with Souad, Mehkennet; they could, all of the terrorists have been worthy citizens, instead of wasteful and cowardly terrorists.

There are specific imperialist connotations to the wrath of ISIS, but the continued Ethnonationalism and discrimination against contemporary minority communities is one of the motivations behind terrorist attacks in Europe.

Ethnonationalism Promoting ISIS

Ben Norton states that political demagogues tend to blame Muslims primarily for terrorist acts. Norton claims that among the European invasions of 2009-13, less than two percent were religiously motivated. He attributes terrorist attacks to Ethnonationalism or separatism. One might take this conclusion with caution and as a biased statement. Considering the nature of ISIS and the caliphate, they place religion at the centre of ISIS activities. Not that their actions reflect a genuine nature of the Muslim faith.

In 2013, more than fifty percent attacks according to Norton were the result of Ethnonationalism, not associated with ISIS. In 2012, the figure was more than three-quarters. According to Norton, the *Muslim blame* is often used as a cover to steer away from real domestic issues, matters ingrained in discontent. Demagogues disengage with the real problems when they for instance flatly told *Black Lives Matter* activists, fighting for fundamental civil and human rights, that their issues are insignificant and not a priority if they are not being held hostage at gunpoint.

Norton finds it unacceptable that it is expected of 1.6 billion Muslims to apologise and distance themselves from terrorist atrocities. He claims that this has become a cold cliché. ISIS's prime goal, according to Norton is to destroy any existence of a *grey-zone;* a zone reflecting Muslim acceptance as part of the Western World. By continuously blaming Muslims induces a split in society. By doing this, the West is playing into the hands of ISIS, reinforcing the divide. The emerging reconciliatory *grey-zone* pose a threat to ISIS. It is paramount to ISIS to retain an absolute separation from the West as the so-called *camp of Kufr - denying the Truth of Islam.*

Shaykh Usamah bin Ladin affirms this by saying: *"Bush spoke the truth when he said, 'either you are with us, or you are with the terrorists'; 'either you are with the Ku fr-crusade, the west or you are with Islam.'"*

Norton points at the following as the flip-side of the double standards coin. When terrorist acts happened in non-Western countries like Turkey, Yemen and Kurdish Stan; the Western Political demagogues remain restrained in their blame. They even stay quiet, conspicuously not blaming the Muslims.

Kinzer and Mitchell on Causal Factors to Terrorism

The following publications by Stephen Kinzer an American author, journalist, academic and *New York Times* correspondent, also touches on the causal factors of terrorism and the origin of modern conflict in Europe. Kinzer comes to the supposition that Europe is stomaching the aftermath of their past imperial and colonial excursions. He states that Britain and France in modern times, primarily have to deal with growing struggle among their authentic citizens. *Home-grown* and the perceived *migrants from abroad* launch terrorist attacks in Europe and Britain. Disturbingly homegrown terrorism, materialise as attacks on their own country and people.

The Arab Spring debacle and civil conflict in ex-colonial African countries resulted in thousands of migrants journeying to Europe. They are escaping the civil unrest in their countries of birth. Because of their colonial history, Europe feels obliged to be tolerant towards these migrants. Violent Islamic militants surface in Europe as home-grown as well as migrant terrorism, threatening European security.

Kinzer states that during the golden age of colonialism, France and Britain were the vigorous conquerors and colonial sovereigns. As occupiers, they procured wealth from the sweat and forced labour of colonised people. The Imperialists became exceedingly wealthy during the colonial era while exploiting the subjugated natives in a Western global empire. He assumes that if European powers did not embark on colonisation; *"... and sown the seeds of hatred, those seeds would not be flowering into the poisonous weeds that are now spreading across Europe."*

Kinzer continues by saying that colonisation not only made Europe lavishly wealthy but it left Europe comfortably assumed. He asserts that the colonists were comfortable: *"Believing that the sins of the past would be forgotten and that countries that committed them would move painlessly into a new era of peace and tranquillity."*

That did not happen, the previously oppressed and colonised countries harbour fanatic fundamentalists, individuals and organised groups, set on revenge and payback; not reconciliation and peace. Kinzer thinks back on how *comfortable* the colonial legacy materialised. The occupation of yesteryear's colonies happened almost unopposed. In modern times the retaliatory vengeance emerges as terrorism and strife for Europe. Kinzer sums it up by proclaiming: *"Cultural conflicts are set in motion by colonialism and have spiralled into anger and violence."* He brings his conclusions home, pointing out that the massacre of Charlie Hebdo cartoonists, was done by two brothers from Algerian descent. The seven people gunned down in Toulouse was killed by an Algerian. All of them French-born to parents living in France, surviving the carnage of the French-Algerian War. Kinzer believes without war and France's colonisation: *"It is unlikely that any of them would have made their way back to France."*

The Manchester bomber Salman Abedi, roots back to Libya, a country colonised by Italy and bombed by Britain in 2011; was this also pay-back? Alarmingly, most of the terrorist onslaughts against European nations or Europeans holidaying or visiting countries abroad, derived from hatred as a result of colonial oppression. Without fail and with few exceptions, the origin of the wrath and revenge finds its roots in imperialism and colonisation.

The author George Mitchell knows how to bring peace to troubled regions. He was the primary architect of the *1998 Good Friday Agreement* for peace in Northern Ireland. In his comments on the planned bombings in London, he recollects that eleven men, arrested in Britain in 2014, were of Pakistani origin. They were planning suicide attacks in Britain, the colonial power that ruled Pakistan for generations as part of India.

The hatemonger British cleric Anjem Choudary that blessed the sacrificial killing of a Jordanian pilot in Syria is also a Pakistani. Britain's other Islamic radical, Abu Hamza al-Masri, life-imprisoned for terrorist crimes, is an Egyptian-born radical. Britain colonised Egypt for more than 70 years.

Mitchell professes that: *"Many factors, personal as well as political, shape the twisted terrorist mind. Religious fanaticism and resentment over social exclusion (Ethnonationalism), are among the most potent. Nonetheless, the legacy of colonialism lurks behind the current wave of violence in Europe."* In effect, Mitchell confirms Ethnonationalism as an additional causal factor to terrorism.

Mitchell points out a discrepant, referring to the legacy of the Belgians that massacred Congolese by the millions but the country is spared extensive terrorism. Portugal represents another discrepant; not frequented by severe terrorism either for its depredations in Angola and Mozambique. However, the decolonisation in these two ex-colonies was extremely violent and vicious. The cruel oppression and exploitation by the Portuguese of African natives, I dealt with in earlier chapters. Mitchell does not rule out the likelihood of terrorism by individuals and groups of immigrants from these formerly brutalised colonies. He surmises that they can still emerge and lead to terror attacks. In fact, Belgium and Portugal did suffer terrorist attacks in recent times. According to *the Guardian of 17 November 2015,* Belgium as a colonial power, which killed millions of Africans during the colonial era in the Congo, is today a prime area for home-grown terrorists in support of ISIS.

The atrocities of the past confirm that European Imperialism probably is a definite contributing factor, but not the sole motivation. Mitchell acknowledges that there are more reasons for committing terrorist attacks.

Mitchell comprehends that Europeans, as former colonisers were hardly aware that immigrants, with deep thoughts of revenge and retribution, arrived on their shores. They pompously assumed that these new citizens would respect the superiority of European values and peacefully abandon their home-grown culture. This pompous and arrogant presumption of Europe was even prevalent in the Imperialistic expansion era when especially British Cecil John Rhodes believed: *"The more of the world we inhabit, the better it is for the human race. What an alteration there would be in them if they were brought under Anglo-Saxon influence."* It seems like Europe's arrogant attitude and egotistical stance did not change over the centuries.

Europe felt it was availing an exemplary humanitarian service to the migrants. In the same way, they had philanthropic undertones to their imperial escapades during colonisation. Europe grants the migrants refuge and welcomes them as displaced and needy people, fleeing from danger and strife in their countries, penniless and distressed. They saw no urgent reason to pay disproportionate attention to care for their welfare or integrate them into their new European society. Europe was happy; they welcomed the migrants, they housed and cared for them. Europe was humanely showing compassion.

Mitchell points out that migrants as foreigners stayed in unfamiliar and sometimes hostile communities. The response of the migrants and their children were an outrage against what they perceived as European hypocrisy. The migrants would link the perceived superior European attitude to preceding European colonial atrocities. Philanthropically Europe promised to *civilise* the oppressed people, the same individuals Europe in the end subjugated and exploited.

Mitchell takes a stand in saying that: *"If France, Britain, and other European countries had resisted the imperial temptation if they had never sent armies to places like Syria, Iraq, India, or North Africa, they would not be facing the terror that afflicts them today. History does not always punish aggressors quickly, but one day, long after the truly guilty parties have moved from the scene, the punishment may come."*

Are we savouring the fruit of colonial wrath today, in the Western World? Are we paying the price for the *sins of the fathers?*

Catastrophically, the generations that caused the anger, those that imposed colonisation, are long gone, dead and buried. The ages of the 21st century are born free from imperialistic wrong-doings. Are they the generations that have to suffer the retribution of colonialism? Do they have to embark on everlasting damage control, *for the sins of the fathers?*

It seems like the wrath of the past do not go away and can be revived and exponentially extrapolated when combined with modern day Ethnonationalism. But there is a flip-side to the coin. If Mitchell's assertions are correct; the so-named *Terrorists ISIS, Boko Haram and Daec* are also free-born, their ancestors were the oppressed the subjugated, not today's generations. Is it their burden to punish the new and innocent free-born generations of European and the World of the West; are they the ones to be punished?

The perpetrators of colonialism and oppression are long-dead and gone. Personally, I am aggrieved by the war criminals like Lords Milner and Kitchener, architects of the Boer Concentration Camps. I have no kind thoughts on them. But, present-day Britain did not send them to Africa, they are the innocent generation, born-free from the atrocities of the past. I prefer to judge people on actions that they control; not the actions of their forebears. In the modern world, if we are not prepared to forgive, I do not say forget, the world will be a terrible place of revenge and wrath. Own up to the wrongs of the past, yes; but, spend your time and opportunity on solutions for the present and the future. Do not become part of a historical wrong.

But, if Europe commits the crimes of Apartheid as Ethnonationalism, the wrath against imperialism will flare up all over again. Furthermore, take into account the revelations of Kabemba as previously expressed. The West should refrain from exploiting developing countries with new-age forms of colonialism and imperialism. By turning a blind eye will extrapolate and re-invent the wrongs of the past; terrorism, decolonisation and de-whiting will continue.

Is it pragmatically possible, to bring opposing born-free generations together, on a middle ground free from terrorism, decolonisation and hate-crime? Draw a line of reconciliation and peace, accept the atrocities of the past as history? Learn from past wrongs and move on, in order and tranquillity? Reconcile for calm and refrain from Ethnonationalism?

To all these questions; the answer is big; *maybe not.* The stakes are too high and deep-seated. Discrimination seems to be part of the modern world. New-age colonialism as induced by capitalists is still rife. The new-age Ethnonationalism reflects all the derogative characteristics of Apartheid and is always present in Europe and Africa. Apartheid has many international faces and appears to be timeless. Within contemporary generations preconceptions and demagoguery remain prevalent. Pseudo-religious instigators, fundamentalists and demagogues continue to groom and brainwash susceptible individuals based on retribution.

Imperialism is not the Sole incentive for Terrorism

Dr Berny Sèbe from the University of Birmingham tries to make sense of the Paris attacks through the prism of colonial history. He concludes that it would be a dangerous reductive supposition. Sèbe claims that ISIS sees France as the: "*Unscrupulous oppressor, past and present of the Muslim world. The Levant, the runaway, leaving unpaid debt emanating from the British and French spheres of influence. ISIS perceives the West as an obstruction in creating a Caliphate as envisaged by Al-Baghdadi."*

According to Sèbe, Jihadi sympathisers hate France as much as they hate the US. They want to build a new-age dispensation. A new caliphate for what they perceive to be the modern Muslim world, divorced from the Western World. He explains that Jihads transpired from former colonies, linked by migratory patterns as a result of imperial connections. He expresses the feeling that France is receiving payback for its colonial past. Added to this, Ethnonationalism, the non-integration of minority communities extenuates shortcomings and causes conflict and terrorism. Sèbe warns that trying to pin the Paris attacks exclusively on colonial history would be dangerously reductive. He claims that since colonialism, new factors came into play.

Firstly, the large-scale attacks; USA twin-towers in 2001, Madrid in 2004 and London in 2005, along with the several Non-Western-States in the Arab world, were not imperialistically motivated. The Jihad's inspiration was to remove and address Western obstacles blocking their vision of the *Caliphate*; is this also a form of decolonisation?

Secondly, according to Sèbe, contrary to the ISIS scenario, the African liberation movements based their drive and origin on Western cultures and values adopted during the colonial past. They apparently do not want to revert to tribalism and old-fashioned fundamentalist values. The 1950s / 60s liberations were a triumph of liberty and equality within a Western political culture. In contrast, the Jihadi groups reject wholesale the benefits of the West; they want sharia law as a political dispensation.

Thirdly, Sèbe refers to the renouncement of the Jihadi actions by members of Muslim communities. The Jihadi can hardly pose as *the voice of the oppressed* when Muslims denounce their actions.

Sèbe, however, considers colonialism as insufficient to pin down the dynamics of present-day Jihadi groups. The Jihadi he claims; *"… have an unprecedented global and fundamentally anti-Western agenda. In their view, the implementation of their political goals relies on the annihilation of the West and its values; an objective which had never been even formulated by anti-colonial activists in the post-war period."*

Modern governments have a solemn responsibility to integrate communities. The West must be careful not to allow Ethnonationalism to fester and develop. If the West continues to allow the exploitation of Africa and the third world, through companies employing new-age formats of colonisation, they will stoke the fire of discontent that will result in terrorism and attack.

Unfortunately, the new-age manifestations as discussed, and prevalent within the socio-political environment are a reality. These incidents affect society and need understanding. They are the intricacies that face modern-day society. They are the barriers that need to be broken down to normalise societies worldwide and specifically within South Africa.

Elif Şafak's take on Majoritarianism in Turkey

Elif Şafak is a Turkish author, columnist, and academic that appeared on *BBC Two's News Night*. Şafak published 15 books and wrote fiction in both Turkish and English. She commented on the April 2017, Turkish referendum. The referendum aimed to give the President more power and to get rid of the position of Prime Minister. Elif stated that democracy is fragile and a country should not let it slip into majoritarianism. Democracy can quickly move into a one-man majority, with unbridled authority. Şafak stated that Turkey historically demonstrated how fragile democracy could be. She said that nations and history do not necessarily move forward. Sometimes countries run in circles making the same mistakes over and over again.

Şafak stated that Turkey declined into total authoritarianism reverting to the foremost jailer of journalism. Whatever you write, a book, tweet or an article you are accused of betraying your country and could be prosecuted. Şafak emphasised that authoritarian rule, unfortunately, results in the literati self-censoring. Their words become thick, preservative and restrained. She stated that the Turkish political elite confuses democracy with majoritarianism. She urges that having the popular vote doesn't mean you can do what you want. Free and fair elections need an essential set of requirements. For instance; respect and maintain the *Rule of Law*, separate the Political- Judicial and Administrative Powers – *Triage Politica*, respect and allow *freedom of speech* through a free media and press, maintain the *independence of the Academia* unrestrained and govern with *accountability* in all matters of State; accountable to the electorate.

Şafak emphasised that the Turkish situation should be a warning to other countries who are vulnerable to the same fate. From India to Hungary, Greece and the Philippines, it can happen elsewhere and anywhere. She followed by saying that we are in a day and age where the traditional left v right divide is no more. Şafak emphasises that the conflict now is tribalism v humanism, wall-builders v bridge-builders. The battle is not between religion and civilisations, but a clash of values within nations.

Şafak concludes by saying that the Turkish political elite might have discarded democracy, but they should know that there are many open-minded individuals, realising their country deserves so much better. The world deserves so much better than authoritarianism.

What Şafak propagates happened in South Africa in 1995, and it is still happening after twenty-two years of democracy. Let's hope that South Africa also have this component of open-minded individuals.

The Growing Threat of Isis

Terrorism in Europe is partially the consequence of imperialism by Europe and the West. Ethnonationalism added to colonialism is a cause of terrorism. The combination of the two re-ignites the wrath of yester-year's enslaved and colonised countries.

Research documentation described a caliphate state as: *"The Islamic State of Iraq and Syria (ISIS) (that) has now officially become a global Islamic caliphate. It took 14 months for its leader, who is known as Abu Bakr al-Baghdadi, to set himself up as a ruler by order of God. He is not only the commander of the faithful now, but also the caliph at large, and the successor of Prophet Mohammed."*

These extremists hate the West they strive to eliminate all Western values from the face of the earth and conquer Western countries. Not that they will succeed, but their fanaticism is evident. Their hatred of the West is absolute and progressed far beyond colonialism and imperialism. The Guardian reported in 2014 on a militant Abu Osama. He waved a black Isis flag in Iraq shouting: *"If and when I come back to Britain it will be when the Islamic state comes to conquer Britain, and I come to raise the black flag of Islam over Downing Street, over Buckingham Palace, over Tower Bridge and Big Ben."*

These diabolic assertions of ISIS and its followers are presently terrorising the West and will do so for some time to come. Islamic extremists the likes of Anjem Choudary started hate preaching in the late 1990's. Were they taken seriously? Apparently not. Considering Souad Mehkennet's interview with Abu Yusaf, it is clear that ISIS is fanatic in their hatred against the West. They will stop at nothing to progress with their caliphate objectives.

What Format of Government

South Africa moved from a stateless tribal rule to colonisation through imperialism, to a Union of two colonies and two Boer Republics, and finally to the Republic of South Africa. Might the format of government be the root of South Africa's problem? To understand the changes it is worthwhile considering the standard forms of regimes. Is a Republic the best form of government for South Africa? The Inkatha Freedom Party in the person of Buthelezi opposed a unitary state and would rather have seen a federal system that would protect the power basis of the different ethnicities. Unfortunately, the central partition of ethnicities was destroyed by colonialism and Apartheid. The South African nation is geographically integrated but ethnically divided. Federalism would have been a disaster especially if the founding motivation was ethnicity. South African ethnicities in modern times intermingle to the point of no-return.

It just seems that the Communist-inclined ANC do not understand the basics of a democratic government, answerable to the people that elected the government. When considering the various forms of government, a Republic format seems to be the ideal democratic state. However, high-jacking democracy as a result of the political phenomena as discussed, democracy can quickly turn into a majoritarianism, autocracy and dictatorship.

Regimes and Governments: Formations and Changes

It might just be that the form of state and government within South Africa is not fit for purpose. Over centuries, the country has undergone changes from tribal regimes to colonisation and ultimately a democratic republic. Unfortunately, democracy has been high-jacked. South Africa is known to be the Democratic Republic of South Africa. But, it shows all the signs of a one-party dictatorship because of populism and majoritarianism. There are a variety of governmental formats worldwide.

Monarchies founded on royal blood ancestry are mostly contemporary constitutional monarchies. These Monarchies retain the Monarch as head of state but elect a representative government to do state administration within statutory guidelines.

Communism is an ideology like the Marx and Lenin philosophy, identifying themselves as *workers of the state or socialists*. It is considered an authoritarian political system, controlling the lives of people with no real freedom.

Dictatorships are similar to Communism, with a Dictator the prime ruler of the country, who makes final decisions. No constitutional or parliamentary restrictions. Military dictatorships run the political system or exert pressure on the government.

Populism and majoritarianism can lead to a one-party dictatorship. Majoritarianism happened in South Africa with ANC rule hijacking democracy and replacing it with a dictatorship.

Plutocracy and Elitism relate to a state or society governed by the wealthy *elite* ruling class. Officials co-opted by the elite ruling class are often the police or military. *Elite groups* will control the news media and also the political parties with their financial wealth. The wealthy will *buy* power through elections using their money to manipulate the media to *brainwash* the electorate known as *demagoguery*. President Zuma's collusion with the wealthy Gupta family is an *elitist* usurpation of power and appears in contemporary news media coined as the *Zuptoid* resulting in unrest and protests. I write extensively on Zuptoid in later chapters.

Republics are governments by the people for the people. The citizens legitimise the government. Formats of republics can be; *crowned* monarchies, *Single Party rule* like the ANC-government, can be *capitalist* governed by capitalism. *Federal states* often referred to as federal republics.

The main characteristic of a Republic is that the elected leaders are replaceable by election or disproof of public will. The balance of power will be the essential component of a Republic. The moment a government usurp power, democracy within a Republic fails, and dictatorial rule takes over.

True Democracies imply *direct democracy* where the citizens directly participate in the governing process. Real democracies suggest freely and informed choices based on logic and untarnished by emotional demagoguery. Such democracies reflect the actual will of the people. The resultant regime incorporates uncompromised decisions and results in substantial opposition. A significant debate ensures adequate checks and balances, preventing the usurpation of power by one person or group.

In modern society real democracies are *pipe dreams*. The power balance will always be challenged by the wealthy and powerful. The nation needs to remain politically active to maintain true democracies. The electorate needs to call the government to account through a strong opposition to the ruling party and efficient checks and balances built into the Constitution. In a *representative democracy,* the citizens elect representatives who make the law. They take up office in government as members of Parliament and rule on behalf of the people that elected them to Parliament. Unfortunately, due to modern-time manifestations like demagoguery, populism and majoritarianism, democracy can be compromised.

Conclusive Comments:
Payback for Imperialism and Colonialism

Imperialism is not the beginning and end to modern day terrorism. There is a myriad of contributing causes and grievances that give rise to terrorism. Although several researchers identify the imperial era as the root-cause of modern terrorism, other political scientists attribute terrorism to Ethnonationalism; understood as discrimination against certain ethnicities. The black-versus-white ethnic divide once again gives rise to conflict.

A crucial question: *Is Ethnonationalism new-age Apartheid? Racism and discrimination based on ethnicity and skin colour?* The features of Ethnonationalism was core to colonialism during imperialism and expansionism. Today, Ethnonationalism is a cause attributed to terrorism; *almost piggy-backing on payback for imperial exploitation.*

The inability to integrate societies, push ethnic groups into a safety bubble of Ethnonationalism. Subjugation and maltreatment of certain ethnicities induce separatism; *Apartheid* once again rears its head on the world stage.

In conclusion, yes, it is payback time for imperialism, but not exclusively. New and age-old factors come into play, and there are also unique discriminatory and exploitive causal factors.

In fact, nothing has changed, racial divide and discrimination, once again cause conflict. It is not only a class system within society; *it is also Apartheid based on ethnicity!*

Added to the dilemma, the Jihadi fundamentalists and ISIS supporters, hate the West and will continue terrorist activities to achieve their goals. ISIS has a different agenda and does not act solely on Imperial disgruntlement; it wants a west free caliphate.

The new-age political manifestations in whatever format they emerge cause world-wide destruction and changes to the political arrangement of societies. In addressing the ills of society, the political power structures need to be aware of these manifestations. The origin and causes of these signs need to be understood to introduce conciliation and correction. It is of the utmost importance that the political leaders know the new-age political expressions and ills within society. Arrogance and ignorance towards the new-age developments will harm modern societies endlessly.

In the next chapter, I will research how these new-age political manifestations, affect South Africa. How they changed the socio-political scenery for the worst.

CHAPTER 11

POLITICAL MANIFESTATIONS IN SOUTH AFRICA

Imperialism and slavery might have happened centuries ago. In modern society, the backlash, or is it pay-back, is a reality. Not only in Europe but also within the ex-colonised countries like South Africa. Political changes manifest within our changing society continuously. The following manifestations influenced and still effect South Africa.

The ANC Majoritarianism and Dictatorial One-Man Rule

The words of Elif Şafak, ring accurate relevant to South Africa: *"Nations and history do not necessarily move forward. Sometimes countries run in circles making the same mistakes over and over again."* For twenty-two years the ANC moved in circles. South Africa as a real democracy did not move forward. It makes the same mistakes over and over again. As a result, the ANC reduced South Africa to a failed state.

The ANC is as bad as Apartheid and even worse. Populism and majoritarianism put an outright majority in power. Too much power breeds corruption, and absolute power delivers a total fraud. To keep the ruling and corrupt ANC governing party in check requires an active and vigorous opposition. Balanced political power dispensation should curtail the abuse of power.

Majoritarianism, Populism and Demagoguery

Majoritarianism, populism and demagoguery are neo-age manifestations. They are phenomena coined to explain changes in the political environment.

Demagoguery is an appeal to people's emotions and prejudices rather than their logical reasoning. A manipulative demagogue associate with dictators and sleazy politicians. The demagogue will appeal to the less appealing nature of the people.

Majoritarianism is a political philosophy or agenda that asserts the will of the majority. Majority support will enable demagogues to introduce changes to societal thoughts and decisions. Often they will support extremism, religion, language and social classification. ISIS, pursuing *sharia law,* might be considered such a movement. As demagogues, they groom young Muslims to become terrorists. The recent Catalonia debacle also incorporates some aspects of majoritarianism. The Spanish government enforce their majoritarian constitution on the Catalonian people. The enforcement tarnishes true democracy. The reverse might even be the case. The Catalonian people use their majority and populism to enforce their will on Spain as a country.

Populism supports the concerns of the ordinary population. It appeals to ordinary citizens, the ones at the bottom of the social ladder. Those perceived to be discriminated against or exploited. Populism often surfaces where, for a part of the population, the *system* does not work. People revolting against the so-called *establishment.* The liberation of Southern African states can be the outcome of populism. In revolution against Apartheid and colonialism, populism indeed prevailed. It played a significant role among the non-whites during the Apartheid era. They felt disenfranchised. The *Apartheid* system did not work for them. The *Apartheid* system born from colonialism rendered them inferior. The oppressive regime threatened their livelihood and culture. They also suffered because of a grotesque wealth-gap. The harsh discriminatory measures under *Apartheid* destroyed their livelihoods.

The Populists perceive themselves to be nationalistic, patriotic and protectionistic. The situational environment will be confrontational, and the charismatic leader or team will not shy away from challenging its rivals. Populism often gives rise to open conflict. Donald Trump threatened Hillary Clinton with jail during the American presidential campaign. Lord Peter Hain and the anti-Apartheid protagonist can resonate as demagogues. He used populism when they rebelled against Apartheid. He supported the liberation struggles of Southern Africa.

During the USA Presidential elections and the Brexit Referendum, the slogan was aggressively propagated *"we want our country back, we will make our country great again."* Demagogues voiced a variety of manipulative deceits in the UK BREXIT referendum. They spread fear relating to European migrants. The Brexit Leavers implied that European Union payments are wasteful and will fund the *National Health Service (NHS).* The Momentum support group of Jeremy Corbin in the UK elections also reflects a hybrid of populism.

The next question that surfaces; how does the modern political changes manifest itself in Southern Africa?

Decolonisation and De-Whiting in Zimbabwe

Just to prompt your memory; Cecil John Rhodes, the master and father of Imperialism and Apartheid, with the support of Britain, colonised the present Zimbabwe and Zambia. I suppose Britain will try to excuse themselves by blaming Ian Smith's Unilateral Declaration of Independence.

That will not wash Great Britain; you declared independence to ex-colonies by the Balfour Declaration. Why oppose Ian Smith when he implemented the Declaration? He did precisely what Britain ruled. His country was declared internally and externally autonomous. Britain should not have interfered.

In 1975, as an outcome of colonisation, almost three hundred thousand white people lived in Zimbabwe. Whites constituted eight percent of the total population. Zimbabwean white population fell in 1999 to one-hundred-and-eight thousand and less than 50,000 in 2002. By 2012, less than thirty-thousand white people lived in Zimbabwe.

It doesn't take a mathematician to tell me that within four decades the percentage whites dropped from eight to one percent; three-hundred thousand to thirty-thousand! The cause of the reduction? Decolonisation and de-whiting efforts speared by farm murders! An organised and concerted orchestration ensued; rid Zimbabwe from the western world symbolism and influence. Farm murders caused the psychosis of fear and distrust. The rest just fell into place; quarter-of-a-million whites left Zimbabwe.

The Mugabe government took the de-colonisation lead. Because of imperial oppression and exploitation, there were ample wrath-ridden blacks to carry out the de-whiting. Mugabe adorned a silent and a blind eye to hate crimes; apart from actively imparting the objective. It is and always was his prime purpose; to get rid of Rhodes' legacy and the West.

He voiced this sentiment in a recent address: *"Zimbabwe will never be yours; (meaning the whites)."* Mugabe is not only cruel and crude, but he is also cunning in his silent support; he did not have to murder the farmers, all done for him.

As recent as the 7th January 2017, the *Telegraph* published an article titled: *"Why white Zimbabwean farmer, Ben Freeth, returned to his farm eight years after it was destroyed by pro-Mugabe forces."* Kent-born Ben Freeth and his family experienced the violence of Zimbabwe's authoritarian regime first hand. They suffered beatings, torture and court battles at the hands of Zimbabwean wrath-ridden-decolonising-hate-criminals. But Ben still care about the hundreds of thousands black farmworkers who lost their livelihoods to Robert Mugabe's atrocities.

Ben returned to Zimbabwe, and as he looks onto the fertile plain of central Zimbabwe in 2017, he remarks: *"It's a little haven of peace."* Along with his wife Laura, they built the farm, the farm Mugabe destroyed. The farm where they raised their three children until Robert Mugabe's war veterans arrived eight years ago and ruined everything. After the destruction, the estate did not produce anything. Producing agriculture lost to decolonisation; the farm left dormant and derelict.

Ben and his family paid the price. They challenged Mugabe to the highest court in southern Africa and won. The Telegraph put it aptly: *"They paid the price for daring to take Mugabe to the highest court in Southern Africa and winning; for being white in the land of a black despot who would rather see his people starve than lose his grip on power."*

Ben comments within *The Telegraph* article: *"It's horrific to see your home in ruins simply because you have the wrong coloured skin; that, ultimately, was our crime."*

The Telegraph in the article states the obvious: *"The decolonisation cost Zimbabwe their vibrant economy."*

Zimbabwe is today one of the many failed states as ex-colonial African countries and shunned by the international community. If the world is a circus, Zimbabwe will be the clown country and Robert Mugabe the fool leading the procession.

Did the western world imperialists and colonial masters intervene to protect the colonists they left behind? That is after they raped Africa from its resources and riches?

No, the West washed their hands off the wrongs of the past. Britain implemented the Balfour Declaration and adorned self-rule and independence on all ex-colonies. Then the Western world started their support for the liberation struggles. They pushed their liberation soldiers into the African fields; the likes of Lord Peter Hain and Ronnie Kasrills. They were let loose on South African soil to create the disaster facing South Africa today.

The riches exported to Europe under imperialism, safe in the coffers of the West. Europe is okay, the whites left in Africa can pick-up the spills.

South Africa is next in line to Zimbabwe. Will the international world care; become involved? The West today and in the past, do not and did not care about Zimbabwe. The West does not and will not care about South Africa. The white people as remnants of the imperial era left behind in Africa is just what it is, collateral damage. Europe has its fallout as a result of imperialism; they have to deal with modern-day migrants and terrorism.

South Africa Next in Line?

I would not be surprised if South Africa is next in Line. Decolonisation and de-whiting are already plaguing South Africa. Surfing Facebook, I daily find evidence of South African whites presently being exterminated. The images are atrocious; rape, assassinations, lynching, disfigured corpses; just too much to contemplate. Evidence rampant, disconcerting and overwhelming. Enough to convince any right-minded white South African that this is not safe. The best option is to get out of Africa. Find a new home somewhere out there where the world is safe and rational.

South Africa is in fact, being decolonised and de-whited, as I write my biography. And, the pattern; farm murders with the aid and guidance of Zimbabwean hate-criminals. Well, one must give them credit; they have been practising killings and hate-crimes for four decades. They must be the experts at this point. And, we are aware of the pattern; criminals learn from each other. Zuma and Mugabe are like two peas in a pod. Mugabe's wife received diplomatic immunity the moment she gravely assaulted a young lady model in Johannesburg, South Africa. No legal consequences, politicians are above the law.

White South Africans represent nine percent of the total population, one percent more than Zimbabwe in 1979. If South Africa follow the decolonisation and de-whiting pattern of Zimbabwe; within four decades the whites will reduce from nine percent to one percent or a fraction of a percentage. Or, to put figures to the drop in whites; four-and-a-half million will leave, and only half-a-million whites will remain.

Let's hope that will never happen.

At the end of September 2017, a lady identifying herself as Hokka Kaiser posted a video on Facebook. She earnestly warns and advises farmers against farm attacks. In the video, she mentions that she works with a colleague Lucas Swartz. Their team deals with stopping and preventing attacks on white-owned farms. Lucas works undercover with so-called *impimpies*. They are the alleged informants on farm attacks.

While reading and listening to Hokka, I realised and recognised; the same things happened in the late seventies right up to my termination as a civil defence officer. The Apartheid government forcefully claimed that civil defence had nothing to do with law and order or military defence. But on the quiet civil defence corps members were trained in armed defence. They were also prompted to be self-sufficient in maintaining law and order via vigilante *farm-watch-groups*. Especially rural farmers established early warning systems via Radio networks on the so-called citizen's band frequencies. The farmers organised *rapid response vigilante groups* that responded when farms were under threat.

Great, I love it when a people revert to every single opportunity to defend itself against any form of risk. That is what civil defence is all about. Pity, the Apartheid government, never got their heads around that bit of reality. Truth be told; everything had changed, but nothing has changed.

Hokka explains in her video clip that the black movements planning and executing farm attacks start their attacks by staking-out farms they target and observe future attacks. Hokka and her team call the stalker the *watcher in the woods*. The people carrying out the attacks call themselves the *hit squads*.

The organisations orchestrating the attacks are known as the *employers*. There is little doubt that the *employers* are the protagonists of decolonisation and de-whiting South Africa; the likes of the *Rhodes Must Fall (RMF), Mass Democratic Movement (MDM) and the ANC Youth League.*

The government of Robert Mugabe actively took part in employing murderers to commit hate-crimes. Jacob Zuma led his followers to *a Kill the Boer chant song.* In my mind, there is little doubt that the ANC is involved in the farm murder campaign. The ANC Youth League vociferously promote the Kill the Boer campaign.

According to Hokka, the farm attacks are inside jobs, not all farm workers will be involved, but at least one will be in cahoots with the hit squad. She advises farmers to keep their dogs inside and always respond to any strange manner among the dogs. The response of dogs can mean that an unfamiliar intruder is in the vicinity; this can be the *watcher in the woods.* Hit squads and all its alliances are most probably being paid. Due to unemployment being an almost fifty percent problem, takers are available aplenty; and they are susceptible due to past atrocities.

Hokka also impresses on farmers to check their windows; hit squads often enter farmhouses through bathroom windows. Never leave windows unclosed and unsecured. She also warns farmers to be vigilant at all times. Farmers are more at risk than police officers in present-day South Africa.

Black maids working for the farmer will try to warn farmers of a planned attack. The housemaid cannot caution them explicitly because of fear that she will be killed if caught informing. By drawing curtains early, say at four in the afternoon, she tries to warn the farming family that they might be *staked-out by a watcher in the wood.*

Hokka warns that the hit squads will try to endeavour to draw the farm family out of the house by knocking on a window or door or setting off a disturbance, like a fire in the farmyard. Farm attacks are meticulously planned. Hokka warns the farmers not to investigate any disturbance. She urges the farmer to sound an alarm on the *farmers watch network* and mobilise assistance immediately.

Hokka emphasises that the hit squads are cowards. The moment they suspect that the farmer believes something is wrong, they will abort and run. She also mentions that whenever her organisation gets a sniff on a planned attack and starts to visit the planned target-farm, the strike will be called off. In all scheduled attacks activities are pre-planned by the *employers* of the attack. The *employers* design rape, murder and robbery in exquisite detail.

The moment one person in the hit squad changes his mind the plan will be aborted. Hokka explains that this is because of witchcraft. The African superstitiously believe that if one turns on the project, they will fail. This behaviour is rooted in ancestral witchcraft.

Hokka also points out that hit squads without fail will include Zimbabweans. The South African black people believe that the Zimbabweans are the masters of farm murders. Zimbabweans have been executing farm murders since the Zimbabwe liberation times, more than three decades.

Hokka also warns farmers to be aware that black farmers involved with *hit squads* will actively befriend the farm dogs. She emphasises that she knows what she is talking about after attending more than three-hundred farm attacks. Hit squads are trained in exquisite detail how to befriend the dogs.

Hokka emphasises that the stuff she mentions in her video is real and relevant. She learnt and experienced it all while interviewing arrested members of hit squads.

The *hit squads* characteristics correspond with the terrorists threatening European countries. They act against the colonial masters of the imperial era. The employer, such as *Isis* and the *ANC Youth League, Rhodes Must Fall (RFM)* and the like will groom the *terrorist cum hate-criminal.* They are cowards that launch stealth attacks on innocent, vulnerable targets.

Zuma-Gupta State Capture: Instigating Racial Tension

Majoritarianism, populism and demagoguery, revealed itself in the Zuma-Gupta debacle. The news media coined the corrupt alliance *ZUPTOID*; a blatant example of how capitalism encroaches on the political landscape. Financial power employed to abuse and destroy democracy. Biz-news asks the question: *"Are we a Zuptoid or a Constitutional democracy?"* And then answers its question saying: *"The ANC-government either holds the Constitution in thinly veiled contempt or is legally short-sighted."* The corrupt ANC government once again showed its autocratic colours. But, let's consider the *ZUPTOID* debacle to understand what happened.

Andrew Harding reported on *BBC News-night* of 20 July 2017. He stated that it is dark times for South Africa. Allegations of high-level corruption pointed at a mix-up in the scandal. A massive leak of confidential emails fuelled the accusations. The charge is that Bell Pottinger the UK-PR company orchestrated racial tension in South Africa. The objective was to distract attention from the wealthy Indian Gupta family in cahoots with President Jacob Zuma. Harding revealed that the scandal is a criminal plot to capture the state itself. *State capture* refers to political interference by private elitist individuals and groups. The instigators chart personal interests to corrupt a state's decision-making process. It can even be on par with a *Coup d'etat.* The objective is to take over the government's decision-making process. The Gupta plot involves money laundering. The Gupta family's proximity to the President gave them the power to sway the political future of South Africa.

Leaked emails suggest how the Gupta family bribed their way into the heart of government. According to Harding the Gupta's offered the Deputy Minister of Finance, Mcebisi Jonas, a bribe of 600 000 Rand cash and 600 million once he complies. The money provided was a bribe. Zuptoid aimed at running a shadow state, led by the Gupas and President Zuma; they denied the allegations. But according to Harding, the *"howls of outrage"* continue to escalate.

Harding continued implicating the spin doctors, in the form of Bell Pottinger PR Company, that *"pitched up in Johannesburg".* The delegation led by the company's founder Lord Tim Bell closed the contract with the Gupta's. Murphy Morobo, ANC veteran, said that the apparent conflict of interest defeated the ends of justice. He described Zuma and the Gupta's as vultures in positions of power. Their influential standings availed them to make a *piecemeal* of the South African democracy.

The Guardian of 5 September 2017 describes the Bell Pottinger company as a high-profile PR company. The company had a catalogue of clients; *"Lord Bell co-founded Bell Pottinger in 1987 as Margaret Thatcher's favourite PR man. The agency over the past three decades has taken on highly sensitive geopolitical PR accounts and controversial clients. These include the Pinochet Foundation, Syria's first lady Asma al-Assad, the governments of Bahrain and Egypt. Oscar Pistorius charged with murder. FW de Klerk when he ran against Nelson Mandela for president and Alexander Lukashenko, the Belarusian dictator."*

According to The Guardian of 12 September 2017, it emerged that Bell Pottinger had been paid £500m to make propaganda Iraq videos on behalf of the US government. The videos had to look like Arabic news videos.

Harding quotes Bell Pottinger's CEO, James Henderson: *"We can get you or your company or government into the media or quietly arrange the opposite. We keep a lot of people out of the press."*

The company also boasts that; *"Where businesses are discreet, ethics are flexible, and rich people with reputations to upgrade are in increasingly plentiful supply."*

Zuma in cahoots with the Gupta's hired Bell Pottinger a UK PR Company to clean up their toxic reputation. The contract was worth a £100 000 per month to Bell Pottinger. Victoria Geoghegan led the deal. She soon became a hated person in South Africa. Her strategy aimed at deviating attention away from the toxic reputation of the Gupta-Zuma alliance. She focussed on racial inequality in South Africa. The primary objective, to highlight South Africa's racial divisions. Instigated ethnic partition reverted attention to the turbulent Apartheid years.

Democratic Alliance's (DA) leader, Mmusi Maimane was interviewed by Harding. Mmusi stated that South Africa suffered racial division for decades. The country finally experienced a relatively short time of democracy and protection of civil rights. Bell Pottinger's intervention made this position vulnerable. Very quickly the instigations started a *"wildfire"* within South African society.

Evidence uncovered by Harding proved that Bell Pottinger wrote the speeches for the *Ancyl National Rally* a group supported by Gupta. The Ancyl demagogues declared civil war in their own words. Their aim was *de-whiting (removing white people) and decolonising* South Africa. Bell Pottinger according to the leaked emails, considered this war cries as *"positive and neutral"* to their campaign. The comments implied that the PR interference is working and has potential.

On the instruction of Zuma and the Gupta's, Bell Pottinger caused friction relating to *white monopoly capital.* They started a social media campaign to stir up revolt. The campaign went viral very quickly and got ugly adding more radical voices. Ferial Hafajee, Editor-at-large of the *Huffington Post* confirmed the existence of the devious plot. She verified that the aim was to deviate attention away from the Gupta-Zuma toxic alliance. 90% of the disadvantaged black and coloured communities have access to social media via mobile phones. The campaign was well-timed and cleverly strategised. Hafajee referred to many journalists, showing interest in the state capture plot. Journalists quickly identified the smear campaign as Bell Pottinger deviating attention away from the Zuma-Gupta toxic reputation.

Harding reported on several websites, as well as *fake Twitter accounts.* Jean le Roux, a media expert, confirmed that there is a definite correlation between Bell Pottinger's campaign and phoney media accounts.

Harding portrays some of the following outcomes among the populace. In part of Harding's video clips, a black lady confronted a white reporter saying: *"Africa is ours, not yours."*

The movement *Black First Land First (BFLF)* aggressively confronted a white journalist telling him: *"We are going to end whiteness."* A spokesperson of *BFLF* challenged the reporter: *"You British because you are the white mono-white-capital, are blaming the Gupta's for organising the black people to take their world-back-campaign. That is why you are organising this anti-campaign of yours."*

The reporter challenged the spokesperson asking what he thinks his role should be in South African politics. The BFLF spokesperson lost it shouting: *"I am not your B***K F***K any more, so shut up."*

Harding reports that it was not long before South Africans started fighting back. Some furious satire clips about the Zuma-Gupta conspiracy appeared on social media. The clips discredited the Zuptoid alliance. The clips portrayed to what extent Zuma was in the pockets and control of the Gupta's.

Bell Pottinger's track record suited the Gupta-Zuma alliance like a glove. Leaked documents imply that Bell Pottinger doctored the Gupta's Wikipedia profile. *The Bureau of Investigative Journalism* in 2011, found that: *"Bell Pottinger had doctored the Wikipedia pages of its clients to remove harmful content and insert positive comments."*

In the later revelations, Victoria Geoghegan, Gupta Account Director, appeared to be aware of the manipulation. She played safe and endeavoured to side-step the allegation. Geoghegan stressed that an employee of the Gupta Oakbay Company should make the changes. The following excerpt from Geoghegan's email confirms the claim. Geoghegan wrote: *"Attached is the final version of the Wikipedia content please, can we have a call at 9.15am tomorrow to brief one of your digital team on how to upload the content? We want to be transparent about the new content we are uploading, so we need to flag that it is an Oakbay employee editing the Wikipedia entry."* Somebody called *Oakbay Rep* edited the page to make the suggested changes. Bell Pottinger's Chief Executive had to apologise for this corrupt action. Under the instruction of ZUPTOID, Bell Pottinger raised unsavoury awareness of gross social inequalities. The equality disparity Pottinger coined as *economic Apartheid.* The move pertains the ultimate manifestation of meddling in politics, *Elitism.* The interference supported state capture. Or shall we call it a *Coup d'état?*

Critics like the *Democratic Alliance (DA)* likewise confirmed the deflection attention campaign from the corruption surrounding President Zuma. Bell Pottinger according to the DA *"left deep scars"* in the country's social fabric. The South African President Jacob Zuma came under new pressure to step down as President.

The Gupta's employed President Zuma's son, Duduzane to negotiate the Bell Pottinger account. President Jacob Zuma instructed that the campaign need to be: *"Along the lines of Economic-Emancipation or whatever; with a narrative that grabs the attention of the grass-roots population who must identify with it, connect with it and feel united by it".*

The ZUPTOID collusion prey on the political sensitivities of the Apartheid era. The campaign actively reflects *populism and majoritarianism* supporting dictatorial rule. Subsequently, Jacob Zuma voiced the concept of *white monopoly capital.* He blamed white wealth on being behind the calls for his resignation. Zuma promised to break up white ownership of land and business. The break-up is similar to what Robert Mugabe did in Zimbabwe. Mugabe destroyed the Zimbabwean agricultural sector with the break-up.

Senior ANC politicians repeated Zuma's sentiments as did *BFLF,* the group connected to the Guptas. The ZUPTOID smear campaign attacked politicians and journalists corroborating the Zuma-Gupta corruption. Zuma labelled politicians and journalists targeted in the assault as: *"Racists masquerading as journalists in defence of white monopoly capital."* Zuma threatened he would *deal with* those journalists and politicians. Pro-Zuma *BFLF* is synonymous with the *Mass Democratic Movement (MDM)*, and *Rhodes Must Fall (RMF)*, campaign groups. They are all set on removing colonial remnants of the West. The movements lobby to *de-white and decolonise* South Africa. Earlier, I dealt with the incidence of hate crimes on primarily white-owned farms.

As a result of the revelations, Bell Pottinger sacked Victoria Geoghegan as Account Director and suspended three others. According to follow-up news flashes, Geoghegan prepared a law-suit of unfair dismissal. Had she been hung out to dry by Bell Pottinger for the company's wrong-doings? The CEO of Bell Pottinger, James Henderson claimed that Management did not know what its employees were doing. Henderson acknowledged that; *"There has been a social media campaign that highlights the issue of economic emancipation in a way that we, having now seen it, consider being inappropriate and offensive. Senior management was misled about what was done."* Henderson in the end also had to resign. His ignorance claim seems suspect. Henderson and Lord Tim Bell procured the Gupta account.

Transparency International UK determines that directors and senior officials can face prosecution if they *turned a blind eye* to wrong-doings. The UK Bribery Act 2010, stipulates that failure by Bell Pottinger to prevent a bribery could leave the UK-based PR firm liable. Bell Pottinger knew about the corruption of the then deputy Finance Minister Mcebisi Jonas.

Two more companies headquartered in Switzerland and China stand accused of kickbacks in Trans-net contracts. Once again the Gupta-family are at the centre of the sticky web.

Bell Pottinger has denied wrongdoing and terminated its ties with Oak-bay claiming it had been the victim of a political smear campaign. Bell Pottinger's excuses did not satisfy the Democratic

Alliance (DA). The DA complained to two regulatory bodies in the UK. The DA's Phumzile van Damme reasoned that; *"If this apology were to be taken seriously, the company would fully disclose all dealings with the Gupta family and President Jacob Zuma."*

The *UK's PRCA Public Relations and Communications Association* during a disciplinary hearing found Bell Pottinger guilty as charged and terminated the company's membership with the PRCA. In an interview with *BBC Two's News-night,* Lord Bell on 4 September 2017, acknowledged that the Gupta account caused the *"flush and demise of the company. "* *BBC News* of 12 September reported that the Bell Pottinger company was put up for sale but attracted no interest, The company went into administration. The Zuptoid debacle destroyed Bell Pottinger. For three decades Bell Pottinger was the high flying PR company in Britain.

The Save South Africa campaign group said that Bell Pottinger *"sowed racial mistrust, hate and race-baiting, and divided society".* Zakes Mda, the South African novelist, commented: *"Bell Pottinger's apology is nothing but offensive spin doctoring. It's like saying: 'I'm sorry for whatever you think I did wrong.'"*

The ANC refused to comment, denying any links to Bell Pottinger. One of the first actions by President Jacob Zuma, to curtail any backlash, was to get rid of the most capable anti-corruption force in government, the *Scorpions.* The disbanding of *Scorpions* paved the way for corruption to continue unscrutinised. The hope is that perhaps, in the future, there might be a political transformation in South Africa to secure a dispensation that can uncover the real picture of what went wrong.

What happened in the Bell Pottinger racial tension and state capture campaign, represents the worst form of elitism. The Gupta family, in cahoots with President Jacob Zuma, abused their financial power and position to manipulate the politics of South Africa. They used populism and majoritarianism to introduce political change in favour of decolonisation and white removal. The manipulation is effectively a coup d'état. An attack and takeover of the state by ZUPTOID. They also used demagogues as spokespeople. The activists in association with Gupta spread their message of *state capture, de-whiting and decolonisation.*

BBC News-night of 28 October 2017 reported that according to the former South African Finance Minister Pravin Ghordin, the Zuptoid scandal had harmed South Africa tremendously. According to Pravin, the Gupta's robbed South Africa of hundreds of billions of Rands, damaging South Africa's democracy and harming the countries international credibility. Naturally, the Gupta's and Zuma denies wrongdoing.

But, according to Andrew Harding as the BBC reporter, the net is widening. He re-iterates that the British Bell Pottinger Company, hired by Zuma and the Gupta's, is already in ruin as a result of their dealings with the Gupta's.

Now it has come to light that the German software company SAP has paid multi-million dollar bribes to a Gupta-linked company. Scotland Yard and American FBI also investigate whether any of their banks or companies were involved. All of the developments are prompting some alarming questions.

The Head of Goldman Sachs South Africa, Colin Coleman, asks the question: *"Is President Jacob Zuma in control or is there a shadow system that is running appointments, procurements and whatever."* Coleman confirms that accountability in Zuma's government is entirely eroded.

According to Harding from the BBC, there is mounting international pressure on President Zuma. He states that the scandal will not go away. Even Ronnie Kasrills ex-minister of the ANC warns that Zuma and his cronies are ruining the state.

These developments evolve in the shadow of Nelson Mandela's dream of a *Rainbow Nation*. Twenty-three years after Nelson Mandela's Rainbow Nation dream, economic inequality between the races remains stark. According to the economist, Thomas

Piketty disparities increased since the end of Apartheid. Piketty confirms my findings that black South Africans earn on average about a quarter of what their white and Indian counterparts can command. Indians and whites are the imported and migrated ethnicities to Africa.

Conclusive Comments: Decolonising and De-Whiting South Africa

Imperialism and colonialism left some derogative traces in the minds of previously colonised countries. African nations are paying a high price for the legacy of the British Empire; injuries inflicted by colonists, resulted in extremists craving revenge. Terrorism and hate crimes surface as a pay-back time for the wrongs of the past. The severe colonial and slavery wounds are not something that some Africans want to forgive or forget.

Capitalism has not relinquished its exploitive capitalistic practices. New-age formats of colonisation are still ravaging developing and impoverished nations.

The West has a long way to go. It has to acknowledge the wrongs of the colonial era. The western world needs to regulate their capitalists. It is essential to maintain acceptable modern practices when establishing mining and industrial operations in developing nations. The West has a responsibility to poor and underdeveloped countries neglected for centuries. Still, in our modern age, the West does not correct their exploitive ways. Capitalism, greed and wealth exploitation is always the driving force behind colonialism. Modern-day exploitive colonisation thrives as a result of Globalisation. The wrong-doings are the same, under imperialism and globalisation.

The four-century-old colonialism is not the only motivation for terrorism. Ethnonationalism, forcing ethnic groups apart, introduces a new age Apartheid. The same unhealthy societal ills haunt society. These troubles plagued South Africa in the Apartheid years and returned in the post-Apartheid years. Reverse discrimination and hate crimes as black-on-white discrimination are rife in South Africa.

The suffering of poor African people in favour of western prosperity often serves as affordable and collateral damage for western expansionists. New-age political developments have a definite effect on South Africa.

The *ZUPTOID* state capture resurfaced the draconian head of *Elitism.* De-whiting, decolonisation and even civil war, were central to the Bel Pottinger campaign. The old wounds of Apartheid were fleshed open and damaged the South African political scene. Amazingly the expertise surfaced from Britain and not the communist East.

In Part Five, I will focus on renewed efforts to decolonise and de-white South Africa. Removing all western world symbols and remnants from South Africa. I will conclude Part Five with the question South Africa *Qou Vadis; where are we heading?*

Part Five:

SOUTH AFRICA, DECOLONISATION: THE FUTURE

Bureaucracy tends to maintain and strengthen its hold on government. The public service is like a leviathan, you can't live without it, but when introducing political reform, you encounter resistance and can hardly live with it. After democratisation, Universities continued curriculums entrenched in Western worldviews, not incorporating the African values and traditions fully. Decolonising protagonists insist that South Africa must rethink, reframe and reconstruct the curriculum, placing pre-colonial Southern Africa and African values at the core of education. Student protests supported the decolonising initiative. The *Rhodes Must Fall (RMF)* and *Black First Land First (BFLF)* activists put decolonisation and de-whiting at the centre of their struggle. To totally Africanise education, ignoring tendencies and developments of the western world will be the ultimate form of reductionism. Africa bears the century-old legacy of being nurtured within a less intelligent environment. The disparity in intelligence poses the very backlog that needs to be addressed and eliminated. The matter of African intelligence I investigated earlier. In Part Five I will examine fundamentally whether decolonisation and de-whiting of South Africa is a rational objective that will produce conditions of quality and prosperity. The decolonising protagonists identify the white population as the remnants of colonialism and imperialism. Not only universities but they also target agricultural for de-whiting and decolonising South Africa. In reality, the white community and all that it stands for is the target of decolonisation. In the final instance and based on the findings of my research I will conclude with an extrapolation on the future of South Africa. I will end Part Five, and my Biography with the question: South Africa *Quo Vadis;* where are we heading?

Part Five consists of the following chapters:

12. Decolonising and De-Whiting South Africa *331*

13. South Africa: A Way Forward *342*

CHAPTER 12

DECOLONISING AND DE-WHITING SOUTH AFRICA

R W Johnson in October 2015 published a paper on decolonisation. Johnson concludes that decolonisation is doomed to fail in South Africa. If decolonisation succeeds, it will have destructive consequences. Interesting Johnson's deliberations are not from the colonial era but the post-Apartheid era. Several news reports from the South African Communist Party (SACP) relating to decolonisation, appeared as recent as April 2017.

Decolonisation and de-whiting South Africa have moved to the forefront of South African politics. R W Johnson deals intensively with the phenomenon of decolonisation. The democratisation of South Africa happened in 1995. But still, a growing communistic inspired urge, to rid South Africa of the colonial past re-appears. The Communistic inclined ANC perceives colonisation as the *Western Capitalistic invasion*. Primarily they want to get rid of white South Africans. To the ANC the white people are seen as the remnants of Western capitalism.

Even after democratisation, the murder of white farmers in Zimbabwe and South Africa is a manifestation of *decolonisation*. This new-age political delusion of the ANC according to Johnson is a concern. South Africa effectively decolonised when it became a Union government in 1910. Question: Was South Africa's democratisation seen as a transformation or a *decolonisation* in the eyes of the SACP? Eight Southern African countries liberated, as discussed in earlier chapters. Only Zimbabwe, Angola and Mozambique decolonised. They drove whites aggressively from the state. Recently, Zimbabwe like some other decolonised African nations welcome the white people back. The very people they pushed out of the state as a form of decolonisation. The other five countries I researched, inclusive of South Africa, did not violently goad the settlers from the liberated state. That was not Mandela's Rainbow Nation dream for South Africa. Neither did Namibia decolonise or incited the whites to move out of the country.

Johnson quotes the 19th-century French politician, Alexandre Ledru-Rollin saying: *"There go the people. I am their leader, and therefore I must follow them"* Like saying *follow me, I am right behind you.* Johnson attributes this attitude to modern-day populism and demagoguery that respond to the people's disgruntlement with ruling establishments, the so-called *system.*

Johnson continues by saying *decolonisation* according to the SA Communist Party, is a *colonialism of a particular type.* The *colonists* are an identifiably separate group living within a society. This kind of segregation results in a *group* ghettoised away from what they perceive as the real *society.* Will the SACP's society be the non-white people? Wealthy and pioneer settlers are the white colonists, *the particular type?* Is the white people not part of the *nation?* Are they the Afrikaner nation? The *identifiable separate western group?*

Johnson points out that there are white settlers still living in liberalised African countries. What are they; *citizens or immigrants?* The Ivory Coast has today more white *people* than before liberation and decolonisation. The SACP is set on a *divide and rule* campaign and not bothered about nation-building. Decolonisation apparently favours disintegration over nation building.

I could not refrain from repeating this perspective in the *Los Angeles Times of 22 July 2016.* The report refers to the failed coup attempt in Turkey: *"Democracy: A train you ride until you arrive at your destination, then you step off."*

The question is; did the ANC ride the *democracy train* and arrived at the *majoritarianism station,* disembarked and governed South Africa corruptly as a dictatorship? It sure seems that way, considering Jacob Zuma's track record!

According to Johnson, the white South Africans, over one-hundred-and-fifty years had built an autonomous nation-state with its cultural parameters, capital investment, industries and economy. That is something the European colonists, Portuguese in Angola and Mozambique and the British in Zimbabwe and South Africa did not establish. The British and Portuguese are not considered African nations, they are still European settlers in Africa.

Decolonisation means the expulsion of white *settlers*, as it happened in Algeria, Kenya, Zimbabwe, Angola and Mozambique. Naturally, decolonisation boils down to ethnic cleansing and extreme racism. According to Johnson, posing decolonisation as democratisation or even non-racism is, delusional and fraudulent. It is as bad an atrocity as imperial oppression. Be it colonialism or Apartheid.

Johnson states that black job reservation in the post-Apartheid South Africa is as wrong as white Apartheid job-reservation. The ANC tolerates job-reservation in the form of blacks-only associations. They discriminate against whites and avail preferential treatment to blacks. All of this is quite flagrant and discriminatory. Is the pot calling the kettle black? South Africa democratised two decades ago. Discrimination is unacceptable.

According to Johnson decolonisation for South Africa in whatever shape or form is a total contradiction to the ANC Freedom Charter, which states that; "*South Africa belongs to all who live in it (inclusive of white people).*" The SACP however, changed *their society* to a Racial Nationalist Party. The stance of the SACP is exact Ethnonationalism. The *decolonisation* of the SACP is intent on delinking South Africa from the West and capitalism. This form of political change according to Johnson is dangerous. The South African Minister for Trade negates investment protection treaties with the West. He would rather keep agreements intact with Brazil, Russia, India and China (BRICS). The BRICS-agreements are bad for trade and investment; why would the ANC harm the country?

Johnson states that the ANC takes great comfort from the fact that China is now South Africa's biggest trading partner. Placing trust in business with China and Russia is an ideal for the ANC. Is this an apparent undertone for decolonisation? Get rid of the West. Johnson claims that when matters go wrong in South Africa blame is often put on the door of colonialism or capitalism. Blaming the West and whites when things go belly-up. Even when the Treasury have to impose austerity measures, the culprit to blame is the so-called and sinister *Third Force from the West*. The SACP and ANC prefer South Africa to reposition itself towards BRICS and move forward as a *developmental state*.

Johnson reports that *decolonisation* in itself, as propagated by this new movement, is fundamentally flawed. South Africa decolonized in 1910, and the country had been independent for more than a century. Since 1948 the complete process of decolonisation petered out when the Apartheid government severed all ties with Britain. Johnson claims any idea of further decolonisation is fraudulent. If continued, it will be detrimental to South Africa on the international and domestic level.

According to Johnson communism features heavily in the decolonisation aspirations of the SACP / ANC conspiracy. Communism displays a lousy track record. Violent disjointedness happened in Russia in 1917, Cuba in 1959 and Iran in 1979. The African liberations of the 1970's were violent. The furious and dictatorial change made it possible to infuse substantial authoritarian political control. According to Johnson, a country's position in the international order is the product of history. Economics, demography and other long-term impersonal factors remain in play. The old saying still rings true: *It is not wise to change horses mid-stream.*

Johnson states that communist inspired changes happened inclusive of violent revolutions. Something South Africa did not experience. Revolutionary decolonisation led to the new regime cutting itself free from the world. Johnson remembers that in the case of the USSR and Cuba, they held their people prisoner with no freedom of movement. The Police State cum Plutocracy had to impose cultural revolutions. Dictatorially they suppress the political opposition. Impeding free speech and restricting freedom of the press. All characteristics are still prevalent in Russia and China. According to Johnson, such re-orientations failed in the long-term. The phenomenon exemplified after over fifty years of communism. In modern times Cuba is repairing its relationship with the USA. The same seems to be true of Iran.

According to Johnson, the SACP/ANC sees decolonisation as a cultural transformation of attitudes, symbols and institutions. Get rid of all the white settlers and their symbolism. But it does not last. Portuguese ex-colonists are returning to Mozambique and Angola. Today, there are more whites in Cote d'Ivoire than before independence.

Johnson points out that South Africa was a Dutch followed by a British colony for over 250 years. Colonial relationship not only sediments within South African architecture. Names of roads and buildings, languages, institutions remain. The particular manner of customs and attitudes continue. History reinforces the Western inference in all walks of South African life. It is so deep-seated that *decolonisation* is unmanageable.

Johnson continues by saying that the colonial experience is integral to South African life. European languages, cricket, rugby, soccer, golf, parliament, trade unions, socialism and Christianity persist. He reflects on the young black demonstrators at Stellenbosch chanting *one country, one language*. They meant English, not Isi Xhosa. Nobody even suggests abolishing or replacing the Roman-Dutch law with tribal law.

Johnston elaborates his appeal further. He states that ever since unification and protection from Britain, dependency on the West has broadened organically. Even without any particular ANC political decision. He continues by saying that South Africa fought three major wars on the side of the West. Allegiance to the West reflects the importance of English. TV, radio, press, music and advertising use English. All embody the West's subtle hold on South Africa. Johnson recaps that we drive on the left, as in Britain. Measurements, standards, certification of skills and professions, all have their roots within Western norms and origin. South African supermarkets, shops, banks and financial institutions are all based on Anglo-American models. South African companies have branches and even headquarters in Britain. Top lawyers have practices in both countries. Historically our top enterprises hire expertise from the Anglosphere. Even ZUTOID hired a British PR company to do its dirty work.

According to Johnson, culturally, South Africa is entrenched in the Anglo-American mould. Under ANC rule English strengthened substantially, signifying that the country is bound to be English speaking. Embedding South Africa even deeper into the Anglo-American culture.

South African students prefer Britain and America for further education. Even as a preference for work experience. South African expatriates gravitate to the UK, US, Canada, Australia, New Zealand and Israel. With a further sprinkling in the United Arab Emirates. All part of the Anglosphere. English books are still central to education. All these manifestations reflect an allegiance that originates from Britain.

According to Johnson, ANC-rule did not change any of the allegiances prevalent before democratisation. Even the centres of ANC exiles, London and Lusaka, were English-speaking. Both Commonwealth countries. The ANC-ruled Durban Council is thrilled to be hosting the Commonwealth Games for 2022; as pleased as they were, hosting the 1999 Commonwealth Heads of Government meeting in Durban. ANC allegiance to Britain remains intact. The British Queen's 1995 visit enthralled the ANC. The SACP cabinet ministers revelled aboard the Royal Yacht Britannia. Johnson refers to the enigma that Verwoerd could not wait to break the colonial ties with Britain and the Commonwealth. The ANC took the country right back into the Commonwealth in 1994; a move that is highly unlikely to change. Commonwealth countries encircle South Africa. Namibia, Swaziland, Lesotho, Botswana, Mauritius, Zambia and Malawi are all commonwealth countries. Even when and despite Mugabe's bluster, Zimbabwe will probably end up back in the Commonwealth.

Johnson remembers ANC officials visiting Durban used the old names, Smith Street, West Street, Stanger Street. Instead of the new denominations celebrating ANC heroes. Any attempt at de-linking and re-centering on communist oriented BRICS will fail. South Africa's allegiance to the Anglosphere is deeply ingrained.

Johnson refers to the introduction of Mandarin to the school's curriculum as a stupid policy. His comment is: *"Well, good luck with that. The private schools might have a chance of success, but schools in Soweto or Thembisa might not find this enticing."*

Johnson states, delinking, within *decolonisation* and courting BRICS is probably a pipe-dream. If decolonisation is to be imposed heavy-handedly, with an authoritarian approach, it will tear the country apart. It will be unaffordable. Decolonisation is bound to fail. Johnson is very critical when it comes to the BRICS allegiance. The ANC government pursue BRICS enthusiastically. But, South Africa is the supplicant in the relationship, playing the role of underdog. He points out that China is destroying the local textile and steel industries. South Africa allows China to build a vast trade surplus with South Africa. In 2014, South Africa showed a negative trade balance amounting to $6.7bn.

South Africa allows large-scale illegal Chinese immigration. Twenty-two Johannesburg shopping malls are Chinese owned. Fantastically, the country gives privileges to the Chinese under the Black Economic Empowerment policy. China promised advice and training. They also assisted Dr Iqbal Survé, Executive Chairman, born and educated in Cape Town, to buy Independent Newspapers.

China pledged to provide Mandarin teachers and schools to South Africa. China advises South Africa on State Owned Enterprise. The SOE system described by the Financial Times as *China's inefficient and debt-ridden state-owned enterprises*. Once again, why does the ANC hurt the South African economy?

Johnson explains that the situation with Russia is even worse. The total trade has yet to surpass $1bn. Russia meddled in Africa for 20 years with liberation struggles. Along with the West, Communism and Capitalism used Africa as a political playground. The West even involved the Apartheid government.

The Apartheid era hosted four university departments with Russian studies. Today there are none. The intense interest of the 1980s evaporated. Once again, South Africa is the supplicant.

Putin visited Russia once. Zuma undertook countless trips to Moscow, worried that one of his wives was poisoning him. He visited Moscow for medical treatment. Apparently, the Russians are critical to Zuma staying alive and in power. Russia has a reputation for supporting Africa only for its selfish, narcissistic advantage. Johnson refers to the ongoing talks of a R1-trillion nuclear contract with Russia without any progress. He evaluates the relationship with China and Russia as highly disproportionate. Johnson concludes, stating that South Africa may grant both countries *most favoured nation* status. But, South Africa can never be of importance to either. China and Russia are bound to value their relations with the United States of America much higher Germany, Japan, Britain, France, South Korea along with the BRICS countries are of greater importance to Russia than South Africa.

The South African mining, manufacturing and agriculture sectors are in retreat; confirming the disproportion and negative trade relations.

Only the tourist industry experience growth. Being an attraction industry, labour intensive with job creation for all races, it is not dependent on communism. Tourism is less oligopolistic and with an enormous future growth potential. Analysis of the tourism sector, according to Johnson is complicated. The vast number of visitors from the impoverished South African Development Community (SADC) from the north African region do not contribute. Over 5.5m visited South Africa in 2010. They usually come to shop or work rather than spend money. Statistics from the West are impressive and high. 338,000 from North America, 120,000 from Central and South America and 128,000 from Australasia. Western arrivals are relatively wealthy and provided the bulk of income to the tourist industry. Russia and China accounted for insignificant numbers of visitors.

The foreign investment statistics from the West, according to Johnson are impressive. 1.33 Million originating from Europe, with Britain top, Germany 3rd, France 5th and Italy 7th. Johnson also refers to Industry and Tourism of South Africa. He proclaims that it is dependent on a steady inflow of Foreign Direct Investment (FDI). 10 to 12% of GDP is needed to pay for trade- and fiscal deficits. Almost exclusively procured from Western countries. An insignificant amount of FDI comes from Russia or China. According to Johnson re-orientation of South Africa away from the West is futile. It is likely to fail.

Communistic states retreated to an authoritarian world and Junta states. South Africa is still a democracy. Still open to the world. South African liberation tainted by the ANC one-party dictatorial government. Johnston suggests that South Arica should rather look at Canada, Australia or the USA. They are all ex-colonies of the expansionist era. They aligned themselves organically and successfully on the international stage. In the long run that is a sensible change for a developing country like South Africa.

When touching on Universities Johnson says that *decolonisation* will do extensive damage. They are the institutions on the front line when it comes to decolonisation. The top four universities in Africa is from South Africa; all built on the British model. The decolonisation attempts in South Africa, are depressing. Present-day symptoms of revenge pose a severe problem. Specifically for white South Africans.

Black Student Movements pursuing decolonisation developed within South African Universities. They gathered momentum very quickly in recent times. It started with Chumani Maxwele throwing human faeces onto the statue of Cecil John Rhodes at the University of Cape Town (UCT). A month later the statue of Cecil John Rhodes was removed. A sister movement *Open Stellenbosch* established and produced the *Luister document, (Afrikaans for Listen)*. Amazing how the English Afrikaans language dominates the struggle continuation. It reflected on the derogatory experience of black students on the Stellenbosch campus. Simultaneously the *Black Student Movement (BSM)* received support from students at Wits, UCT, and Fort Hare. *Reform-PUK* strengthened support at North-West University. The *Wits-Fees-Must-Fall* ignited a movement backed by several universities.

Decolonisation at university level aims at dismantling the western imperialism influence and legacy. Western institutions, systems, symbolism, and standards in the higher education want removal.

Steve Biko discussed the ideas of liberation, decolonisation, pride and black consciousness. He refers to an inferior status given to Africans. A state of *denigration and derision* under Apartheid. Biko identified two stages in the *Black Conscious Movement's Psychological Liberation* a positive change in mindset and *Physical Liberation* removing the physical remnants of colonization. Biko claimed that: *"We (blacks) cannot be conscious of ourselves and yet remain in bondage. We want to attain the envisioned self, which is a free person."*

The KwaZulu-Natal University (UKZN), was forced down the road of *decolonisation*. Decolonisation resulted in the flight of students and faculty. Administrative chaos ensued, and benefactors and donors disappeared. That ruined UKZN and left it bankrupt. The same fate is awaiting the four top universities should they give way to the likes of the *Rhodes Must Fall group (RMF)* and *Black First Land First (BFLF)*.

Africa has a history of wrecks of once-good-universities. The University College of Rhodesia, Makerere, Ibadan, Algiers and Kinshasa are grave examples. Universities are easy to destroy, very hard to revive. The loss of educational institutions is wrong for any country. It robs them of opportunities and growth.

According to Johnson, the era of *decolonisation* will without doubt pass. But there will be severe collateral damage?

Conclusive Comments on Decolonisation

The legacy of Imperialism causes a revenge vendetta in South Africa. Decolonisation has emerged prominently on university campuses. The extreme measures taken on university campuses derives from colonial retribution, targeting Cecil John Rhodes' legacy as a colonist. It is doubtful whether this secondary stage of decolonisation contributes to a better society. Burning down and disrupting student facilities are contra productive. It amounts to the very dilemma that South Africa is facing. A psychosis of societal distrust, disenfranchisement and fear increasingly grips the nation.

Historical colonialism and all it entails is part of Africa. It can not be erased or ignored. Not all of it was wrong and can be forgotten. Sure, we need to consider the mistakes. But, *don't throw the baby out with the dirty water*.

Some good came from the Imperial expansion and Western invasion. Learn from the errors of the past. But importantly, retain the excellence from the past. Build a better future for all.

Capitalism and exploitation started in the fifteenth century. But, it did not end with decolonisation as a Union or democratisation in 1995. The ANC government controlled by communism in 2017 embarked on a new-age decolonisation voyage.

The following chapter will deal with the way forward. South Africa Quo Vadis.

Chapter 13

South Africa: A Way Forward

South Africa Quo Vadis: Where are we Heading?

Cape Town often named as the most beautiful city in the world is truthful. The growing tourism industry reinforces this worthy accolade. There is nothing wrong with the country. Every province, city, town and rural area contribute to the magnificence of the country. The problem lies with the Communist-inclined ANC government.

The ANC followed onto the racist Apartheid government. Both regimes let the country down. After almost a quarter-of-a-century in power, the ANC can no longer blame Apartheid or colonisation. Or for that matter the *phantom third force from the West.*

Almost a quarter century of ANC rule and governance is lacking. Surely twenty-two years is ample time to show some progress. Apartheid South Africa had severe political shortcomings. But, economically it was never a failed state. At least the Coloureds and Africans were better off. They maintained a higher standard of living.

Is South Africa's Rainbow Nation Repairable?

The prognosis set out above seems dire, is it that bad? Do I come to this conclusion unsubstantiated and without reason? No, the terrible situation reverberates in the news media. According to Bulelani Mfaco: *"South Africa burns. Something has gone wrong with the vision of a new South Africa if black people can set alight buildings that are meant to serve them. Society is wrong."*

Max du Preez seems to think South Africa can survive, there is hope, but he has doubts; *"Zuma's opponents have smelled blood, and this will test our patience. Should the ANC have had a bloody revolution? The banana republic cum failed state, another Zimbabwe or an Arab Spring-type revolution. Perhaps we should just slit our wrists before the year is out."* Du Preez corrects himself saying, *"What nonsense"* stating that his condition for survival is to get rid of the psychosis of fear and mistrust, or as he puts it: *"The paralysing, dark pessimism."* Du Preez trusts the ability of the South African people. He believes they will weather the storm.

South Africans lost hope of a better future according to the Democratic Alliance (DA) leader Mmusi Maimane as the official opposition. Maimane states that people are disillusioned. They will not register to vote in the next election. He might be wrong. The 2016 municipal elections predict a likely shift away from ANC domination. It might just be that the next general election will result in change. The country seems to make progress towards a healthy opposition as a counter to the ruling ANC. The DA made gains at the expense of the ANC, some of the larger cities came under DA rule.

The Economist: Cry, the Beloved Country

The *Economist* points out that Apartheid South Africa produced a Gross Domestic Product (GDP) equal to 40% of that of 48 countries south of the Sahara. South Africa had an opportunity to transform into a sound state after the transition to democracy in 1994. But, the Economist, labels South Africa as *"The hopelessly failed state."* The growth rate dropped from 6 to 2%. Foreign debt downgraded to a Baa2-rating, recently to *junk status*. Education standards lowered to 132nd out of 144 countries. Almost half of the country's under 25 year-olds are unemployed. All the indicators maintain pessimisms, projecting a calamitous and unwelcome future perspective. One gets utterly despondent looking at the news media reports on South Africa. Reports are all bad news, expecting terrible prospects for South Africa. Even where hopeful stories surface, it is a case of wishful thinking. The projections always have a precondition before the situation improves, claiming that:

- If the balance of power shifts and a stronger opposition surfaces, then it will restore growth.

- If we can curtail the President's usurpation of power, then the political dispensation could balance out.

- If the administration is held to account, then things will improve.

- And, if corruption reduces, the government could be purified and corrected.

The future of South Africa seems *to be* a *maybe. If this happens then perchance, it will* improve.

Skills migration and the brain drain of South Africa

The *Brain-drain* along with the ANC Government's maladministration and corruption is the leading causes of South Africa's downfall. To lose highly skilled citizens, need to be a grave concern for any developing country. Consider the cost of procuring skilled labour in the medical community. It cost close to R 250 000 (£ 15 000 at an exchange rate of R17 to the £) to train a physician in South Africa. According to the British Medical Association, the cost for Britain is £ 540 000. According to CBS News, the charge in the USA amounts to $166 750. What a bargain to poach a doctor from South Africa at a fraction of the training cost. All paid for by the South African economy. What a deal and a steal for the West to poach medical staff from South Africa. Or, what a loss to South Africa when a doctor finds the living conditions in South Africa unbearable. Close to one million relocated since democratisation. They moved to one of the western world states for a better life since democratisation. Instead of serving the South African economy they are adding value to western industrialised countries.

The actual extent of the skills loss due to migration holds a significant underestimation according to the Human Research Council of South Africa. Political upheaval is the driving force behind the exodus of professionals. Recently the motivation for emigration was ascribed to:

- Increased crime, deteriorating public sector conditions and lowering of the standards of living.
- More lucrative salaries and working conditions in other countries.
- South Africa's adverse currency exchange rate.

These are high incentives for skills migration. Over half of the skills migration are economically active. More than two-thousand of them are in professions like engineering, medicine and teaching. The real cost of losing skilled labour is enormous when one considers that a million white population left the country. Most of them highly qualified and in the prime of their working life.

One of the so-*called unpatriotic dese*rters is Ms Elise Hugo. She migrated to Canada with her young son and civil engineer husband. She *said: "I can finally sleep easy with the back door open at ni*ght." Can you blame her? The most significant challenge for the South African Government, is to turn the country into a developed country. Retain highly skilled professionals. That will uplift South Africa from a failed state to a developed country.

I investigated the reduction of whites in South Africa earlier. At this rate, the number of whites might decrease to a fraction of a percentage point. Or, even strip the country of white intelligence.

Will saving South Africa from a failed state require improvement of safety and security and improved delivery of services? Will it require the development of sound policy to attract the highly skilled from other parts of the world? Will it need responsive and accountable governance to allow highly skilled workers to move to South Africa?

Yes! If South Africa's government want to succeed, it will have to provide a safe and prosperous environment, responsive and accountable to the nation. It is a dire situation requiring drastic measures.

Winning the Hearts and Minds of South Africans

Sun Tsu declares: *"If you know the enemy and know yourself, you need not fear the result of a hundred battles. If you know yourself but not the enemy, for every victory gained, you will also suffer a defeat."*

It is strange quoting a typical war strategy to address peace and prosperity. In times of war, we consider invading forces, with disillusion, distrust, disrespect and disenchantment. Does that sound familiar? South Africa fits the bill. We ascertained that already! I can almost verbally apply Sun Tzu's words: *'If you, the ANC-government, know yourself but not the nation (enemy), then for every victory, corruption and mismanagement gained, you the ANC-government, will suffer a defeat in the form of demonstrations, destruction and civil disorder'.*

That is conclusively a description of the hearts and minds of the people of South Africa. We turned into a country of disillusion, distrust, disrespect and disenchantment. Did the situation in South Africa deteriorate that badly?

Is it a far-fetched metaphor even to think let alone verbalise? Is it possible that the government can become the enemy of the nation? We came full circle, from Apartheid as the oppressive enemy to the *ANC government as a corrupt maladministration.* An ANC adversary, an enemy to the country.

How to address the problems, pose a myriad of obstacles. Not an easy task. An initiative on a national scale that addresses the shortcomings might be the obvious solution. But, every single ethnic group can have different expectations with real and diverse perspectives. Problems not solved, will reduce any initiative to failure and drive the situation back into Ethnonationalism and segregation. Any scheme of restitution needs to have the respect and acceptance on all tiers of the South African society, formal and informal. From the President inclusive of the lowest grass-roots level.

346

The Apartheid government used the civil defence initiative in much the same manner. Through a program of co-optation and information management, towards a state of preparedness and safety. They involved the white population primarily, to retain a minority rule. It failed because it was not transparently democratic. The program did not reflect the will of the entire nation. The government must take the people along with any policy of the state. If they do not, they will fail.

The aim of a process, rectifying the wrongs within the South African society, will be to protect all citizens. To make them safe and to restore trust in the future.

May just be that there is something positive to learn from Apartheid civil defence, as a process, program and mechanism. The answer lies in addressing the distrust, fear and discontentment within a corporate programme that reflects the will of the people and maintains full democracy.

The Priorities that need Serious Attention

Priorities that need addressing are fundamental. It should start at the top. The pinnacle of government, the State President. It needs to work its way down applying these priorities throughout the public and the private sector. It should start and end with South African citizens. The electorate does not elect politicians so they can enrich themselves. Chosen as servants of the people, politicians should serve diligently.

• *Base political justification* on character, integrity and allegiance instead of skin colour and hatred from the past.

• *Restore, respect and trust in the Rule of* Law. Nobody should be above the law. The government in its entirety should set the example. Equality and fairness maintained for all, unprejudiced. Violations must transparently be brought to justice and punished. Set an example and voice the message – *nobody is above the law.*

- *Comply and maintain the core principles of democracy.* Demos implies the people and Kratos power: Democracy. The political power rests with the citizens. Politicians are the servants of society. Politicians are just representing the will of the citizens. Insist in all walks of public life on the principle of open accountabi*lity*.

- *Restore and respect the trust in the Judicia*l System. Recog*nise the Triage P*olitica, separation of powe*rs. The politica*l forces make th*e laws, administrative bur*eaucracy manage policy *and the j*udiciary, review and hold all to account. The divisions within government should function independently and free from interference by polit*icians.*

- *Prevent the usurpation and concentratio*n of power. Provide for checks and balances to hold all accountable for their *actions.*

- *Provide for the basic needs of the* whole nation. Secure fundamental human rights for every individual. Ensure access to food, water, shelter clothing, proper sanitation, education, and healthcare for all. Strive to get the majority of citizens above the poverty threshold.

The above are the essentials. Only once they are met and sustained, will it be possible to restore the trust of the nation in the public sector. When confidence in the government returns, it will make life bearable. The government can then work on the economy and the growth rate of the country. The conditions set out above are the foundation of a healthy society. Applied correctly it will serve as a starting point towards a new democratic and responsible society. South Africa needs dedication, setting high standards, and strive towards restoration. Impart excellent and fair governance.

But as I prepare my manuscript for publ*ication the Huffington Post of 15 Se*ptember 2017, has got exciting news. In 2016, the North Gauteng High Court decided to proceed with corruption charges against President Jacob Zuma. Previously it covered up claiming that it was illegal and irrational; no case will render a verdict.

Now the president is seeking leave to appeal against the ruling because the *National Prosecution Agency* ruled that Zuma must answer to the charges.

Zuma is in the position of being prosecuted for this criminality. Should he succeeded in his appeal, he will not be prosecuted at all.

The question on everyone's mind in South Africa is: are we at a point where Zuma has to face his charges? What is certain, South Africa is in for real drama. Zimbabwe and the removal of Mugabe gives hope to South Africa. As one person satirized: *"The South Africans prayed for Zuma to be removed but then the prayers were answered in Zimbabwe."*

Conclusive Comments on the Future of South Africa

Western countries like America, Canada, Australia and New Zealand, are today governed as white man's land. They moved on and became formal Western countries. *Successful* colonialism by the West happened elsewhere in the world, not in Southern Africa. There is a difference between Southern Africa's decolonisation and ex-colonies elsewhere in the world. The eight countries I considered in Southern Africa, reverted to be ruled by its original natives, the black-skinned majority. They are not European and Western colonies anymore. The concern for South Africa is *decolonisation threats, de-whiting and the cross colour black-on-white hate crimes.*

South Africa needs a turn-around plan. Make people of all ethnicities and skin tones welcome in South Africa. It is wrong to make some ethnicities, like the white people, feel unsafe and unwanted in their country of birth.

A continuous exodus of well qualified and established professionals is dangerous; it cannot be afforded or tolerated. One can easily say *let the white professionals go*. But, they are skilled and shape the real intellectual core to the country. The bulk of them is in the most productive years of their lives. They can make valuable contributions to a knowledgeable environment. Developing nations like South Africa need a creative and intelligent environment to grow and prosper. Africa has suffered centuries of intelligence backlog. To isolate, de-white and decolonise the whites from the country is a massive failure for the future of South Africa. The intellectual advance of whites is an asset to South Africa. Not to be flaunted or ignored. The brain drain consists of the upper echelon of intelligence and also the young, up and coming individuals. It will require concerted efforts for restitution, on both sides of the colour spectrum. It is time to set the disparities right with an excellent education and a creative environment that will benefit the South African nation as a whole.

The worth of the white South Africans is undeniable. The white migration of Europeans transformed South Africa into a powerhouse in Africa with advanced knowledge. The exploited labour, people of colour, need to be acknowledged for its part played in the success. Without their input, none of the industries would have functioned. The growth would not have been possible.

The country cannot afford the loss already incurred. The script is on the wall, and the proof is already prevalent! Apart from the *Brain-drain*, there is also the financial cost of training that goes to waste. The Western Industrial nations are reaping the benefits, at the peril of South Africa.

Under Apartheid, there was an economic success. It should be retained and used to shape a new South Africa. It is unthinkable that, what even people like Peter Hain describe as the *cleanest development in the world,* need to be destroyed and obliterated in decolonisation efforts.

South African history is what it is, it cannot be erased or cognitively ignored. Do not tolerate the destruction of South Africa. Take the good from the past, get rid of the evils and build South Africa's future on the best foundation possible. Do not try to carve South Africa's future from the imperial gravestones of the past. Do not look to the future through a tunnel vision of colonial hatred based on grievances. Replace hatred and retribution with hope and reconciliation.

Base the political will on character and allegiance to South Africa as a country and a unified nation. Heed the words of Libby Lane the first woman Bishop in the UK; *"Driven by fear our lives spin out of control, what we need is hope, hope that nurtures our lives enabling society to believe in the future."*

So, the way forward:

• Define a sound and workable plan as an all-encompassing corporate management programme.

• Address the wrongs of society and deploy the program on every level of the nation, from the President, through the public and private sector, right down to the grassroots level.

• Implement the program nationwide, supported and honoured by the government and the whole country.

Maybe, Jacob Zuma is at the end of his corruption tether. Perhaps the Law will catch up with him. Just Ma*ybe*?

OR

JUST SIT BACK AND ACCEPT FAILURE. C'est La Vie! That's life, let it be. SOUTH AFRICA IS A FAILED STATE. ANOTHER AFRICAN FIASCO! **WHATEVER!**

EPILOGUE: SOUTH AFRICA TODAY IN TURMOIL:

Demonstrations, Riots. April 2017: Violent demonstration by students protesting. Millions of Rands lost to demonstrating factions destroying institutional buildings and facilities.

February 2017; Time Magazine Cover: President Jacob Zuma Corrupt: A Fraud who cannot read or count: Five wives, 20+ children and he shagged his best friend's daughter. The dickhead who sold his country to the wealthy Indian Gupta family in a *STATE CAPTURE. More damaging to South Africa than Apartheid Verwoerd?*

Mass Anti-Zuptoid, the Zuptoid Protests: Zuma in cahoots with the Indian family Gupta and British PR firm; a state capture. Bribe-selling the nation out to the wealthy *Elite*. But, There is hope the *National Protection Authority* has after years of covering for Zuma decided to prosecute on his notorious '783' charges against him. Zuma will stand trial; at last, justice might prevail!!

IMAGE: With full accreditation to BIZNEWS, the article: "OUTA lays treason, racketeering charges against Duduzane Zuma, Guptas" on August 3 2017.

Mandela's Vision for South Africa Wasted. *A full 27 years of jail for Madiba –22 years for Zuma to mess it all up.* Instead of a Rainbow Nation, we have a *Failed State* with a *junk credit rating*. South Africa, is in a state of fear, distrust, disillusion and disenfranchisement.

ACKNOWLEDGEMENTS

Expansionists, Colonists, Philanthropists and Criminals

Ever since the first European set foot on African soil, there were criminals and kind people, heroes and vagabonds. They shaped South Africa over three and a half centuries. They are the criminals and the crooks. As history unfolded, some were great. Some were evil. The imperialists, colonists, settlers, oppressors and exploiters.

On the flip side of the coin, South Africa is indebted to the philanthropists and the do-gooders. All of them, I have to acknowledge. If they did not come to Africa in the imperial era, my book would not have happened. They imposed their will on the indigenous natives of South Africa. On the other hand, if colonisation did not occur, the Khoikhoi, might still live their tribal ways. I would not have been in Africa. History is not something that you can change. It is axiomatic and set in stone. I am proud to be an African, Afrikaner and Euro-African.

Most importantly, I acknowledge the born-free generations of all ethnicities in South Africa. They should not be culpable for the sins of the fathers.

The Internet and Publishers of Resources

I pay tribute and acknowledge the creators of the world-wide-web, the internet. They established a forum for information exchange second to none. I used it extensively. The publishers of papers, articles and books, I have to acknowledge as the source of my research. Without them, my biography will be dead in the water. I referenced them extensively at the end of my book and within the text.

My Family

It was not my choice to be in this world. You decided for me. You made me part of this beautiful world and specifically South Africa. You enriched and cursed my life in so many ways, passing down the *sins of the fathers*. But, thankfully, you provided me with a rich cultural inheritance. I acknowledge and respect your contributions. I still experience an enjoyable life. I revel in writing about the past in my somewhat critical perspective. Where you as my forebears did go wrong, it was not in malice. Your actions were in good faith and the will to survive. You only did what you believed was right.

Thanks to my wife Melanie and my son Handré for their support and patience that created and sustained an active and inspired environment for me to write in. I know you might have felt that I entered into a *writers affair*, intrusive to family life. I love you for your support and endurance.

Melanie, you have a way of saving me from myself. I know I will always be safe. When I go wrong, you have such a lovely way of putting me right. I do sometimes get a bit OTT. Thanks for reading and bettering me and my book.

Handré I value your comments and critical approach to my writings and ramblings. You always bring me back on track with your excellent English. Thanks for critting my book. You made it superior to what it was.

To my friends and crit-readers, I am ever so grateful for your time and effort.

- Jenny Newberry
- Anne Atkinson
- Anne de Waal
- Sandra Malan

I know your better halves also made contributions. I acknowledge the composite contributions. Your feedback I value, it inspired me and contributed to the final product.

Spiderwize: My Publisher and Promotional Agents

I realise that you are business partners. But my book success is not possible without you. Thank you and let's make it happen. I value and respect the vital role you play in putting my biography out there.

My Final Comment

Do not treat my book as a research document. It is not that. I publish my Biography as my life perspective on Apartheid. Where I formulate conclusions and recommendations, they are my convictions and only mine. I do base my deliberations on published papers and books that I reference. But once again, they only reflect my perceptions. I do not profess my viewpoints, as the be all and end all. The events and phenomena I touch on are real and recent. I sincerely hope you will find the contents relevant to life in the 21st century and pertinent to your life.

THE AUTHOR - JAN CRONJE

Born in April 1945, I was too young to know about the 2nd World War. The Germans surrendered on 7 May 1945. When I celebrated my third birthday, the Afrikaner Apartheid Government came to power. When I turned seventeen, Apartheid imprisoned Mandela for treason. They jailed him for twenty-seven years. Throughout my formative years, my family supported the Apartheid Government. At the age of sixteen, South Africa became a Republic. Harold Mac Millan warned, Britain could not support the South African racial policies. In the same year, the South African Police killed sixty-nine black demonstrators in the Sharpeville massacre. At eighteen I became a soldier in the South African Defence Force, under the conscription campaign to defend South Africa in a border war, fighting the liberation Terrorists. When I turned twenty-nine, I became one of the first Civil Defence Officers in South Africa, to protect the white people of South Africa. The only enemy was the so-called black terrorism onslaught. At the age of forty, I studied International Politics researching liberation movements and dictatorial governments, especially oppression worldwide. At the age of forty-five, the Apartheid government freed Nelson Mandela from Polls Moore prison. I lived half an hour's drive from Polls Moore Prison. When I turned forty-six in 1992, I published my Master's Degree Thesis. I criticised the Apartheid Civil Defence and acknowledged the Terrorist Movement's civil defence successes. When I turned forty-nine, after twenty-two years of service, the Apartheid regime underhandedly blacklisted me for exposing their failure. Shortly after early retirement at age forty-nine, South Africa democratised. I was jobless. My thank-you after 22 years' service. I entered the private sector to sustain my family. For half a century I lived through Apartheid. For additional twenty-two years, I experienced Post-Apartheid South Africa under the African National Congress Government. They are governing South Africa to a failed state. After seven decades I decided to write my book: *Apartheid: The Blame, Past and Present*

Feel welcome to visit my Website www.apartheidandme.com

You are welcome to leave a comment, share a thought or even submit some personal experiences related to the contents of my book.

References & Resources

Chapter 1 and 2 as well as pages 3 and 4

https://en. wikipedia. org/wiki/History_of_Botswana#

http://spartacus-educational. com/

http://www. britishempire. co. uk/

https://en. wikipedia. org/wiki/British_Empire

http://www. sahistory. org. za/people-south-africa/

http://abolition. e2bn. org/slavery_45. html

https://en. wikipedia. org/wiki/National_WomenMonument

http://www. sahistory. org. za/topic/concentration-camps

http://cronierwines. com. my/our-story. html

http://www. telegraph. co. uk/news/ Tutu

https://africacheck. org/reports/

http://www. bbc. co. uk/history/british/victorians/boer_wars

http://www. sahistory. org. za/people/cecil-john-rhodes

http://www. britannica. com/biography/Cecil-Rhodes

http://spartacus-educational. com/FWWinBritain. htm

http://www. christianity. com/church/history/huguenots

http://www. britishempire. co. uk/maproom/capecolony. htm

http://www. avclub. com/article/new-web-series-highlights

http://news. bbc. co. uk/local/cornwall/hi/people_and_places/

https://v1. sahistory. org. za/index. html

http://www. rfc-rnas-raf-register. org. uk

http://www. thebirdman. org/InhumaneBoerWarConcentration

http://www. sahistory-. org. za/topic/women-children-.

https://en. wikipedia. org/wiki/-Herbert_Kitchener'

http://aboutworldlanguages. com/afrikaans

http://www. sahistory. org. za
http://www. sahistory. org. za/people/cecil-john-rhodes
https://en. wikipedia. org/wiki/Prynnsberg_Estate

Books:

Kamp Hoer: Author: Francois Smith
Of Warriors Lovers and Prophets: Max du Preez

Chapter 3

http://www. sahistory. org. za/topic/national-party-np
http://africanhistory. about. com
https://www. nelsonmandela. org/
http://spitfirelist. com/
https://en. wikipedia. org/wiki/List_of_terrorist_incidents
http://https://www. cuba-solidarity. org. uk/news/
http://www. sahistory. org. za/topic/national-party-np
http://www. sahistory. org. za/article/state-policies-and-social-
protest http://africanhistory. about. com/Ossewabrandwag. htm
http://www. sahistory. org. za/topic/national-party-np
https://en. wikipedia. org/wiki/Arthur_Goldreich
http://www. german-foreign-policy. com/
https://en. wikipedia. org/wiki/Genocide_of_
indigenous_peoples
http://www. nr. edu/chalmeta/151/Mth_151_
Section_5. 1_notes
http://samilitaryhistory. org/lectures/aftermath. html
https://en. wikipedia. org/wiki/Wind_of_Change_ (speech)
http://conservativepapers. com/news/2015/12/24/israel

Chapter 4 and 5

http://scholar. sun. ac. za/Johannes Andreas Cronje

https://www. nelsonmandela. org/ https://www2. warwick. ac. uk/fac/soc/pais/people/

http://www. disaster. co. za/

http://www. sahistory. org. za/topic/state-emergency

https://en. wikipedia. org/wiki/Uri_Davis

https://www. theguardian. com/news/2006/nov/southafrica

http://www. independent. co. uk/lifestyle/southafrica

http://www. news. com. au/finance/economy/

https://blogs. spectator. co. uk/2017/02/rhodes-must-fall-

https://en. wikipedia. org/wiki/South_-African_farm_attack

http://www. raptureready. com/2017/03/12/white-genocide

https://newamerican. com

http://www. walesonline. co. uk/news/politics/anti-apartheid

Chapter 6

http://listenmusicfm. net/track/Fanie-En-Jabulani

http://www. businessinsider. com/life-during-apartheid

http://www. theinitialjourney. com/life-in-apartheid-

http://www. sahistory. org. za/article/land-labour-

http://overcomingapartheid. msu. edu/multimedia

http://newlearningonline. com/apartheid-education.

http://www. rugby15. co. za/shosholoza-the-south-african-rugby

http://www. sahistory. org. za/sa-prime-minister-verwoerd http://www. nr. edu/chalmeta/151/Mth_151

https://stiffkitten. wordpress. com/2010/08/1/pre-colonial-africa/

https://theinitialjourney. com

Chapter 7

http://newafricanmagazine. com/mozambique

https://en. wikipedia. org/wiki/Cecil_Rhodes#Rhodesia

https://en. wikipedia. org/wiki/Ian_Smith

http://www. historyworld. net/

http://thecommonwealth. org/our-member-countries/lesotho/

http://thecommonwealth. org/our-member-countries/
swaziland/

http://peoplesworld. org/today-in-history-mozambique

https://qz. com/458137/mugabe-is-asking-back-the-white/

http://www. sahistory. org. za/people/cecil-john-rhodes

Chapter 8

http://discoveringbristol. org. uk

http://allafrica. com

http://www. bbc. co. uk/-news/world-africa-34580862

http://-www. bbc. co. uk/news/world-africa-34580862

http://www. npiamerica. org/research/racial-differences

https://africacheck. org/2015/03/12/black-brain-white-brain

http://www. oxforddictionaries. com/lingua-franca

http://www. merriam-webster. com/dictionary/Bantu

http://www. localhistories. org/aftime. html

https://en. wikipedia. org/wiki/HistoryAfricaSouthern_Africa

http://allafrica. com/stories/200710250639. html

http://www. nytimes. com/books/first/j/jencks-gap. html

http://dailystormer. com/how-is-it-possible-that-africans/

https://en. wikipedia. org/Watson#Controversial_comments

http://www. independent. co. uk/news/science/africans-are-less

https://en. wikipedia. org/wiki/Vereeniging#History

https://thelife. com/if-you-want-peace-prepare-for-war
http://www. npiamerica. org/racial-differences-in-intelligence
https://africacheck. org/2015/03/12/analysis-black-brain-white

Books

Guns, Germs, and Steel: The Fates of Human Societies by Jared Diamond. Originally published: 1997 ISBN: 0-393-03891-2

Chapter 9

https://www. uct. ac. za/dailynews/? id=9004
http://www. news24. com/SouthAfrica-/
Newsstudentauditorium
https://www. telegraph. co. uk
https://www. bbc. co. uk/news/world-africa
http://www. telegraph. co. uk
http://www. telegraph. co. uk
http://fin24. com/economy/nine-corruption-scandals
http://www. moneyweb. co. za
http://moneyweb. co. za/news
http://researchspace. ukzn. ac. za
http://citizen. co. za/news/news
http://businesstech. co. za
http://fin24. com/Econom
http://mg. co. za/article
http://dailymaverick. co. za
http://opensecrets. org. za
https://politicsweb. co. za
https://pressreader. com/south-africa/business-day
https://files. ethz. ch/isn/123917/2006_05_29. pdf
https://files. ethz. ch/isn/-123917/2006_05_29. pdf

https://independent. co. uk/news/world/africa

https://welections. wordpress. com/guide-to-the-2014

https://en. wikipedia. org/wiki/Ethnic_South_Africa

https://africacheck. org/2014/09/17/crime-and-violence

https://wikipedia. org/wiki/Sexual_violence_South_Africa

http://businesstech. co. za/news/general/corruption

http://businesstech. co. za/news/wealth/zuma-pay-back

http://www. bdlive. co. za/opinion/2013/08/22/apartheid

http://www. uct. ac. za/dailynews/? id=9004

http://www. bbc. com/news/world-africa-36997461

http://www. bbc. co. uk/news/world-africa-37655939

http://www. telegraph. co. uk/news/2016/04/29/Jacob_zuma

http://www. politicalsciencedegree. com/political-systems

Books:

Into The Cannibal's Pot: Lessons for America from Post-Apartheid South Africa by Ilana Mercer.

A Time Traveller's Guide to Our Next Ten Years Paperback – 1 Apr 2014 by Frans Cronje (Author)

Chapter 10 and 11

https://www. theguardian. com/media/2013/dec/09/bell-pottinger-tim-bell-pr-interview

https://books. google. co. ukI_Was_Told_To_Come_Alone.

https://www. bostonglobe. com/opinion-colonialism-bred

https://wikipedia. org/wiki/Decolonisation_higher_educ

http://www. salon. com/2015/11/14/stop_blaming_muslims

http://www. bbc. co. uk/news/av/south-africa-s-gupta-

https://www. biznews. com/bell-pottinger-kleptocracy/

http://www. -politicsweb. co. za/south-africa-decolonized

http://www. news24. com/columnists/archive/tumomokone

https://wikipedia. org/Democratic/Alliance(South Africa)

http://www. economist. com/news/

http://www. dailymail. co. uk/news/NHS-poaching-doctors

https://www. highbeam. com/doc/1G1-60696289. html

http://www. poa. gov. za/news/

https://www. ft. com/content/

https://www. bostonglobe. com/french-british-colonialism

http://www. birmingham. ac. uk/research/paris-attacks. aspx

https://oppidanpress. atavist. com/decolonisation

https://en. wikipedia. org/wiki/Decolonisation/Fanon

https://www. theguardian. com/politics/2005/aug/20/past.

http://www. osisa. org/economic-justice/blog/undermining

http://www. open. ac. uk/researchprojects/makingbritain/
content/imperial-conference

http://fpif. org/payback_for_colonial_sins/

Books:

'They asked me to come Alone' by Souad Mehkennet –
The Art of War by Sun Tzu

Chapter 12&13

http://www. news24. com/Travel/Cape-Town

http://english. al-akhbar. com/node/20378

https://www. theguardian. com/uk-news/2014/black-flag

https://clarionproject. org/uk-poll/isis-supporters-britain

http://www. -independent. co. uk/british-people-muslims-uk

https://www. imf. org/en/News/Articles/

http://www. survival-international. org/campaigns/

http://www. huffingtonpost. co. za/2017/09/14/its-been-a-long-road-and-president-jacob-zuma-is-almost-out-of-tricks_a_23209440/

https://reutersinstitute. politics. ox. ac. uk/risj-review/journalism-democracy-and-state-south-africa

http://www. thejournal. org. za/index. php/thejournal/article/view/9/31

Royalty free images online:

https://www. shutterstock. com/? kw=royalty%20free%

http://www. istockphoto. com/gb/stock-photos?

South African History online Images and Excerpts

Article by Emily Hobhouse as quoted and accompanying image. "Lizzie Van Zyl who died in the Bloemfontein concentration camp, 1902" from South African History Online, www.sahistory.org.za.

http://www.sahistory.org.za/policy

Pinterest

Image from www.pinterest.co.uk as used in Part 1 Chapter 2: "Boer child in a British Concentration Camp, Anglo-Boer War…"

https://www.pinterest.co.uk/pin/423338433698135104/

Biznews

Imageused in Epilogue with full accreditation to the article: "OUTA lays treason, racketeering charges against Duduzane Zuma, Guptas"on August 3 2017.

https://www.biznews.com/undictated/2017/08/03/outa-lays-treason-racketeering-charges-dududzane-zuma-guptas/